D1624176

Crime and Inequality

364.941
G91

Crime and Inequality

Chris Grover

WILLAN
PUBLISHING

Published by

Willan Publishing
Culmcott House
Mill Street, Uffculme
Cullompton, Devon
EX15 3AT, UK
Tel: +44(0)1884 840337
Fax: +44(0)1884 840251
e-mail: info@willanpublishing.co.uk
website: www.willanpublishing.co.uk

Published simultaneously in the USA and Canada by

Willan Publishing
c/o ISBS, 920 NE 58th Ave, Suite 300
Portland, Oregon 97213-3786, USA
Tel: +001(0)503 287 3093
Fax: +001(0)503 280 8832
e-mail: info@isbs.com
website: www.isbs.com

© Chris Grover 2008

The rights of Chris Grover to be identified as the author of this book have been asserted by him in accordance with the Copyright, Designs and Patents Act of 1988.

All rights reserved; no part of this publication may be reproduced, stored in a retrieval system, or transmitted in any form or by any means, electronic, mechanical, photocopying, recording or otherwise without the prior written permission of the Publishers or a licence permitting copying in the UK issued by the Copyright Licensing Agency Ltd, Saffron House, 6–10 Kirby Street, London EC1N 8TS.

First published 2008

ISBN   978-1-84392-329-9 paperback
       978-1-84392-330-5 hardback

British Library Cataloguing-in-Publication Data

A catalogue record for this book is available from the British Library.

Project managed by Deer Park Productions, Tavistock, Devon
Typeset by GCS, Leighton Buzzard, Bedfordshire
Printed and bound by T.J. International Ltd, Padstow, Cornwall

#236434186

Contents

For my Mum and Dad, Ronnie and Brian

Acknowledgements

There are many people whom I would like to thank for their support in the researching and writing of *Crime and Inequality*. Keith Soothill, Emeritus Professor of Social Research, Department of Applied Statistics at Lancaster University encouraged me to write the book and when I had completed it he read it all. Sue Penna of Lancaster University's Department of Applied Social Science also read a complete draft. Others – Janet Jamieson of Liverpool John Moores University and Linda Piggott of the Department of Applied Social Science, Lancaster University – read and commented on several chapters, while individual chapters were also read by Paul Iganski and Gill McIvor who also work in the Department of Applied Social Science, Lancaster University. Thanks must also be extended to the anonymous reviewers who helped to focus the book. Of course, any omissions or mistakes are mine. I would also like to thank Lancaster University for allowing me sabbatical leave in the winter of 2007 during which time a good proportion of the book was written, and thanks must once again be extended to Sue Penna, Linda Piggott and to Dave Smith for covering or taking over my administrative duties during this period. Finally, I would like to thank my partner Karen for her love and support.

Preface

You can't say it's a problem and then do nothing about it: Ministers now accept the gap between rich and poor is too wide, but still refuse to face the political costs of action to narrow it. (*The Guardian*, 16 August 2007)

Inequality is the most pressing concern that is currently facing Britain, but as the quote above suggests, there is little political commitment to do much about it, despite the fact that there is a wealth of evidence that suggests it is related to a host of socio-economic problems. Inequality structures all life chances and outcomes: those at the lower end of the income distribution are likely to be the most poorly educated; to suffer more ill-health and to die in childhood and, if they reach adulthood, to die younger than richer people; to be in low-paid and casualised sectors of labour markets; and are more likely to be involved with criminal justice agencies as both the perpetrators and victims of crime. In some of these examples – most notably education and health – the disadvantaged life chances of poor working-class people is often acknowledged. However, relationships between crime and economic inequality are at worst ignored or at best downplayed. There is, then, a need to re-emphasise the fact that crime is structured through social status; it is something that disproportionately affects poor people.

While connections between inequality and poverty, and crime are often unspoken relationships they have been known about for many years. However, as Ian Taylor (1999) argued in his last book *Crime in Context*, recent years have been marked by the rise of individualistic and commonsensical criminologies. His observations are as equally applicable today as they were a decade ago. In fact, in Britain in relation to crime and criminal justice policy things have deteriorated further with the capturing of debates about crime, as well as a range of other socio-economic phenomena, by discourses that emphasise personal responsibility and duty to others above all other considerations. In these discourses individuals are held responsible for phenomena that are actually better understood as having social and economic antecedents and it is a concern with such developments that provides the context for the writing of *Crime and Inequality*.

In fact, there were three issues that contextualised the writing of *Crime and Inequality*. First was a concern regarding academic boundaries. Although I would not describe myself as a criminologist, I am, after teaching for several years on the criminology degree course at Lancaster University and, earlier in my career, working on projects examining the press reporting of crime, sympathetic to the concerns of criminology. However, I would like it and social policy, the academic discipline that I feel more comfortable with, to have more fluid boundaries through which ideas and analyses can be developed. This is because social and economic inequalities are crucial to the two disciplines, although they differ in both the extent and the nature of their engagement with them. As we shall see, it is poorer people who are most likely to be in contact with criminal justice agencies and to face the greatest socio-structural pressures to offend. They are also most likely to be the victims of crime. For me, this means that criminology cannot adequately explain offending and the operation of criminal justice without reference to economic and social inequalities, while social policy cannot engage with the ways in which inequalities are experienced without focusing upon crime as a substantive topic.

The second issue encouraging me to write *Crime and Inequality* was a frustration with contemporary politics where the main political parties are seemingly in agreement that greater levels of authoritarianism, control and surveillance are required for a more ordered society. We see this in a range of social and criminal justice policies that are concerned with disciplining the perceived miscreant to encourage conformity to an increasingly narrowly conceived citizenship that is structured through individual responsibility and duty, and paid work. While some of the indicators were visible when 'old' Labour was in the transition to New Labour, particularly with the abolition of the former's Clause 4 commitment to the social ownership 'of the means of production, distribution and exchange', there was still surprise at the whole-hearted embrace of the economic and social policies of previous Conservative governments that had exacerbated levels of inequality and poverty in Britain. Particularly shocking was the embrace of the free market as being 'natural' and inevitable, and the courting of big business whose ambassadors have been central to New Labour's restructuring of social policy, especially those related to social security and labour market policy, since its election in 1997 (Taylor 1998) and ideas for it in forthcoming years (Freud 2007). While such policy areas have since industrialisation been structured through the capitalist logic, this has taken on a more urgent significance under New Labour's policies aimed at getting people into 'low-paid' work.

Third, I was concerned with the detail of policy and policy debates. Often in policy-related publications the detail is lost to more general claims about, for instance, what changes in policy mean for our understanding of state welfare and criminal justice. However, for me, it is important to get a sense of the detail of policy – and there are no apologies for those parts of *Crime and Inequality* that are very detailed – for it is only through analysing such detail that one can fully understand the material context that structures the lives of people and how expressions of collective responsibility for various social groups are being fractured through developments in social and criminal justice policy that differentiate between people according to their age, their alleged moral character and their material circumstances.

My concern with these three issues should become clear in *Crime and Inequality*. I have tried to write each chapter so that it makes sense in its own right, dealing with a stand-alone topic, as well as being part of the whole book.

Chris Grover
Bolton le Sands
Lancashire

List of abbreviations

AHC	After Housing Costs
ASBO	Anti-Social Behaviour Order
BBC	British Broadcasting Corporation
BHC	Before Housing Costs
BME	Black and Minority Ethnic
CAB	Citizens Advice Bureau
CCTV	Closed Circuit Television
CPAG	Child Poverty Action Group
CPRS	Central Policy Review Staff
CTC	Child Tax Credit
CYPA	Children and Young Persons Act
DETR	Department for the Environment, Transport and the Regions
DfES	Department for Education and Skills
DSRM	Diversity Sector Relationship Manager
DWP	Department for Work and Pensions
EMA	Education Maintenance Allowance
EMAG	Ethnic Minority Achievement Grant
EMETF	Ethnic Minority Employment Task Force
EMFF	Ethnic Minority Flexible Fund
EMO	Ethnic Minority Outreach
ESA	Employment and Support Allowance
EU	European Union
FC	Family Credit
FPN	Fixed Penalty Notice
GCSE	General Certificate of Secondary Education

HAP	Homelessness Action Plan
HB	Housing Benefit
HM	Her Majesty's
HMRC	Her Majesty's Revenue and Customs
ILO	International Labour Organisation
IS	Income Support
JSA	Jobseeker's Allowance
LEA	Local Educational Authority
LPC	Low Pay Commission
MP	Member of Parliament
MUD	Moral Underclass Discourse
NACAB	National Association of Citizens Advice Bureaux
NACRO	National Association for the Care and Resettlement of Offenders
NAPO	National Association of Probation Officers
NDLP	New Deal for Lone Parents
NDYP	New Deal for Young People
NEET	Not in Education, Employment or Training
NMW	National Minimum Wage
NNI	Neighbourhood Nurseries Initiative
NVQ	National Vocational Qualification
NWS	New Workers Scheme
OFSTED	Office for Standards in Education
PND	Penalty Notice for Disorder
RED	Redistributionist Discourse
RSI	Rough Sleepers Initiative
SBR	Stricter Benefit Regime
SEA	Specialist Employment Adviser
SEU	Social Exclusion Unit
SID	Social Integration Discourse
SRR	Single Room Rent
TUC	Trades Union Congress
UK	United Kingdom
WTC	Working Tax Credit
YOP	Youth Opportunities Programme
YT	Youth Training
YTS	Youth Training Scheme
YWS	Young Workers Scheme

Chapter 1

Introduction

That the British criminal justice system deals with and processes poor working-class men and women is widely accepted. Even the government's own research on connections between crime and social exclusion points to this. In the report *Reducing Re-offending by Ex-prisoners* (2002), for instance, the Social Exclusion Unit (SEU) noted the following observations. Of the prison population in Britain:

- 72 per cent were in receipt of state benefits immediately before their entry to prison, compared to 13.7 per cent of the general population.

- 48 per cent have a history of debt, compared to 10 per cent of households with difficult or multiple debts.

- 4.7 per cent were sleeping rough immediately before their imprisonment, compared to just 0.001 per cent of the general population.

- 67 per cent were unemployed in the four weeks before their imprisonment, compared to 5 per cent of the general population.

- 27 per cent had been taken into local authority care as a child compared to 2 per cent of children in the general population.

- 49 per cent of the male and 33 per cent of the female prison population were excluded from school compared to 3 per cent of the general population.

- 52 per cent of the male and 71 per cent of the female prison population have no educational qualifications, compared to 15 per cent of the general population.

While these observations point to the poor material and social circumstances of offenders, the SEU report gives no indication of how these factors that structure offending should be addressed. This is because it is concerned with reducing offending among ex-prisoners, rather than with addressing the reasons why people engage in offending behaviour in the first place. These observations, however, demonstrate that if offending is to be addressed then relationships between crime and inequality must be taken seriously. Related to this, they also suggest that in order to tackle offending, areas of policy intervention that are not necessarily or usually associated with criminal justice need to be considered for their potential to address the social and economic circumstances that contextualise offending. It is these two issues – relationships between crime and inequality and social policy interventions as a means of managing offending and anti-social behaviour – with which *Crime and Inequality* is concerned.

Economic inequality has been part of criminological analyses since the development of structurally based explanations in the early decades of the 20th century. From the Marxist-inspired work of Willem Bonger (1916) explaining crime as a working-class survival strategy through the Chicago School's (Shaw and McKay 1942) analysis of the patterning of crime and Merton's (1938) attempt to explain the propensity for crime, to the neo-Marxism of the 'new criminology' (Taylor *et al.* 1973), inequality has appeared, most often, implicitly in criminological analyses. It has also been part of more recent attempts to place crime within its wider social and economic context (for example, Taylor 1999; Hillyard *et al.* 2004).

However, in such analyses the issue of inequality is often not dealt with to any great extent; the fact that societies are unequal is often taken for granted, with little discussion of the evidence of inequality, why it occurs and what, if anything, is being, or can be, done about it. In contrast, *Crime and Inequality* makes the issue of inequality much more explicit in its analysis of relationships between inequalities and various aspects of offending. In brief, while this book is in a tradition of criminology that locates the contextual factors of offending in socio-economic structures, it more closely focuses upon the nature of inequality, how it is linked to offending and how, through the constraints of patriarchal and racialised capitalism, interventions of the state help to construct economic inequalities and often exacerbate them. In the level of detail that it offers, it is also distinguishable from analyses (for example, Taylor 1999; Young 1999, 2002) that acknowledge that wider social policy changes may impact upon offending. Both Taylor's (1999) and Young's (1999, 2002) recent analyses are broad in approach. Taylor (1999), for instance, is accused of 'painting on a large canvas' (Haggerty 2001: 131), while Young's analysis (although he refutes this – Young 2004) is criticised for its methodologically flawed pairing of the inclusion/exclusion dichotomy leading to sweeping claims about modern and postmodern societies (Yar and Penna 2004). What this means is that both Taylor and Young tend to gloss over the detail of policies, many of which may not have criminal justice as their focus, but nevertheless are thought of, at least in the policy imagination, as having potential impacts upon offending and anti-social behaviour. So, for instance, several of Taylor's (1999) nine crises, most notably the job crisis, crisis of material poverty and social inequality and the crisis of inclusion and exclusion, are structured through and arguably exacerbated by state interventions, but he wrote very little about those interventions.

It is at this juncture that *Crime and Inequality* becomes important, for it examines the state of inequality in contemporary society and its relationship to offending and social policy developments that are, at least in part, thought of as having potential impacts upon offending.

Crime, inequality and social policy

In the previous section we saw that the prison population is marked by indicators of inequality, poverty and exclusion. That is one reason for examining the connections between, on the one hand, crime and, on the other hand, inequality and social policy. There are, however, a number of other reasons why the interconnections of crime, inequality and social policy need examining. First, while we have seen that there is statistical evidence suggesting that the criminal justice agencies basically manage poor people, those statistics cannot explain why this is the case. The structure/agency debate is important here, because those observations could be explained through structural arguments that suggest we need to understand offending behaviour in its wider socio-economic environment (this is the underlying approach that *Crime and Inequality* takes). However, there are other approaches that we shall be discussing along the way where the focus is upon the behaviour of individuals; the argument being that poor material circumstances cannot be used as a reason to condone offending and anti-social acts because, no matter what their circumstances, individuals can always act as responsible moral agents (see Deacon 2000, 2002). In such arguments offending is committed by people who either do not know how to act in a law-abiding manner, or actively choose not to act in such a manner (Grover 2005a).

Second, and related, there is an argument that the relief of poverty and its causes (most notably, worklessness) actually encourages criminal and anti-social behaviour by eroding the responsibility of individuals. Such arguments were the crux of the behavioural 'underclass' thesis and are also visible in the more individualistic and morally prescriptive versions of communitarianism that New Labour subscribe to (Deacon 2000). Such arguments have a long and infamous history. Chambliss (1964), for instance, demonstrates how the 1349 Vagrancy Act that criminalised the giving of alms, an activity previously seen as being part of the moral economy, to those of 'sound mind and body' who were unemployed was driven by a concern that such alms discouraged vagrants from working and encouraged them to engage in theft and other criminal activity. In what is now termed the 'economic model of crime' – that individuals 'choose between crime and legitimate work depending on the opportunities, rewards and costs of each' (Hale 2005: 328) – the suggestion is that there is a direct correlation between not engaging in paid employment and offending.

Third, there is an argument, supported by the statistics quoted at the beginning of this chapter, that the criminal justice system has the role of controlling what are seen as 'problem populations'; those which:

> disturb, hinder or call into question ... capitalist modes of appropriating the product of human labour ... the social conditions under which capitalist production takes place ... patterns of distribution and consumption in capitalist society ... the process of socialization for productive and non-productive roles ... and ... the ideology which supports the functioning of capitalist society. (Spitzer 1975, cited in Box 1987: 128)

When Spitzer was writing the main 'problem population' was unemployed people (cf. Box 1987; Crow *et al.* 1989). While unemployed people continue to be problematised because their worklessness is associated with fecklessness (cf. Crow *et al.* 1989), they have been joined by other groups lacking paid work, most notably lone parents (hereafter, referred to as lone mothers as about 90 per cent of them in the UK are female – National Statistics 2006a) who are seen as being particularly threatening because they have the potential to subvert not only the capitalist order (many are not in paid work and those who are not are likely to be receiving state benefits) but also the patriarchal order (they are outside the control, and therefore threaten the power, of men). In this context, it is argued that lone mothers are incapable of raising their children, especially their male ones, unless they are in paid employment (Grover and Stewart 2002).

Fourth is the observation that social policy, particularly social security and labour market policies, act partly to manage anti-social and criminal behaviour. There are different ways of approaching this argument. Piven and Cloward (1972), for example, argue that during periods of high levels of unemployment relief programmes are expanded to maintain order. In the case of Britain we might point to youth training programmes and active labour market policies to support their argument. In a more abstract account, Claus Offe (1984) argues that social policies are crucial in effecting what he describes as 'active proletarianisation'; the ways in which unemployed labour offers itself for sale to capitalist enterprises. The state is involved in this process because it cannot be assumed *a priori* that unemployed labour will offer itself for sale. In contrast, workers could find other means of survival: for example, begging, crime or the adoption of an 'alternative' lifestyle (*ibid.*: 93). The implication of this argument is that the state's role in active proletarianisation is crucial to maintaining the supply of labour for capital by preventing workers from taking forms of subsistence other than paid work. In doing so, it also prevents offending and other behaviours that are defined as being problematic.

Fifth, some areas of social policy, in particular social security policy, are increasingly being used as a means of punishing offenders. So, for instance, the 1991 Criminal Justice Act made it possible for magistrates to apply to have fine and compensation payments deducted from the benefit payments of those people receiving *Income Support* (IS), the benefit for the very poorest people in Britain. Similarly, the 2000 Child Support, Pensions and Social Security Act allowed in pilot areas IS and means-tested *Jobseeker's Allowance* (JSA) to be reduced or withdrawn from individuals who break the conditions of their community orders (see Knight *et al.* 2003), while the 2006 Welfare Reform Bill will allow the withdrawal of *Housing Benefit* (HB) from those tenants who do not take recommended measures to address their anti-social behaviour after they have been convicted of it (for discussion see Deacon 2004; S. Lister 2004; Rodger 2006).

Sixth, there are conceptual issues that link social and criminal justice policies. In the criminological literature many recent developments in criminal justice are explained through the concepts of responsibilisation and remoralisation. Drawing, sometimes unacknowledged, on the work of Gamble (1988) the former is explained through reference to neo-liberalism, in particular, a reordering of responsibility for crime prevention from the public to the private; while the latter is explained by reference to neo-conservatism. It is argued (Muncie and Hughes 2002; Gilling 2001) that there is a tension between responsibilisation and remoralisation because the neo-liberalism of the former implies a lesser role for the state, while neo-conservative remoralisation demands a greater degree of state intervention in the 'regulation, surveillance and monitoring of entire families and neighbourhoods' (Muncie and Hughes 2002: 9). While we should not overstate the extent to which the state has withdrawn from the provision of welfare and related services in Britain (cf. Pierson 1994; Powell and Hewitt 2002), it is the case that trends towards responsibilisation and remoralisation are equally visible in social policy developments. Since the 1980s there has been a concerted effort to 'responsibilise' individuals by encouraging them to provide for their own social and economic needs through the purchase of financial products, such as private pensions, insurances to cover sickness, ill health and unemployment, and protection schemes to cover mortgage payments in the event of unemployment and other forms of worklessness (Farnsworth and Holden 2006). There has also been a concerted effort at remoralising state-dependent poor people, particularly through policies aimed at making them compete for and take paid employment (Rose 2000).

Undoubtedly, there are other connections that could be made between crime, and inequality and social policy, but those outlined above provide a fruitful basis for examining their relationships, something that we will do in the following chapters. More immediately, they seem to lend support to the idea that over the past two decades or so we have witnessed a criminalisation of social policy.

Criminalising social policy?

The idea of the criminalisation of social policy is used to describe an expansion of criminal justice concerns into areas of policy traditionally described as social policy. In this sense, it is argued that the boundaries between criminal justice and social policy are becoming blurred (for instance, Muncie and Hughes 2002; Rodger 2006) or merged (Gilling 2001). The criminalisation of social policy is often applied to understanding the operation and strategic concerns of criminal justice partnerships at a local level (see, for example, Crawford 1997, 1999 on crime prevention, and Gilling 2001 on community safety) and refers, according to Crawford (1997), to ways in which statutory and voluntary groups concerned with social policy issues are drawn together through such partnerships around the issue of crime. While crime may not be the substantive concern of the organisations, the focus of their partnerships and the available funding is upon crime-related issues. In brief, the idea is that welfare-orientated policies are being developed for their potential to tackle crime, in particular youth offending (for example, Muncie and Hughes 2002; also Rutherford 2002; Phoenix 2003; Smith 2005; Tidsall 2006; Muncie 2004). While such trends are mostly observed at a local level, Muncie (2006: 242; Muncie and Hughes 2002) points to the ways in which centrally organised policies and initiatives, such as the various New Deal schemes (discussed in detail in Chapters 3 and 5), have been drawn into 'a broader criminal justice agenda' concerned with the management of risk. Indeed, it is the issue of the management of risk that Gilling (2001: 382) argues has enabled the conjoining of criminal justice and social policy, noting that 'addressing risk factors and insecurity is something traditionally associated with social policy: the risk factors may be things like unemployment, bad housing and low educational attainment'.

It is argued that the criminalisation of social policy is particularly worrying because 'fundamental public issues may become marginalised, except in so far as they are defined in terms of their criminogenic qualities' (Crawford 1999: 527). Crawford, for instance, highlights the potential to 'view poor housing, unemployment, poor schooling, the lack of youth leisure opportunities and so on as no longer important public issues in themselves' (ibid.). In this context, Smith (2005: 12) argues that the criminalisation of social policy involves the redefining of power imbalances as 'problems of disorder and criminal justice' and that it focuses upon individual behaviour, rather than the socio-economic antecedents of behaviour (Bannister et al. 2006).

The observations of Smith (2005) and Bannister et al. (2006) point to one of the contradictory pressures that structures the criminalisation of social policy. This relates to the argument we have made that some social policies have been co-opted as mechanisms to deliver punishment (point five above). It is the case that punishments can only be delivered through those areas where the state has some leverage; this is most likely to be income and housing (Grover 2005a). Indeed, it is these two areas through which aspects of punishment for crime and anti-social behaviour are being delivered through social policies. Such actions might be defended through popular appeals (holding poor people responsible for their actions) and, more philosophically, through debates about balancing rights and responsibilities by means of the conditions attached to the receipt of welfare benefits and services (see, for example, Deacon 2004 on sanctioning HB).

However, we should not overestimate the crime-related antecedents of social policy developments. We need to bear in mind that social policies have many roles, of which addressing law and order-related issues may be one, and not necessarily the main one. This is an important observation because the fact that social policy has various roles creates further tensions that will be examined in this book. Here, the focus is upon the ways in which social policy interventions have traditionally been, and continue to be, concerned with issues that can be considered outside of direct concerns with managing crime-related risks. The New Deals, for instance, that Muncie (2006) points to as being an example of the criminalisation of social policy are as much, if not more, concerned with the governance of economic growth – for instance managing wage inflation pressures – as they are with managing offending and anti-social behaviour (Grover and Stewart 2002; Grover 2003, 2005b). The labour discipline required in post-industrial society has required a retooling of the state apparatus (cf. Jones and Novak 1999), with new penalties for those who, for whatever reasons, are unable to engage with the demands of the state that they play a full role in the flexibilised and casualised 'knowledge' economy. These penalties have been extended to a range of claimant groups who are increasingly being defined as unemployed labour (Grover 2005b on lone mothers; Grover and Piggott 2005 and 2007 on sick and disabled people).

The consequence of these developments – the criminalisation of social policy and the regulation of the free market through social policy – is the impoverishment of already poor people. This observation relating to the inconsistencies between social policy developments and the material antecedents of offending and anti-social behaviour forms one of the main foci of this book which will argue that contemporary configurations of social policy interventions at the national level are inconsistent with addressing crime and anti-social behaviour because they often have the effect of making poor people poorer.

Although in *Crime and Inequality* we will discuss aspects of education and housing policy where relevant, the main focus is upon labour market and income maintenance policies. While this may be seen as being rather narrow in approach, it is these two social policy areas that recent governments have seen as having particular potential not only to reduce poverty and exclusion, but also to address various aspects of offending and anti-social behaviour. In order to explore these relationships we focus upon and examine how policy developments in the two areas are thought to relate to offending behaviour and how it is thought they are able to tackle it. Their likely success in doing so is also explored in *Crime and Inequality*. Before we examine briefly the content of each chapter, it is necessary to examine some of the concepts that will be used throughout the book.

Inequality, poverty and social exclusion

Throughout the book reference will be made to the concepts of inequality, poverty and social exclusion. While all three are related, they are analytically distinct. This section examines how the concepts are defined and how they are operationalised in policy interventions.

Inequality

There are different forms of inequality that relate to different aspects of everyday life. Economic inequality is perhaps the better known and refers to financial and material inequalities. It usually refers to differences in income (mostly, but not exclusively wage income) and wealth (for instance, property, shares and savings). Social inequalities refer to those inequalities that are the consequence of imbalances in power and status; for example, inequalities of class, gender, 'race' and disablement. We shall take economic and social inequalities separately.

Neo-liberalism and inequality

The inequalities and their causes, and the social policies that *Crime and Inequality* are concerned with, are related to the massive economic and social shifts that Britain has witnessed since the 1970s. Central to this have been the ways of understanding, talking about and governing the British and global economy. Regulation theorists (see, for example, Jessop 1994a, 1994b, 2002) have argued that in Britain the economic crisis of the 1970s resulted in a shift, facilitated to a great extent by the Thatcherite New Right, in the predominant economic paradigm away from the planned economy of Keynesianism to 'free' market neo-liberalism. This shift in ideas of economic governance had profound social and economic implications in Britain, for central to neo-liberalism was (and is) a privileging of competition, private ownership and the need to keep inflationary pressures in check. What this meant in practice was a wholesale rejection of the idea that the state could plan for economic growth and development. Most notably the Keynesian idea that the state could and should ensure full employment through interventions that sustained the demand for labour was rejected and replaced by the idea that in order to encourage the 'free' market to create jobs a focus upon the supply side – the character, attitudes, skills and financial cost – of labour was required. Jobs would only be created if labour was competitive and flexible. Labour would have to do the types of work that capitalist enterprises were offering, at wages that were not artificially high because of institutional interferences, and in conditions dictated by the market. A raft of policy developments (many of which are discussed in more detail later in the book), from the destruction of trade union powers to the erosion of social security benefit levels – particularly, but not exclusively, for young people – were consistent with the neo-liberal agenda of (re)asserting the importance of the market in framing relations between capital and workers.

The consequence of these developments was an increase in unemployment driven by job losses in those sectors, most notably the extractive and heavy manufacturing sectors, that in the 'transnationalization of production' (Dicken 1992: 430) were relocated to countries where labour was cheap and where it was offered little protection by trade unions or legal frameworks governing employment practices. In Britain this process, coupled with the rejection of demand management, led to a collapse in demand for male workers in particular in what are commonly understood as semi- and unskilled occupations, the consequences of which continue to structure the experiences of many men in those areas of Britain that were most closely associated with extractive and heavy industries. In contrast, the main areas of employment growth over the past two or so decades has been among women in services sector jobs, many of which are characterised by 'flexploitative' practices (cf. Gray 1998); part-time, casualised and low paid (see Chapter 5). Hence, it is argued that the shift to neo-liberalism has resulted not only in high levels of economic inactivity, but also in a polarisation between a core of relatively well-paid people in relatively secure full-time work, and a periphery of low-paid, casualised workers (see Young 1999 2002) who, as we shall see, are increasingly reliant upon the state to subsidise their wages in order to bring them up to a politically defined minimum.

While in opposition 'old' Labour was particularly critical of the New Right's belief in neo-liberalism as the solution to the economic dilemmas facing Britain. However, the replacement of Clause 4 of the Labour Party's constitution that had committed it to the common ownership of the means of production was indicative of the direction that New Labour was to pursue in the years following its election in 1997. New Labour confirmed the New Right's argument that neo-liberalism was *the* means of securing Britain's economic position in the global economy. The then Chancellor of the Exchequer (and now Prime Minister) Gordon Brown acknowledged this when he argued that:

> ... the new economy will need more competition, more entrepreneurship, more flexibility ... reform was needed in the 1980s to create more flexibility and that modernisation is continually needed to upgrade our skills and create a more adaptable workforce. (Brown 1999: 4 and 5)

In political terms there is now a consensus that neo-liberalism is the only viable economic paradigm if the desire is for global economic prosperity. From our perspective this is important because there is a disjuncture between, on the one hand, the 'architecture of governance' (Penna 2001: 1) that constructs global neo-liberalism as being the only way forward and, on the other hand, pretensions at a national level to tackle social exclusion. This is because social exclusion, 'particularly those dimensions resulting from an income polarisation ... is constantly being produced by the operations of the contemporary [neo-liberal] political economy' (*ibid.*: 4). It is just not possible, as the architects and supporters of New Labour argued in a discourse referring to the 'third way' (Blair 1998; Giddens 1998, 2000, 2001), to have a successful marriage of social justice and global neo-liberalism. The 'third way' has been about the buttressing of neo-liberalism and securing the position of the 'free' market, rather than being concerned with social justice. This, as we shall see in *Crime and Inequality*, has resulted in increasing levels of inequality and stagnantly high levels of poverty.

Social inequalities: the importance of culture

Economic and social inequalities are not mutually exclusive. So, for example, on average, women are more likely to be poor compared to men (Flaherty *et al.* 2004) and black and minority ethnic (BME) people are more likely to be poorer than white people (Platt 2002).

Fraser (1997, 2000) argues that such observations are the consequence of economic and cultural injustices. In brief, collectivities of people – for instance women and black people – are differentiated 'by virtue of *both* the political-economic structure *and* the cultural-valuational structure of society' (Fraser 1997: 19, original emphasis). In the case of women, for example, the inequalities they endure compared to men are a reflection of a political economy that demarcates between 'productive' labour and 'reproductive' labour, the latter of which women are assigned primary responsibility for, and which clearly distinguishes between 'men's' and 'women's' paid employment through the fragmentation of labour markets. This means that women are exploited as women under capitalism in different ways to men because of their gender (for example, Massey 1984; Beechey and Perkins 1987). However, in addition and closely linked, women's inequities are also the consequence of a cultural-valuation system structured through androcentrism and sexism that privilege traits which are associated with masculinity and which devalue and disparage activities and acts – such as caring – coded as being 'feminine'. Similarly, in the case of 'race', the inequalities faced by BME people are the consequence of their position in political economy which means that they are seen as a pool of labour that can be exploited on 'race'-specific lines. What this means, Fraser (1997) argues, is that BME people are often seen as superfluous to the economy (witness the higher rates of unemployment among particularly black and Pakistani and Bangladeshi people – Platt 2002) and are concentrated in areas of employment that are low paid and have poor conditions attached (Platt 2002; Low Pay Commission 2005). However, the inequalities of BME people are, in Fraser's analysis, also the consequence of a cultural-valuation dimension that constructs norms that privilege whiteness (Eurocentrism) and devalues those things that are coded in society as, for example, 'black' and 'brown'. Here, for instance, one can point to stereotypes that link blackness with crime and (sexual) deviancy (Gilroy 1987a, 1987b; Grover and Soothill 1996).

For our purposes Fraser's arguments are important because of their focus upon not only the political economic position of men, women, BME and white people, but also their cultural position, in particular the disadvantages of BME people and women through the privileging of traits associated with masculinity and whiteness, and through racist and sexist discrimination. Such observations are pertinent to studying relationships between crime and inequality because of the interconnections between the two sites of injustice. It will become apparent, for instance, that many working-class people are poor because of their marginal status to economic production and because of moral judgements, rooted in a cultural distrust and fear of them, that construct such people as having character and behavioural weaknesses. In addition, the chapters on young men (Chapter 3), women (Chapter 5), BME people (Chapter 6) and street homeless people (Chapter 7) demonstrate interconnections between the economic and cultural positions of these various groups and their position as characters in the pantheon of crime.

Inequality, opportunity and outcome

Inequalities can be considered in relation to opportunities and outcomes. In the case of the former the focus is upon equality of access to various opportunities that affect life chances. Here, for instance, the focus may be upon equality of access to activities such as paid work and to services like education and health which have a significant impact upon the quality of life of individuals. In the case of the latter, the focus is upon the ways in which desirable life chances (for example, wealth and income) are distributed throughout society.

New Labour has not to any great extent focused upon equality of outcome, preferring instead to focus upon equality of opportunity. It is generally accepted that it abandoned the redistributive policies of 'old' Labour that would lead to greater equality of outcome in order to capture the political support of 'middle England' (cf. Hills and Stewart 2005). In fact, the focus upon equality of opportunity is an example *par excellence* of what Goldson and Jamieson (2002) describe as the 'double speak' of New Labour, for the focus upon 'equality' is attractive to New Labour's more traditional political supporters, whereas the focus upon 'opportunity' is held to be attractive to its more recent supporters. As Margaret Hodge MP (then Under Secretary of State at the Department for Education and Employment) noted in 2000:

> [Equality of opportunity] allows us to position ourselves as promoting both individual ambition and prosperity, while still tackling inequality. That appeals to middle Britain. (cited in Hills and Stewart 2005: 15)

What Hodge fails to mention is that the focus upon equality of opportunity is also attractive to middle Britain because it is structured through a concern with individual responsibility. For us, the danger of emphasising opportunity is that those people unable to take advantage of existing opportunities are held to be responsible for their ensuing exclusion. In brief, the focus becomes a concern with the morality and lifestyle choices of poor and excluded people. Callinicos (2001: 62) succinctly makes the point with reference to paid work:

> There is ... an important sense in which New Labour authoritarianism is a consequence of Gordon Brown's version of neoliberal economics ... if macro-economic stability is secured and the right supply-side measures are in place, any further unemployment is voluntary. Unemployment is in these circumstances a consequence of the dysfunctional behaviour of individuals who refuse to work, and this behaviour must in turn be caused either by their individual moral faults or by a more pervasive 'culture of poverty'.

Poverty

Poverty is not the same as economic inequality, but it is a 'close relative' (Howard *et al.* 2001: 9). Alcock (2006: 6) argues that poverty can be understood as the 'unacceptable face of inequality'. He goes on to note, however, that being poor is about more than just being at the 'bottom of the distribution of resources' (*ibid.*). In contrast, poor people 'are those who have too few resources to live within society. Poverty means not having enough'. The most problematic aspect of the concept of poverty, however, is attempting to measure what poor people do not have enough of. The answer may seem blindingly simple: money. However, this raises the more difficult question of what poor people should be able to afford. Traditionally, such concerns led to debate about whether poverty should be defined in absolute or relative terms (see R. Lister 2004: Chapter 1). However, it is now recognised that even those definitions of poverty considered to be absolute are structured through a sense of relativity; measures of what is necessitous are always relative to time and place (Veit-Wilson 1986). This has led to the claim (Howard *et al.* 2001: 20) that: 'Neither absolute nor relative helps our understanding of poverty.' In contrast Howard *et al.* (*ibid.*: 26) call for 'better ideas and research tools with which to study poverty'.

Inequality and poverty also differ in the ways that it is thought they can be addressed. Alcock (1987), for example, notes how analyses of poverty tend to take place within Fabian or social democratic frameworks. This means it is thought that poverty can be tackled through the piecemeal intervention of the state. Alcock is right. If poverty could be defined, and the state had the ideological and economic willingness, it could be eradicated. However, while the tackling of poverty is likely to have some effect upon extremes of inequality, it will not abolish it because, as more radical analysts (for example, Ginsburg 1979; Gough 1979; Novak 1988) and the supporters of free markets (for example, Hayek 1960; Friedman 1962) inform us, economic inequality is fundamental to the operation of capitalism. To tackle economic inequalities contemporary British society would have to be reordered. It would require commitment to an egalitarian way of arranging the economic enterprise. At the least, this would involve intervention in (i.e. limiting) the wages of higher paid people and a more progressive (redistributive) system of benefits and taxes.

None of the mainstream political parties though is committed to engineering greater equality through restricting the wages of the highest paid and/or introducing a more progressive taxation regime. Seventeen years of Thatcherism and Majorism taught us that the Conservatives have very few problems with inequality, even in their supposedly more compassionate guise under the leadership of David Cameron MP (Norman and Ganesh 2006; Toynbee 2006). Furthermore, while some New Labour politicians have aired concerns about the need for the redistribution of wealth to tackle inequality of outcomes (for example, Peter Hain MP [then Leader of the House of Commons] in 2003 and Yvette Cooper MP [then Parliamentary Secretary in the Office of the Deputy Prime Minister] in 2004), their comments have been distanced from the mainstream of New Labour thinking that suggests wage and material inequalities are not particularly problematic. Little, if anything, has been done, for example, about the incomes of the highest wage earners (Hills and Stewart 2005) and little is likely to be done. The architects of the New Labour project believe in an economic orthodoxy that suggests that, beyond what it describes as a 'fair' minimum wage – 'a matter of common decency' (then Prime Minister Tony Blair MP, cited in *The Guardian*, 29 January

1998) – wages should reflect the value of individuals to enterprises they work for and, therefore, should be set by market rather than through state intervention (Grover 2005c).

In Britain, the idea of poverty and practices of its relief have historically been structured through moral typologies of poor people. R. Lister (2004: 102) notes: 'the bifurcation of "the poor" into "deserving" and "undeserving", each with their associated stereotypes, has had a profound impact on their treatment by the welfare state and its antecedents.' In critiques of the *Elizabethan Poor Law* the distinction between poverty and indigence was clearly drawn. Jeremy Bentham (1796, cited in Poynter 1969: 119), for instance, argued that poverty was something that *all* those who had to labour to secure their subsistence endured. In contrast, indigence was something endured by those 'destitute of property ...[and] *unable to labour*, or unable even *for* labour to procure the supply of which he happens thus to be in want' (*ibid.*, original emphasis). The indigent, Bentham argued, should be relieved at a level just above starvation in 'industry houses'. What this meant was that the indigent, or the pauper as they became once they received poor relief, should be relieved at a level below the poorest independent labourer. This, the principle of 'less eligibility', even if the term is no longer used, still structures many social policies, most notably income maintenance policy. Now the talk is of 'work incentives', but they amount to the same; ensuring that people in receipt of state benefits should not receive an income that discourages them from 'independence' gained through the wages of paid work.

Such distinctions and the concept of less eligibility had an economic function; they were aimed at ensuring that people would labour in order to secure their subsistence. However, they were also held to have a moral function in that they drew distinctions of character. Pauperism 'spelt degradation and infirmity of character' (R. Lister 2004: 105). The role of poor relief was to prevent poor people from being paupers 'by making that prospect repugnant' through the delivery of poor relief through workhouses (Himmelfarb 1995: 142). It is generally argued that workhouse relief (what was called 'indoor relief' under the *New Poor Law*) involved the distinction between the 'undeserving' (able-bodied) and the 'deserving' (impotent) pauper, a distinction that under various labels has 'subsequently been deployed to categorize "the poor" more generally, most notably in the US as well as the UK' (R. Lister 2004: 105). Most recently, such distinctions were made with reference to the behavioural 'underclass' by right-wing American commentator, Charles Murray (1990: 1) when he argued:

In a small Iowa town where I lived, I was taught by my middle-class parents that there were two kinds of poor people. One class of poor people was never even called 'poor'. I came to understand that they simply lived with low incomes, as my own parents had done when they were young. Then there was another set of poor people, just a handful of them. These poor people didn't lack just money. They were defined by their behaviour. Their homes were littered and unkempt. The men in the family were unable to hold a job for more than a few weeks at a time. Drunkenness was common. The children grew up ill-schooled and ill-behaved and contributed a disproportionate share of the local juvenile delinquents.

We shall see below that the morally prescriptive and authoritarian brand of communitarianism that structures New Labour's social and criminal justice policies also has resonances with this moral underclass position (Young 1999, 2002; Deacon 2002). Here, I want to focus upon the rather narrow definition of poverty that New Labour is wedded to.

At a lecture in memory of the architect of the post-Second World War welfare state, William Beveridge (see Beveridge 1942) in March 1999, the then Prime Minister, Tony Blair, committed New Labour to eliminating child poverty within a generation (by 2020) (Blair 1999; HM Treasury 1999; for discussion, Fimister 2001; Dornan 2004; Brewer *et al.* 2006). Most of the debate about this pledge has focused upon whether or not it is likely that child poverty will be abolished by 2020. Given that the interim target of reducing child poverty by 25 per cent between 1998/99 and 2004/05 was substantially missed, and more recently child poverty has increased (Brewer *et al.* 2007), it is unlikely that it will be without substantially more investment. The Institute for Fiscal Studies (*ibid*), for instance, estimates that to have a 50:50 chance of halving child poverty by 2010–11 (the government's next interim target) it will cost an additional £4 billion per year. There is little indication that New Labour has the political commitment to finding this amount of money.

However, what is of more interest to us is the fact that New Labour's main concern is with *child* poverty, to which it added, in 2002, pensioner poverty. By focusing upon these two groups – children and older people – New Labour is in many ways reproducing distinctions between the 'deserving' and 'undeserving' poor based upon demographic characteristics that are accepted as being legitimate reasons for not engaging in paid employment (the individuals are held to be either too young or too old to work). In contrast, people of working age, particularly single people and childless couples, are cast out as being less deserving of state support. These distinctions have concrete consequences for poverty and inequality, for they mean that the social security benefits for children and people of retirement age are increasing at a faster rate than those of people of working age. In April 2005, for instance, JSA increased only by 1 per cent (55 pence per week for a single claimant over the age of 24), compared to the state pension which rose by 3.1 per cent (£2.40 per week for a single pensioner) and the *Child Tax Credit* (CTC) that rose by 4.0 per cent (£1.25 per week). Average earnings were increasing by about 4.4. per cent at the time. What this means is that inequality was increasing not only between benefit recipients and workers, but also between benefit recipients; single and childless unemployed people in particular were becoming poorer compared to those in work and other benefit recipients.

While these distinctions have a moral history in the relief of poverty, New Labour's justification for focusing efforts on child poverty relates to its concern, outlined above, with equality of opportunity. In this line of thinking, children from poorer households can only hope to enjoy the life chances of children from more affluent households if their formative years are not adversely affected by poverty (HM Treasury and Department for Education and Skills 2005). However, the equality of opportunity of children is being pursued at the expense of the poverty and inequality of other social groups, most notably adults of working age.

Social exclusion

The concept of social exclusion has its antecedents in classical sociology (see Levitas 1996, 1998; Born and Jensen 2002; O'Brien and Penna 2007). However, more recently, its employment has been political rather than sociological (R. Lister 2004; O'Brien and Penna 2007). Burchardt *et al.* (1999: 228; see also Evans 1998), for instance, note how the concept of social exclusion 'probably originated in France where it was primarily used to refer to those who slipped through the social insurance system; the socially excluded were those who were administratively excluded by the state'. In the 1980s the idea of social exclusion became an important dimension of the European Union's (EU) anti-poverty programmes. Alcock (2006) notes that the term appeared in the second EU anti-poverty programme in 1988 and notes how from 2000 'all member states [of the EU] have committed themselves to drawing up and regularly reviewing National Action Plans to combat social exclusion'. It is argued that the EU partly adopted the term in order to accommodate the reluctance of some governments (including Britain's) to use the word 'poverty' (Veit-Wilson 1998; R. Lister 2004). While this suggestion is discarded as cynicism by some (Atkinson 1998), there is concern that the term is treated as an alternative to poverty (cf. R. Lister 2004). In this context, it can legitimately be asked how the concepts of poverty and social exclusion differ. R. Lister (*ibid.*) points to two main issues; breadth and dynamism. The argument is that the concept of social exclusion has a greater breadth than that of poverty and, in contrast to poverty which focuses upon an outcome (a lack of income), social exclusion emphasises dynamism, including the processes involved in excluding particular individuals or groups from contemporary society and the need for forward-looking indicators of what people can expect in the future (Atkinson 1998).

It is fair to say, there is lot of scepticism about the use of the concept of social exclusion. Øyen (1997), for example, is critical of what she defines as a 'political rather than analytical concept' (R. Lister 2004: 87). R. Lister (*ibid.*: 98) seems to be less sceptical, but sceptical nevertheless, when she argues that it is 'better understood as a potentially illuminating concept and as a set of political discourses with a range of policy implications'. With regard to the latter, the worry is that through its potential replacement of the concept of poverty the need for more financial resources – the cause of poverty – will be deflected. Fairclough (2000), for instance, points to the way in which Tony Blair in his speech at the launch of the Social Exclusion Unit (SEU) in December 1997 moved from defining social exclusion as being about more than just income to a position which suggested that it was in contrast to poverty and, therefore, it had nothing to do with money at all, an observation also made by Lister (cited in Pantazis 2000: 7).

The concept of social exclusion is also held to be problematic for its potential to individualise exclusion rather than examining it as a structural phenomenon. Atkinson (1998: 14) points to this when he notes that 'in terms of failure to achieve the status of inclusion, we may be concerned not just with a person's situation, but also the extent to which he or she is responsible'. Veit-Wilson (1998) takes the analysis forward in his argument that there are 'strong' and 'weak' versions of the social exclusion discourse. The 'strong' version focuses upon the role of those doing the excluding and, if it is to be tackled, how the power of those who are able to exclude others can be reduced. In contrast, the 'weak' version of social exclusion discourse involves a focus upon the character of the socially excluded. In this scenario policy is aimed at overcoming the character flaws of the excluded.

R. Lister (2004) picks upon such observation when she notes, as we have seen above, that social exclusion is a 'set of political discourses'. The most well known explication of such an argument is Levitas (1998) who argues that there are three ideal typical social exclusion discourses:

- The redistributionist discourse (RED) constructs social exclusion as an issue of social justice and rights. In policy terms the focus is upon tackling structural inequalities.

- The moral underclass discourse (MUD) constructs social exclusion as essentially being the consequence of individual pathology. It is the character, attitude and lifestyle of the excluded that is the problem. Policies structured through MUD take an individualistic approach aimed at including people through changing their attitudes and behaviours.

- The social integrationist discourse (SID) is perhaps the most narrowly focused discourse, for its concern is with unemployment and economic inactivity. Social cohesion can be achieved through the inclusion of workless people in paid employment.

New Labour's social and criminal justice policies reflect a combination of the elements of some or all three discourses. Levitas (*ibid*.: 28), for instance, argues that New Labour has moved 'significantly away from RED towards an inconsistent combination of SID and MUD', while R. Lister (2004: 78) notes that New Labour's 'approach to tackling social exclusion reflects a shifting amalgam of the three'. The centrality of paid work to New Labour's policies most usefully helps to explain why this is the case, for not only is employment held by New Labour to be the most effective means of tackling poverty (and, therefore, reducing the worst excesses of inequality), it is also held to be the most important indicator of social inclusion (Giddens 1998; for discussion see Grover and Stewart 2002). Gordon Brown MP (then Chancellor of the Exchequer), for instance, argued that: 'the most serious cause of poverty is unemployment' (HM Treasury 1997a) and that: 'Lack of work is the most important pathway into poverty and work is the best way out' (Chancellor of the Exchequer 1998: 54). However, it is also the case that worklessness, as we saw above through the argument of Callinicos (2001), is held to be the consequence of the pathological failings of workless people. In this sense, not only is paid work held to be the solution to a range of economic problems for individuals and the British economy, it is also held to have a range of social benefits, including the tackling of offending and anti-social behaviour, that we shall be discussing in this book. Hence, since its election in 1997 New Labour has developed various authoritarian social policy interventions aimed at ensuring that individuals take the opportunities for paid work that are available. The problem here is that the main socio-political concern is with the political economic position of non-employed people. It takes little account of cultural position but, as we shall see, cultural processes are often experienced as exclusionary (O'Brien and Penna 2007).

Outline of the book

There are eight further chapters in this book. Chapter 2 explores theoretical approaches that explain connections between crime and inequality and the evidence that suggests a link between the two. This chapter sets the context for the rest of the book by concluding that while it may be difficult to know exactly what the relationship is between crime and inequality, the former cannot be addressed without focusing on the latter.

Chapter 3 focuses upon young men. In the context of a historically enduring concern with their actions the chapter argues that the predominant explanation of the offending and anti-social behaviour of young men has in recent years been various versions of the 'crisis of masculinity' thesis. The chapter suggests that this has led to a conservative agenda that aims to re-establish the patriarchal family in poorer communities. This, it is hoped, will in a control theory-type argument, help to focus the attention of young men upon paid work and providing for their dependants. The chapter then goes on to examine the social security and labour market policies that have been introduced in the recent past which have attempted to get young men into paid work so that young working-class women can have more confidence in them as 'breadwinners'. The polices are critically discussed and it is argued that attempts to get young men into paid work have not been particularly successful, with the most worrying trend being young people leaving the New Deal for Young People (NDYP) with no indication of what they are doing. Hence, it is argued that, in contrast to engineering the conditions for lowering offending among young men, state interventions may actually be exacerbating them.

Chapter 4 examines the current political and policy interest in relationships between parenting, and offending and anti-social behaviour. This interest is placed in the context of a historical concern with poor working-class families and their alleged inabilities to socialise their young people. The chapter then goes on to examine contemporary concerns with such issues through an examination of the particular form of communitarianism – Anglicanised communitarianism – that helps to structure New Labour's thought. The centrality of the idea of the 'parenting deficit' and the focus upon moral responsibility in all material circumstances are discussed in criminal justice, education, housing and income maintenance policy. The focus upon parenting is problematised, first, because of epistemological issues related to relationships held to exist between offending and anti-social behaviour and parenting; second, because of the consequences of attempting to tackle anti-social behaviour through social policy interventions in the material circumstances of poor people and their families; and, third, because of the punitive impact such policies have, in particular on poor women.

Relationships between women, crime and inequality are examined in Chapter 5. The chapter is divided into three sections. The first explores through the work of Carlen (1988) and Phoenix (1999) relationships between women's offending and their material circumstances. This section demonstrates the complex and sometimes contradictory nature of these relationships, but follows Carlen's argument that the offending of poor women can be explained through the class and sex 'deals' that structure the lives of poor women. The second section discusses the ways in which, as lone mothers, poor women are problematised as being a threat to social order because of an alleged innate inability to provide their children, especially their male children, with the 'correct' role models. The third section discusses the ways in which the state has attempted to manage this issue through attempts to get lone mothers into paid work. Policies that have been developed to accomplish this are critically discussed, and it is argued that, rather than improving the poor material conditions of women, the approach taken by New Labour may exacerbate them, thereby reproducing the material circumstances that help to structure female offending.

Chapter 6 explores relationships between crime, inequality and ethnicity. After demonstrating the inequalities endured by BME people, the chapter goes on to examine relationships between BME people and the criminal justice system. The main focus is upon two periods of uprising: in 1981 in Brixton and in 2001 in some of the former mill towns of West Yorkshire. In this context, the chapter examines relationships between the material conditions of BME people and ideas related to the desirability of multiculturalism in the 1980s and its perceived undesirability in the first decade of the 21st century. It is argued that recently the emphasis has been on improving the material condition of BME people through an approach that does not take account of 'race' or ethnic differences; policies that are relevant to improving the material condition of white people are equally applicable to BME people. Hence, the emphasis upon the importance of paid work and ways of tackling unemployment through education and skills training and connecting BME people to labour markets through policies such as the NDYP. Such developments are problematised because of their relative neglect of workplace racism and because there are indications that the receipt of social security benefits for BME people is likely to become more closely linked to ethnically dependent criteria, such as being able to speak English.

In Chapter 7 we examine the victimisation of poor people by focusing upon a group – street homeless people – that is particularly vulnerable to crime. By using Young's (1999, 2002) work on the 'gaze downwards' of relative deprivation, the chapter argues that offences against street homeless people that are predominantly committed by the 'respectable' can be explained with reference to a vindictiveness that is structured through a moral and financial concern with people who might be a charge upon the public purse through their use of state-sponsored benefits and services. The chapter then goes on to examine recent approaches to tackling street homelessness through the Rough Sleepers Initiative (RSI) and, later, the Homeless Action Plan (HAP). The chapter argues that these strategies have been less successful than recent governments have suggested because they are located in historically familiar discourse that problematises street homeless people as a threat to social order, and because these approaches are also structured through a concern with the responsibilities of street homeless people to help themselves and a desire to demonstrate measurable outcomes of policies that are supposed to address street homelessness.

Chapter 8 focuses upon the use of financial penalties. The chapter examines in the context of Barbara Hudson's work (1995, 1998, 1999, 2000, 2003) attempts in England and Wales to link fines – the most prevalent form of punishment for those convicted of offences – to the income of offenders through unit fines and, later, day fines. The chapter demonstrates that such efforts to formalise links between income and fines have been unsuccessful because they are seen as a challenge to liberal notions of law; they are accused of being unfair for better-off people. The chapter then goes on to examine the ability given to courts in the 1991 Criminal Justice Act to deduct from some social security benefits the fines of those who had defaulted. While this move was introduced in an attempt to reduce the number of fine defaulters who were imprisoned, the chapter argues that the loss of control of what can be a substantial part of the income of benefit recipients helps to reproduce the material basis of offending. This is a point that is also made with reference to the 2000 Child Support, Pensions and Social Security Act that allowed, in pilot areas initially, for the withdrawal of benefits from those people who were held not to be complying with their community punishments.

Chapter 2

Crime and inequality

Introduction

This chapter focuses upon three issues: inequality in contemporary society, evidence of relationships between crime and inequality and its indicators, and theoretical explanations of connections between crime and inequality. The chapter demonstrates that the UK is a deeply unequal society, with recent policy developments, such as the *National Minimum Wage* (NMW) and the emphasis upon paid work, having done little to arrest inequality. The focus is primarily upon economic inequalities. The gendered and racialised aspects of inequality are discussed in following chapters (5 and 6 respectively). However, in order to set the context for Chapter 3 there is a particular focus in this chapter upon the socio-economic position of young people, who, because of a conjunction of economic orthodoxy and cultural assumptions about their relationships to their birth families, face particularly acute economic disadvantage.

The chapter then goes on to examine evidence of relationships between crime and inequality. The focus is upon economic inequality and crime, and crime and unemployment, one of the strongest predictors of low income. This section demonstrates that there are close relationships between crime, income and wage inequality, and unemployment and crime. One of the main problems with this evidence, however, is that it cannot explain why inequality and crime are related. Hence, the next section focuses upon theoretical explanations of why inequality may be associated with crime. This section examines absolute deprivation and its relationship to rationality, control theory, relativities (anomie and relative deprivation) and cultural criminology. The contribution of each of these to understanding associations between crime and inequality is examined. The chapter concludes that relationships between crime and inequality are complex and that while it may be difficult to prove a causal link between the two, inequality is nevertheless an important contextual factor in explaining crime and this is enough for it to be concerning to policy-makers charged with addressing crime as a socio-economic problem.

Inequalities in contemporary society

Economic inequality

The United Kingdom is a deeply unequal society. In 2002 the wealthiest 1 per cent of the population owned a quarter (24 per cent) of the UK's marketable wealth, while the wealthiest 50 per cent owned the vast majority (94 per cent) of it. This, of course, means that the poorest 50 per cent owned only 6 per cent of marketable wealth. Wealth is also increasingly concentrated among the very rich. In 1976, for example, the wealthiest 5 per cent of the population owned over a third (38 per cent) of marketable wealth. By 2002 they owned 45 per cent.[1] These observations are reflected in changes in the Gini Coefficient (a measure of income inequality). According to the Gini Coefficient, between 1996/7 and 2005/06 there was a statistically significant increase in inequality (Brewer *et al.* 2007). This should, perhaps, not be surprising given that in the decade between 1994/5 and 2004/5 the income of the poorest tenth of the British population increased by about a quarter, compared to over 40 per cent for the richest tenth (Palmer *et al.* 2006, Table 4A: 34).

Poverty: the unacceptable face of inequality

As the 'unacceptable face' of inequality, poverty is notoriously difficult to define, but even on one of the government's own relative definitions of poverty – 60 per cent of the median income after housing costs (see box) – there were 11.4 million people (one fifth of the UK's population) living in poverty in 2001/02 (CPAG 2006). While the number of people living in poverty has been falling in recent years (from, for instance, 13.5 million in 1997/98 – Flaherty *et al.* 2004, Table 2.2: 43), the figure of 11.4 million is still 60 per cent higher than the number of people who were recorded on the same measure as being poor in 1979.

Measuring poverty

The government uses as its headline measure of poverty those people living in households that have an equivalent income below 60 per cent of the median. Figures demonstrating the number and proportions of such households can be found on the Department for Work and Pension's website at http://www.dwp.gov.uk/asd/hbai.asp.

The median household income is the one in the middle of the income distribution. Hence, if you were to list all household incomes the median would be the one with an equal number above and below it. It is not an average.

The median income is measured in two ways: before housing costs (BHC) and after housing costs (AHC). The BHC measure is the net income of all members of a particular household. The AHC measure is the BHC measure less payments made by the household for its housing costs (for instance, rent and mortgage interest payments) and some related expenses, such as water charges and insurance for the structure of the building.

The AHC measure gives a higher proportion of the people living in poverty compared to the BHC measure. So, for instance, in 2005/06 3.8 million (30 per cent of children) were living in poverty according to the AHC measure, while 2.8 million (22 per cent) were living in poverty according to the BHC measure.

It is, therefore, perhaps difficult not to conclude that in its drive to tackle child poverty the government has moved from the AHC measure in relation to its first target that it missed in 2004/05 to the BHC measure for its next target in 2010/2011 to make the target easier to achieve. The target in 2010/2011 is to reduce child poverty by a half compared to the 1998/99 baseline figure. On the BHC figures this will mean a reduction of 1.7 million children living in poor households compared to 2 million under the AHC measure.

Poverty, unemployment and worklessness

As we noted in the previous chapter, the immediate cause of poverty is an inadequate income. The causes of inadequate incomes arise 'primarily from worklessness, and inadequate wages and benefits' (PAG 2006: 2). Of those people in households where the adult(s) are unemployed, it is estimated that nearly three-quarters (71 per cent) are income poor, compared to only four per cent in households where all the adults are in full-time work. It is estimated that there are now more people in paid work in the UK than ever before (National Statistics 2006b, Table D.1) and over the past 15 years, using the International Labour Organisation (ILO) definition, unemployment has fallen by just over 40 per cent from 2.83 million in 1992 to 1.68 million in 2006. Long-term unemployment (defined as that lasting 52 weeks or more) has fallen by an even greater extent, reducing by nearly two-thirds from 990,000 in 1992 to 360,000 in 2006. However, the focus upon unemployment gives a somewhat distorted view, for those recorded as unemployed are not the only people without paid work. In recent years a great deal has been said and written about worklessness (in contrast to unemployment) after it was realised there was a divergence between 'work rich' and 'work poor' households (Gregg and Wadsworth 1996, 2000), denoted by increasing worklessness among working age households. In many ways, New Labour's 'welfare to work-welfare'[2] policies have been concerned with reducing the number of workless households. However, this has only been moderately successful, for despite 10 years of intervention, the proportion of such households has only fallen from 17.4 to 15.8 per cent of working age households. In 2006 there were 2.97 million workless households in the UK containing some 4.20 million people (all figures from National Statistics 2006c).

The extent of worklessness is of concern because of its relationship to poverty. For most people not having paid work means having to claim benefits, many of which are inadequate to bring people to the 'poverty line' if defined as 60 per cent of median (after housing costs). So, for example, in 2004/05 this measure of poverty was £100 for a single person, whereas IS for such a person (over the age of 25) was only £55.65 per week, and was £268 for a couple with two dependent children, whereas the IS rate for such a family was only £160 per week. In this sense, *out-of-work benefit* receipt is easily equated with living below a poverty level income.

We saw in the previous chapter that New Labour has focused upon two groups that are seen as deserving of state support: children and retirement pensioners. The concentration of resources on these groups means that there was a fall in the proportion of them who were poor between 1994/5 and 2004/05 (Palmer *et al.* 2006, Table 3A: 33). However, the number of working age adults without dependent children living in poverty has remained consistent at about a fifth. By 2004/05 a third of all people in low income households were of working age and without dependent children. Indeed, over the last decade while the level of IS for pensioners and families with two or more children has increased relative to earnings, it has fallen sharply for couples with no dependent children and after increasing in the early years of the 21st century, was back to its 1998 level by 2006 for couples with one child (*ibid.*, Table 6A: 36).

A large proportion of workless individuals are claiming *Incapacity Benefit* (IB), a benefit for those deemed too sick or disabled to work. In a critique of political claims that unemployment is a problem that has essentially been solved, Beatty, Fothergill and colleagues (Beatty and Fothergill 2002, 2005; Beatty *et al.* 2000; Fothergill 2001) argue that regional disparities in IB receipt point to a 'diversion from unemployment to sickness benefit' (Beatty and Fothergill 2005: 838). This, they argue, has occurred on a massive scale: over a million people (650,000 men and 470,000 women), suggesting that 'Britain has more "hidden" unemployed among sickness claimants than "visible" unemployed on the claimant count' (*ibid.*: 845). Their explanation of this is a combination of differences in the requirements for receipt, and levels, of benefits for unemployed and sick people that conjoin with a lack of demand for workers in those geographical areas (mainly those previously dominated by primary production and heavy industry) to disadvantage those people with conditions and illnesses that impair, but do not prevent, them from working.

Paid work: the best route out of poverty?

One of the mantras that has structured New Labour's welfare reform agenda is that 'work is the best route out of poverty' (Alan Johnson MP, then Secretary of State for Work and Pensions, cited in Department for Work and Pensions 2005). However, the validity of this claim is questioned by the fact that over half (54 per cent) of children living in poverty are in households where at least one adult is in paid work (CPAG 2006) and that half of working-age adults in poverty are living in households where at least one adult works (Palmer *et al.* 2006: 17). Palmer *et al.* (2006) argue that these observations reflect, in the case of children, a failure in government to recognise the extent of in-work poverty and, in addition, in the case of adults, a lack of clarity on the part of the government regarding who can be classed as being 'unable' to work and to what extent their security should be addressed. In addition, it is also the case that there is confusion at the centre of the government's policy, for arguably its main policies – the NMW and in-work benefits (tax credits that subsidise paid work) – that together New Labour describes as its 'making work pay' strategy are more concerned with maintaining financial less eligibility than they are with tackling poverty (Grover and Stewart 2002; Grover 2005c). This line of argument is related to changes in the wage dispersion from the mid 1970s; the stagnation of wages at the lower end of the earnings distribution was held to clash with levels of out-of-work benefits (cf. Lilley 1994). Hence, there was need for intervention to raise the potential income from entry-level jobs. This is very different to tackling in-work poverty, for the focus is upon providing distance between in-work and out-of-work incomes rather than bringing people up to a particular level of income.

The first ever NMW in the UK was introduced in April 1999. The claim that this was a historic occasion was blunted by its low level (£3.60 per hour for workers aged 22 or over) and lower rates for those aged 18–21 and no wage protection at all for workers under the age of 18. However, since its introduction, the 'adult' rate has increased by nearly one half, so that by October 2006 it was £5.35 per hour. The evidence suggests that the NMW has increased at a rate above the median wages of the lowest paid (Butcher 2005). Since its introduction though it has done little to reduce wage inequalities between the highest and lowest paid (Dickens and Manning 2004). So, for example, between April 2004 and April 2005 it was only the lowest paid 4 per cent and highest paid 25 per cent of workers who saw increases in wages above the increase in the median (Low Pay Commission 2006). Moreover, and as we have already noted, even with the introduction of the NMW, having paid employment is not a guarantee of an above-poverty income. Indeed, a person on the NMW working the average number of hours (32) in 2006/07 (*ibid.*) would receive a gross income of only £171.20 per week; below, for example, the poverty line (defined as 60 per cent of the median, after housing costs) for childless couples, and for both couples and lone parents with two dependent children (CPAG 2006).

New Labour believes, however, as governments before it have done, that capitalism will not pay wages high enough to ensure the social reproduction of children and other dependents of workers. Hence, the 'making work pay' strategy through in-work benefits (tax credits) seeks to subsidise low wages and/or part-time employment of 16 hours or more per week. In 2004/05 wages were subsidised through tax credits by over £11 billion, a growth of over 10 per cent on the 2003/04 figure[3] (extrapolated from National Statistics 2006d, Table 2.1). While it is argued that the subsidisation of low pay made a significant contribution to the fall in the number of children living in poverty between 1998/99 and 2004/05 (Brewer *et al.* 2006), it is also the case that in the longer term, it is feared that it will help establish the NMW as a maximum, rather than a minimum wage (Grover 2006).

Young people: particularly disadvantaged

In the previous section we examined different aspects of inequality in contemporary society. Little attempt was made to disaggregate the data by demographic factors. In this section, however, we begin to do this by focusing upon the position of young people in order to provide the context for the following chapter and because we know that young people are responsible for a large amount of offending and anti-social behaviour. As in the previous section, we focus upon unemployment, wages and benefit entitlements.

Unemployment

While we must not underestimate the fragility and unpleasantness of the work performed by working-class young people in the post-Second World War period (Mizen 2004), it is fair to say that until the 1970s unemployment was not a great concern for them. As Kemp (2005: 140) notes: 'For much of the post-war period up to the mid-1970s, the majority of young people left school at 16 with relatively few qualifications and entered a restricted range of occupations.' However, all this was to change with the global economic upheavals of the 1970s. Young workers have always had a more precarious relationship with paid employment compared to older workers. However, it is possible to argue that unemployment has a disproportionate effect, or as Mizen (2004: 53) describes it, a 'calamitous impact' on young people. This is particularly worrying because unemployment is concentrated among young people.

In the early 1980s, the increasing number of young unemployed people was a cause of popular and political concern. Mungham (1982) demonstrates how the press, for example, was full of stories about a 'time bomb' of youth unemployment. In short, young unemployed people were seen as a threat to social stability, a threat that was realised in the urban disturbances of 1981 and 1984. By 1985 about four in 10 (38.5 per cent) of unemployed people were aged under 25 (Department of Employment 1985, Table 2.5). This figure remained remarkably constant for many years, for by the year 2000, despite investment in the *New Deal for Young People* (NDYP), young people, according to the ILO definition, still accounted for over a third (34.6 per cent) of all unemployed people (National Statistics 2006e, Table C.1). In more recent years, the position of young people *vis-à-vis* unemployment has worsened. By 2006 people under the age of 25 accounted for over four in 10 of unemployed people (*ibid.*). This is twice as many as might be expected if unemployment were spread evenly across age cohorts.

Perhaps more importantly, young people are also adversely affected by long-term unemployment. In the mid 1980s, for instance, they accounted for nearly one in three (27.7 per cent) of long-term unemployed people (Department of Employment 1985, Table 2.5). While, in the late 1990s and early years of the first decade of the 21st century, the proportion of long-term unemployed accounted for by young people did decrease to a level that one would expect if it were spread evenly across ages, in more recent years, it has once again increased. By 2006, as a proportion of all long-term unemployed, it was at a similar level (26. 7 per cent) to that of the mid-1980s (extrapolated from National Statistics 2006e, Table C.1). The number of long-term unemployed people of all ages is a lot lower in 2006 compared to the mid 1980s. However, the proportion who are aged under the age of 25 contradicts the claim the government makes that it has 'eradicated long-term unemployment' among young people (Blair 2006a: 2)

Wages

Young people have not enjoyed increases in wages over the past 30 years to the same extent as older people, for their wages have lagged behind increases in the average. So, for example, between 1980 and 2005 the average weekly wage for full-time adult male workers increased by approximately 475 per cent. However, for those male workers aged 16 to 21 years the average increase was 378 per cent (extrapolated from Department of Employment 1981 and National Statistics 2005). These changes are reflected in the proportion of wages earned by young workers compared to all workers. As Table 2.1. demonstrates, in 1980 male workers aged under 18 and working full time could expect to earn a little over 40 per cent of the average for all workers, while those aged 18–20 could expect to earn about two-thirds (63.6 per cent) and those aged 21–24 years over 80 per cent. However, by 2003 the figures had decreased for all workers aged under 24 by about a fifth (19.3 per cent in the case of under 18-year-olds, 23.7 per cent for those aged 18–20, and 19.8 per cent for workers aged 21 to 24 years).

Orthodox economic arguments would suggest that the wages of young people have not kept pace with earnings more generally because of a lack of commitment to, or a lack of human capital for, paid work among young people. However, as we shall see below,

Table 2.1 Changes in the proportion of the average weekly wage paid to young workers (male, full time) 1980 and 2003

	1980	2003	Per cent change
Under 18 years	40.4	32.6	–19.3
18–20 years	63.3	48.3	–23.7
21–24 years	81.8	65.6	–19.8

Notes: extrapolated from Department of Employment (1981, Table 10) and National Statistics (2004, Table F7).

there has also been concerted efforts in policy interventions to reduce the wage expectations of young people, arguably providing the most convincing explanation of why young people are particularly poorly paid.

The relatively poor position of young workers in relation to wages has been institutionalised through the introduction of the NMW. When first introduced in April 1999 there were two rates for the NMW; a main rate of £3.60 per hour and a 'development rate' of £3.00 per hour, payable mainly to workers aged 18–21. Economic considerations framed the level of the development rate. The lower rate for younger workers was justified as reflecting the fact that younger people accept lower wages in return for on-the-job training. However, given that many available jobs require few formal qualifications or training (Felstead *et al.* 2002) and that a fifth (21.4 per cent) of workers feel they required less than a month to 'learn to do [their] job well' (Performance and Innovation Unit, 2001, Figure 9), it is difficult not to conclude that this was a spurious justification for a policy that was consistent with that of the preceding two decades, of placing downward pressure on the wages of young people (Grover and Stewart 2002; Mizen 2004) and which certainly helped maintain wage differentials between younger and older workers.

At least 18–21-year-olds had some protection from very low wages through the introduction of the NMW. The youngest workers (aged 16 and 17) had to wait another five years for a NMW of £3.00 per hour in order to: 'prevent [their] exploitation and encourage young people to view themselves as valued members of the workforce' (Low Pay Commission 2004: para. 4). By October 2007 a situation existed whereby 18–21-year-olds had a minimum wage rate (£4.60 per hour) that was about four-fifths (83.3 per cent) of the main NMW of £5.52 per hour, while 16–17-year-old workers had protection (£3.40 per hour) of about three-fifths (61.6 per cent) of the main rate. However, it is not just national governments that are guilty of institutionalising unfair and unfounded wage differentials between younger and older workers. For example, the Greater London Authority's (2005a, 2005b, 2006) call for a 'Fairer London' through the development of a living wage is structured through similar concerns: '£7.05 per hour as a living wage for London' (Greater London Authority 2006: v), except for young (aged 16–20) Londoners for whom the Greater London Authority recommends a living wage of £6.00 per hour (15 per cent below the main rate). As with the justification for the lower rate of NMW for young workers, it is argued that this lower rate reflects the fact that young people have 'relative labour market inexperience and that they are acquiring training, whether formal or on the job' (Greater London Authority 2005a: 6).

Benefits

We have noted that unemployment is a phenomenon that is dis-proportionately concentrated among young people. This is problematic in a social sense, but also financially because young people receive less in benefit payments than older people do. So, for example, in 2006/07 IS and income-based JSA, the main social assistance benefits were a fifth lower for 18–24 year olds than they were for those aged 25 and over. Young people aged 16 and 17, except in tightly drawn circumstances that are related to familial separation, are excluded from receiving such benefits altogether. Where 16- and 17-year-olds do qualify for benefit – and these will be some of the most vulnerable in society – they are entitled to only three-fifths of the main 'adult rate' of IS and income-based JSA.

Poverty

Given these disadvantages that young people face, it is perhaps not surprising that Iacovou et al. (2007) found a poverty rate[4] of nearly 1 in 5 (18.8 per cent) for those people aged 16 to 30 years. However, within this group, younger people were those who were more likely to be living in poverty. So, for example, 16–19-year-olds had a poverty rate of 22.7 per cent compared to 14.3 per cent for 25–29-year-olds. Iacovou et al. explained these findings with reference to factors that structure child poverty, such as lack of parental employment for the younger cohort of youth (aged 16–19) and leaving the parental home for the older cohort of youth (aged 25–29). However, events such as leaving home do not have to be associated with poverty. As we shall see in Chapter 3, social policy in Britain has developed over the past couple of decades partly as a means of deterring young people from leaving their parental home and setting themselves up independently of their parents. Iacovou *et al.* (*ibid.*) though, do rightly highlight that if poverty among young people is to be successfully tackled then it is not enough for them simply to obtain paid employment; they need stable jobs that have a degree of longevity.

Crime and inequality

We saw in the previous chapter that the prison population is made up of people who come from a background of poor material and financial circumstances. However, it is also argued that the connection between crime and inequality is at best tenuous, and at worst non-existent. There are empirical and theoretical reasons for such arguments. With reference to the empirical reasons, analysts point to the existence of white-collar crime (see Sutherland 1949; Braithwaite 1984; Nelken 2002), which is often committed by those who might not be considered as deprived. Furthermore, self-report studies demonstrate that offending, particularly among children and young people, is undertaken by people from all socio-economic backgrounds (Anderson *et al.* 1994; Graham and Bowling 1995). In essence, the argument is that to focus upon inequality and poor material circumstances as an explanation of offending and anti-social behaviour over-predicts the crimes of the socially and economically marginal. However, the following sections that discuss empirical and theoretical approaches to exploring relationships between crime and inequality will demonstrate that the two are, in fact, closely linked.

Crime and Inequality: the evidence

Income inequality

Box (1987: 96) notes that: 'Income inequality is strongly related to criminal activity – with the exception of homicide. It should be emphasised that no existing research has produced results which contradict this.' This observation was premised upon a review of 16 studies conducted between 1975 and 1984. More recent research supports Box's conclusions. This research has tended to focus upon the relationships between wage inequalities and crime. This is perhaps not surprising, given the observations noted above, because, by the beginning of the 1990s, Britain had the greatest levels of wage inequality since records were first kept in the late 19th century (Balls 1993; Osbourne and Nichol 1996). Witt *et al.* (1999: 398; see also Witt *et al.* 1998) concluded that: 'high crime is associated with ... high wage inequality associated with the distribution of weekly earnings of full-time manual men.' Others have focused upon low wages. Machin and Meghir (2004), for instance, found that the relative decrease in the wage of low paid workers between 1975 and 1996 led to increases in property crime. The general thrust of their argument – that wages are closely related to crime – was buttressed by Hansen and Machin (2002) who examined the effect of the introduction of the NMW in England and Wales in April 1999. In line with the predictions of the economic model of crime – that individuals 'choose between legal and illegal work on the basis of their relative reward' (Hale 2005: 335) – Hansen and Machin (2002) found there was a statistically significant link between changes in crime and the extent of low pay before the NMW was introduced, despite the fact that the largest proportion of beneficiaries of the NMW were women (Low Policy Commission 2001) who, generally speaking, are less likely to commit crime compared to men. Such findings are not unique to England and Wales. Research in the USA, for instance, suggests that 'falling real wages may have been an important determinant of rising youth crime during the 1970s and 1980s' (Grogger 1998: 756) and that wage inequality is linked to violent crime (Fowles and Merva 1996; Wilkinson 2004). The implication of these findings is that although paid work is held up as being one of the most important solutions to crime, the structure of contemporary labour markets means it is unlikely to have as powerful an effect as it is often thought to do in terms of addressing crime (Downes 1998).

Benefit receipt and crime

Given the parameters of the economic model of crime, it might be expected that changes in benefit levels will impact upon levels of crime. While there has not been research into the effect of the general relationship between benefit levels and offending, the introduction of the JSA in October 1996 did give Machin and Marie (2006) the opportunity to consider the effect of a major change in benefit provision on crime levels. They found that crime rose by more in the areas most affected by JSA, and, hence argued, 'that toughening the benefit regime can have an unintended consequence, namely increases in crime' (*ibid.*: 149). The findings of Machin and Marie are particularly relevant to our concerns because benefits for other claimant groups, most notably lone mothers and disabled people are to be increasingly structured through *benefit sanctions*. In the future, for instance, lone mothers will have to submit to the JSA regime in order to claim benefit (discussed in Chapter 5), while a new *Employment and Support Allowance* (ESA) is to be introduced for sick and disabled claimants from 2008. The ESA introduces benefit sanctions for sick and disabled claimants who are thought capable of work, but not making enough effort to enter it. Further empirical work is required to examine the likely impact on crime of these changes in income maintenance policy.

Unemployment and crime

Hakim (1982: 450) argued that the literature she reviewed (published between 1925 and 1981) suggested that:

> Three processes appear to operate: unemployment increases recidivist crime; parental and youth unemployment increase juvenile delinquency (which can form the basis for eventual adult criminality); and unemployment increases reconviction, the rate of imprisonment and the size of the prison population.

In the mid 1980s though, Hakim was in a minority. Her argument, that there was clear evidence of important relationships between crime and unemployment, was contradicted by other claims that suggested either the relationships were weak (Long and Witte 1981; Box 1987), or remained unproven (Tarling 1982; Carr-Hill and Stern 1979). Hence, Chiricos (1987: 188) describes there being a 'consensus of doubt' regarding the relationships between crime and unemployment between the mid 1970s and mid 1980s.

However, Chiricos goes on to argue that evidence of a positive relationship between crime and unemployment is more common in studies using data after the 1970s (the work, for instance, of Carr-Hill and Stern and Tarling had been based upon pre-1970s evidence). In many ways, this should not be surprising, for unemployment rose to unprecedented levels in the mid 1980s. In addition, long-term unemployment became a particular problem. This is important if, as Pyle and Deadman (1994: 339) highlight in the context of Box's (1987) work, 'those who feel that unemployment is a purely temporary phenomenon may view the possible acquisition of a criminal record as a rather heavy price to pay for avoiding a few weeks of economic hardship'. While Field (1990) could find no evidence of a statistical relationship between unemployment and crime at a general level, his analysis did suggest 'that unemployment – perhaps long term unemployment in particular – and the material deprivation that goes with it may be a causal factor in crimes of violence against the person' (*ibid*.: 8). Using data from the 1992 British Crime Survey, Elliott and Ellingworth (1996: 86) found 'positive, but not necessarily significant relationships between unemployment and measures of crime, employing cross-sectional data'. Two years later, after further developing their statistical techniques, they (Elliott and Ellingworth 1998: 529) were able to conclude that there existed a 'significant positive relationship between male unemployment and property crime'. Hale's (1998: 694) analysis observes that if 'unemployment increases year to year then other things being equal the models show that burglary and robbery will increase'. Disaggregating the official crime statistics to a regional level, Carmichael and Ward (2000: 559) found a 'systematic positive relationship between burglary rates and male unemployment, regardless of age'.

There are, however, at least two critiques of the strand of quantitative criminology that the above studies are located within. First, it is argued that it is inherently sexist. With the exception of Box and Hale (1983, 1984, 1985) and Box (1987), Naffine and Gale (1989) point to the lack of interest in examining relationships between women's unemployment and the crimes committed by women. This lack of interest, they suggest, is due to cultural assumptions about the role of women in society, in particular what is imagined as their relatively marginal role in paid employment. Unemployment is seen 'as such a calamity that it provokes criminal activity' (*ibid*.: 144) only when men are its victims. However, they suggest that their evidence from Australia creates problems for those who claim that unemployment is a cause of crime, for they could find little evidence of a relationship between female unemployment and crime.

Second, Farrington et al. (1986: 336) argue that aggregate studies of relationships between unemployment and crime are problematic because they say little about 'which might cause which' (does unemployment cause crime or vice versa?) and 'even if unemployment rates and crime rates are correlated over time or place, this does not necessarily mean that unemployed individuals are more likely to commit crimes than employed individuals'. In contrast, Farrington et al. (*ibid*.) suggest that 'in order to draw conclusions about individuals, it is necessary to carry out research based on individuals'. Their own work – the Cambridge Study in Delinquent Development – found that crime rates were higher for periods of unemployment compared to periods of employment, particularly for crimes involving material gain.

Dickinson (1995) highlights results found by Northumbria police who, in their study of the employment status of offenders, found that unemployed people accounted for a number of offenders that was disproportionate to their number in the population more generally. So, for example, in 1980 56 per cent of burglaries involved unemployed people when unemployed people accounted for only 12.1 per cent of the population in the north of England. This study, however, is problematic because it focuses upon those crimes that were known about and cleared up. So while it might be the case that unemployed people accounted disproportionately for those crimes that were known about, it is not known what proportion of those crimes that were not cleared up were committed by unemployed people. Studies such as that carried out by the Northumbria constabulary say more about the operational biases of the agencies that make up the criminal justice system than they do about whether unemployment is a cause of crime.

The material circumstances of offenders

It is clear from other studies that the material circumstances of offenders is marked by acute socio-economic disadvantage. Stewart and Stewart (1993), for example, focused upon the socio-economic circumstances of 1,389 young people who had committed various offences, but mainly crimes of dishonesty. Their findings were stark: 64 per cent of their respondents were unemployed (10 times the national average rate of unemployment of 6.7 per cent), ranging from 51 per cent in the West Midlands to 76 per cent in Northumbria (*ibid.*: 21). Unemployed 17-year-olds in the study had the lowest incomes; four in 10 (38 per cent) of such young people said they had no weekly income at all. In total, two-thirds of respondents had an income of £40 or less a week. For offenders, 'financial difficulties were more often characterized by the interviewees as a factor directly related to their offending behaviour' (*ibid.*, para. 5.10). This was made clear in qualitative interviews with 59 of the survey respondents and in notes provided by probation officers. Probation officers considered the poor financial situation of offenders, coupled with addiction, to be the most important aspects of young people's social circumstances related to their offending. Female and younger offenders (17-year-olds) were most likely to be described by probation officers as offending for reasons related to their poverty. A related exercise (Smith and Stewart 1997) compared the socio-economic condition of young probation clients in the early 1990s to that of probation clients in the mid 1960s. It demonstrated how the material circumstances of such people have become markedly worse. In 1991 only 21 per cent of clients were employed compared to 59 per cent in 1965, while the proportion of probation clients with no income at all was four times higher in 1991 than it was in 1965.

Explaining connections between crime and inequality

In the previous section we examined the evidence of relationships between crime and inequality. On balance, this research suggested that crime and inequality are closely linked, even if it is not clear if inequality causes crime. However, the studies that we focused upon did not and cannot explain why crime and inequality are linked. Hence, in this section we focus upon criminological theory to illuminate why we might expect crime and inequality to be closely related.

Absolute deprivation: crime as a survival strategy

The idea that crime might have its roots in absolute deprivation is something that is not really countenanced in contemporary criminological thought. There are several reasons for this. First, such arguments were undermined when crime rates increased alongside increasing affluence. So, for example, Taylor (1997) argues that the work of the Marxist criminologist, Willem Bonger (1916) that suggested crime was the consequence of the spread of 'egoistic' sentiments among the working-class, evidenced by 'the relative willingness of workers to engage in crime for material survival, particularly in response to periods of unemployment or penury' (Taylor 1997: 273), 'lost power and influence when improved economic circumstances in the mid to late 1930s failed to produce any radical reduction in the scale of the problem of crime' (ibid.: 274). Similar arguments might be made of the fact that crime rates increased in the post-Second World War period, a period that was marked by increases, on average, in wealth. Second, to suggest that crime might be explained as a response to absolute deprivation implies that it is a rational response to a particular set of material disadvantages. However, the view of crime as a utilitarian response to material circumstance is criticised as being overly deterministic and partial (Young 2003).

It can be argued though that such critiques of relationships between absolute deprivation and crime do not take account of the lived realities of poverty and low income. General increases in wealth, as we have seen, are not necessarily the best measure of how people at the lower end of the distribution are faring and we know from research with poor families that being in receipt of benefits is often experienced as a period of extreme hardship when individuals and families barely have enough money to cover even their subsistence needs (Cohen *et al.* 1992; Beresford *et al.* 1999). Hence, it might be premature to dismiss possible links between absolute deprivation and crime. The point is perhaps best made by people engaged in criminal activity. In her study of the role of poverty in the lives of female offenders, for instance, Carlen (1988: 114) quotes two women who linked at least some of their offending to what might be considered absolute levels of need.

Donna, for instance, told the judge at her trial for prostitution-related offences: 'I don't do this just for money or to buy myself gold and clothes. I do it to be able to eat and sleep somewhere for the night.' While a cynic might suggest that Donna was making such comments to engender a sense of sympathy in light of her court appearance, there is nothing in her biography and that of the others in Carlen's study to suggest that this was the case. Similarly, Carlen (*ibid.*) quoted Jean as saying:

We used to sign on Thursday and get his money on a Saturday. Sometimes it never used to come till Monday. So we was left starving. How can you tell my kids – one's 5 and one's nearly 6 – when they're crying and hungry, that they have to wait 'til Monday? If I didna pinch it, we'd have to go round scrounging. It were horrible.

'Inadequate' and 'unreliable' are familiar complaints about social security payments (Beresford *et al.* 1999), and here Jean is directly linking these factors to her offending. While, of course, what one eats and where one sleeps may be considered relative experiences, these two women were not talking about the quality, or otherwise, of the food they had to eat or where they lived. In contrast, they were arguing that they could not afford either in the case of Donna, and the former in the case of Jean.

Relativities: anomic strain and relative deprivation
The origins of concerns regarding relationships between relativities and crime can be traced to the work of Robert Merton (1938). Merton's focus was upon what he saw as contradictions in American

society of the 1930s; between culturally defined goals emphasising the importance of material and financial success (the 'American Dream') and a social structure that meant many people could not obtain these goals legitimately. America in the 1930s was characterised by high levels of joblessness and poverty. Four years after the Wall Street Crash of 1929 and in the midst of the Great Depression, about 15 million men, one-third of the work force, were unemployed (Piven and Cloward 1972: 49). By the winter of 1934, 20 million people (one-sixth of the population) were on the 'dole'. In 1933 the federal government did intervene with the introduction of the Federal Emergency Relief Act. However, even after this not all states intervened to relieve poverty (*ibid.*: 74).

It was this contradiction (or 'strain') between the focus upon material and financial success on the one hand, and a lack of opportunity to legitimately gain these success goals on the other hand, that Merton argued led to anomie, a condition of normlessness. To manage this process of strain, Merton argued, individuals could take one of five adaptive strategies, the most important of which for our purposes are conformity and innovation. Despite the tensions, Merton argued, the vast majority of Americans were conformists, accepting both the goals and the institutionalised means of gaining them. According to Downes and Rock (1988: 126), the 'mass of middle America remained small-town Puritans, wedded to cautious advancement but with an eye to the main chance. Their conformity ensured some social stability.' The innovative adaptation 'basically involved the adoption of illegitimate means to the attainment of the cultural goal, "money-success"' (*ibid.*). Merton's ideas were particularly influential in the 1950s and 1960s, providing the theoretical basis for further developments in criminological thinking, including some versions of sub-cultural theory (for instance, Cohen 1955; Cloward and Ohlin 1960) and, according to Box (1981), Matza's (1964) refutation of sub-cultural theory in his ideas on delinquency and drift.

Merton's work was focused upon relative notions of deprivation. People may have felt deprived because they were unable to access legitimately those life chances upon which most emphasis was placed in the 'American Dream'. In this sense, Merton was clear that absolute deprivation was unlikely to lead to deviant adaptations. He quoted, for instance, the poor countries of south-east Europe which, he argued, did not have the deviancy rates of the USA because, while they had more poverty and deprivation, they did not have the American Dream mentality. Hence, Young (1999: 81) notes of Merton: 'it is not material deprivation per se, *nor* the lack of opportunity which give rise to crime, but deprivation in the context of the "American Dream" culture where meritocracy is exhorted as open to all.'

It is often argued (Yar and Penna 2004; Jones 2006) that Young uses Mertonian strain theory in *The Exclusive Society* (Young 1999) and its condensed version (Young 2002) to explain offending in late modern society. However, Young (2006) argues that he actually uses relative deprivation as the basis of his explanatory framework, rather than strain theory. The difference between the two is their differing points of reference. In the case of Mertonian strain theory it is a 'general goal' of culturally defined successes (*ibid.*: 350). In the case of relative deprivation the point of reference is between groups. In this sense, relative deprivation 'occurs where individuals or groups subjectively perceive themselves as unfairly disadvantaged over others perceived as having similar attributes and deserving similar rewards' (*ibid.*: 349–350).

Relative deprivation is the explanatory tool of Left Realists, of whom Young is the leading proponent. Young (1999: 9) notes how:

> Relative deprivation is conventionally thought of as a gaze upwards: it is the frustration of those denied equality in the market place to those of equal merit and application. But deprivation is also a gaze downwards: it is dismay at the relative well-being of those who although below on the social hierarchy are perceived as unfairly advantaged: they make too easy a living even if it is not as good as one's own.

Following on, relative deprivation helps explain both high crime rates (the gaze upwards) and the authoritarian response – what Young (2002, 2003) describes as vindictiveness – to the crimes of a structurally explained underclass (the gaze downwards). In this sense, Young argues that contemporary society can metaphorically be understood as bulimic; it 'consumes and culturally assimilates masses of people through education, the media and participation in the market place' (1999: 82), but 'systematically in the job market, on the streets in day-to-day contacts with the outside world practises exclusion' (2002: 469). While the language of New Labour may be around inclusion, Young points out the contradictions of attempting to include people through such practices as paid work and its enforcement through policies such as the New Deals; practices that many people experience as being exclusionary.

In contrast to many theorists, from both the Left (Wilson 1987) and the Right (Murray 1984, 1990, 1994), who define crime in terms of a breakdown of culture, Young (2002: 468–469; also Young 2003) argues that poorer people are fully incorporated into mainstream culture. In the case of the USA, for instance, he draws on Nightingale's (1993) ethnography of the Black Philadelphian ghetto, to argue:

> Here is full immersion in the American Dream: a culture hooked on Gucci, BMW, Nikes, watching television eleven hours a day, sharing mainstream culture's obsession with violence, backing (at the time of study) Bush's involvement in the Gulf War, lining up outside the cinema, worshipping success, money, wealth and status – even sharing in a perverse way the racism of wider society.

It is through such observations that Young (2003; Hayward and Young 2004) has examined the possibilities of inflecting his approach with arguments from cultural criminology.

Cultural criminology

Among other things, cultural criminology is concerned with the attraction of transgression and law breaking. Following Katz (1988), one strand of cultural criminology is concerned with the aetiology of offending by engaging with its emotionality. For its advocates, this focus offers advantages – particularly the depth of understanding of offending and transgression – over other criminologies, especially those in administrative and positivistic traditions. Young (2003), for instance, argues that the view of crime as an essentially utilitarian act in positivistic criminologies is unable to account fully for law breaking and transgression. He also suggests that such criminologies are structured through assumptions and narratives that 'jump from deprivation to crime' without attempting to explain the processes involved. In addition, cultural criminology is said to be able to deal with the overly deterministic nature of posivistic criminologies by explaining through the emotionality of offending why, under shared social conditions, not all people engage in offending and transgression (Hayward 2002), although O'Brien (2005) casts doubt upon whether it is actually able to do this.

It might also be argued that cultural criminology can explain offending in all social classes, for there is little to make us suppose that better off people do not themselves seek the 'adrenalin and excitement, terror and pleasure' of criminality (Ferrell 1998, cited in Hayward and Young 2004: 264). This claim needs to be understood in the context of the argument that for large numbers of people the 'chaotic and uneven' world of late modern society 'throws up feelings of melancholia and uncertainty' (Hayward 2002: 84).

The point though should not be overemphasised, for while such feelings may be widespread, it is also the case that legitimate pursuits to address such feelings are income-dependent. Higher incomes, for example, brings access to activities, such as hang gliding, sky diving and skiing, that Lyng (1990) describes as 'edgework' (voluntary risk taking). However, and in an argument that although focusing upon access to securing particular feelings, has resonances of strain theory, Hayward (2002: 86) points to the fact that licit avenues to 'risk, hedonism and excitement' are contingent upon class, gender and neighbourhood and, because of this, 'if one is not able to escape one's social environment to engage in licit risk taking or edgework activities, one has to find alternative outlets to play out these emotions.'

For people who are marginalised in contemporary society this takes on particular significance as:

> the run-down estate or ghetto becomes the paradoxical space; on the one hand it symbolizes the systematic powerlessness so often felt by the individuals who live in such environments, and on the other the sink estate serves as a site of consumption that provides numerous illegal activities. The ghetto becomes a 'performance zone' in which displays of risk, excitement, masculinity and even 'carnivalesque pleasure' in the form of rioting are frequently perpetuated. (*ibid.*)

It is this theme that Young (2003: 408) extends, for in criticising earlier expositions of cultural criminology, in particular Katz (1988), he argues that the structural factors that Katz asserts are background in explaining crime, need to be foregrounded, alongside the emotionality emphasised in cultural criminology:

> the structural predicament of the ghetto poor is not simply a deficit of goods – as Merton would have it – it is a state of humiliation. And crime, because it is driven by humiliation not by some simple desire to redistribute property is transgressive. The theory of bulimia which I have proposed involves incorporation and rejection, cultural inclusion and structural exclusion, as with Merton, but it goes further than this emphasizing that this combination of the acceptance followed by rejection generates a dynamic of resentment of great intensity. *It is Merton with energy, it is Katz with structure* [emphasis in the original].

45

Social control theory: the ties that bind

> Well, there is crime where I live ... there is a lot of poverty and
> there's crime. How you tackle it I don't know because if people
> haven't got enough money to live on, what else do they do?
> They get to the end of their tether and then they think, 'Well,
> what have I got to lose by taking something that belongs to
> somebody else? What have I got to lose? Nothing.' (Beresford
> *et al.* 1999: 112)

While this quote may be interpreted as being overly deterministic, it
points to social control theories that, rather than focusing upon why
people commit crime, question why people obey rules and laws.

Downes and Rock (1998: 235) note that the antecedents of control
theories have a 'formidable pedigree. They can be traced back
through Durkheim to Hobbes and to Aristotle.' However, Hopkins-
Burke (2001) argues that the most important contribution to modern
social control theories came from Travis Hirschi (1969). For Hirschi
(1969: 16) 'delinquent acts result when an individual's bond to society
is weak or broken.' Hirschi identified four elements of the social
bond:

- attachment: sensitivity to the opinion of others (Taylor 2001: 372);
- commitment: the extent to which an individual is committed to
  conventionality;
- involvement: the extent to which an individual is involved in
  conventional activities;
- belief: the extent to which people believe they should obey society's
  rules.

> These four elements: interact to produce an ideal-typical portrait
> of a non-delinquent who is strongly attached to conventional
> others, strongly committed to conventional activities, heavily
> involved in them, and imbued with a strong belief in the need
> to obey the rules. The delinquent is relatively free from such
> controls, and hence more at risk of deviation. (Downes and
> Rock 1998: 240)

With resonances of Matza's (1964) work, Downes and Rock (1998: 240)
argue that even if a person is relatively free from controls, 'deviation
is not ... automatic or determined: it is simply no longer ruled out
as a possibility'.

While social control theory is criticised as lacking an explanation of the motivation (beyond the lack of control) for offending (Smith 1995) and Hirschi later developed his own ideas, emphasising self-control over social control (Gottfredson and Hirschi 1990), the idea that offending is related to the strength of the social bond is particularly pertinent to examining relationships between crime and inequality. This is because arguably the poorest people have the fewest reasons for accepting societal rules and being wholly committed to them.

Some expositions of relationships between social exclusion and crime have resonances of social control theory. Blair (2006b: 3, emphasis added), for instance, argued in the context of announcing the need for a Minister for Social Exclusion:

> We intervene too late [in the lives of children]. We spend without asking how effective is the spending. These are the children who are the clients of many agencies of Government but the charges of no-one, prey to drugs, into crime and anti-social behaviour, lacking in self-belief, *lacking a basic stake in the society into which they are born*. It isn't good enough. This is not a caring country whilst we allow such hopelessness to go unchecked.

Blair's comments are tainted by economic and administrative concerns (cost and the effectiveness of services) and are overly dramatic. However, they do point to potential relationships between not having a 'stake in society' and offending and anti-social behaviour.

To understand what happens when that stake or bond is weakened or non-existent, we can point to the work of Carlen (1988). Carlen (1988: 11, original italics) employed social control theory to understand the relationships between poverty and female offending. She analyses 'the particular combinations of circumstances at the specific points in their criminal careers when [the] thirty-nine women [in her study] felt that they had absolutely *nothing* to lose (and maybe *something* to gain) by engaging in criminal activity'. Carlen's work demonstrates the complex interaction of social and economic factors involved in processes that can lead to the social bond weakening. As she notes, the scarring of the lives of the women in her study by poor material circumstances, violence and abuse, and brutalisation through institutional care, meant that they had little to lose by engaging in offending behaviour.

Willott and Griffin (1999) examined the interconnections between masculinity, the state and offending behaviour by interviewing 66

47

working-class men who were serving custodial sentences or who were on probation orders. The authors were interested in how the men explained their criminal actions. In doing so, the men drew on a discourse of breadwinning masculinity to argue that they were expected to provide for their families. When they were unemployed they could not fulfil this role and therefore saw crime as a way of being able to express their 'real' or hegemonic masculinity. However, the importance of offending in the construction of their masculine identity could not be separated from what they saw as their distant relationship to the state. In this respect the men argued that the state had broken its promises (for example, in terms of managing employment levels) and they were suffering because of it. Because they were suffering the broken promises of the state they should not be expected to conform to its rules. The majority of the men talked about earning through crime as being a last resort, their actions framed by a Robin Hood-type narrative of 'what they did to whom'. In other words, the men essentially positioned 'themselves as decent folk who are forced into "crime" by a knowing and unjust State system' (*ibid.*: 451). In this scenario, the breaking of the social contract between the state and the individual had the effect of releasing the men from their part of the contract that included acting in a law-abiding manner.

Conclusion

This chapter has shown the deep inequalities that exist in contemporary society. It has also examined the research evidence that demonstrates relationships between crime and inequality, and theoretical explanations that help us to make sense of those empirical findings. Stewart and Stewart (1993, para. 8.5) warn that with regard to offending and material circumstance it is not possible to draw 'a simple and generally applicable causal relationship ... [that can] be statistically established: the obvious cannot necessarily be proved in a scientific sense to the satisfaction of those who hold contrary beliefs'. It is perhaps best not to seek a single cause of offending, or even to seek a causal relationship at all. Critical criminologists, for example, argue that it is more useful to think of crime as having a number of 'determining contexts' (see Chadwick and Scraton 2001). The evidence and theories in this chapter suggest that inequality can be understood as a determining context. Hence, it is something that needs to be taken seriously in understanding offending and the state's reaction to it. It is upon these issues that the following chapters of this book focus.

Notes

1 All figures are from HMRC (n.d.): http://www.hmrc.gov.uk/stats/personal_wealth/table13.5.pdf (accessed 27 February 2007).
2 Following Grover and Stewart (2002) the term 'welfare to work-welfare' is used as a critique of New Labour's term 'welfare to work', for it is clear that many people can only afford to take entry-level employment because of the payment of *in-work benefit*. Hence, the 'independence' of paid work cannot be dichotomised with the 'dependence' of unemployment.
3 The figure of £11 billion excludes payments equivalent to, or below, the *Family Element*.
4 Iacovou *et al.* (2007) took into account three indicators of disadvantage in calculating the poverty rates of young people. These were income poverty (household income below 60 per cent of the median); monetary deprivation (a continuous measure ranging from 1 for those at the top of the income distribution to 0 for those at the bottom); and non-monetary deprivation, which was calculated from 24 variables that included not being able to afford 'basic requirements' (such as keeping one's home adequately warm and buying new, rather than second-hand clothes); an ability to afford certain items (including a car or van, and a telephone); a lack of particular household facilities (a bath or shower, an indoor flushing toilet and hot running water); problems with housing (having a leaky roof, damp walls, floors and/or foundations and rot in window frames and/or floors); and factors related to environmental problems (including, shortage of space, vandalism or crime in the area).

Chapter 3

Young men

Introduction

We know that young people account for a large amount of crime in contemporary society and that young men are likely to be engaged in offending behaviour more than their female peers (Graham and Bowling 1995; Goldson 1998; Flood-Page *et al.* 2000). The reasons why young men and women engage in crime are complex and 'defy simplistic explanations and solutions' (Jamieson *et al.* 1999: 1). Hence, Jamieson *et al.* (*ibid.*) note that monocausal explanations of offending do not explain adequately the offending of young men and women, and provide little basis for understanding or tackling it. However, despite such arguments, and the current influence of risk-based approaches (see, for example, Farrington 2006; Wilson *et al.* 2006) that, even if they are conservative in nature (cf. Brown 1998), do point to a multitude of factors that may influence offending, monocausal explanations of the offending behaviour of young men in particular still seem to predominate. In this context, this chapter focuses upon relationships that are held to exist between a lack of paid work and the offending of young men. First, the chapter explores arguments of analysts and commentators who, despite having differing intellectual and philosophical outlooks, come to similar conclusions about the importance of paid work in managing the behaviour of young men. The chapter then goes on to examine how central governments have developed policies aimed at getting young men into paid employment. In discussing these two issues, the chapter argues that this particular agenda is socially conservative, involving by its very design, a need to reassert the patriarchal privileges of men as a means of managing their behaviour. The chapter also highlights the contradictory nature of attempts to get young men into paid work, for they have arguably been structured through policies that exacerbate their poor material circumstances.

The problem for young men

It is now widely accepted that the view of young men as being problematic is not new (Pearson 1983). The reason why young men are defined as being problematic is because they are a metaphor for social change. They are, as Davis (1990) suggests, the 'screen' on to which the hopes and fears relating to the contemporary and future condition of society are projected. Hendrick's (1990) work on the 'male youth problem' of the late 19th and early 20th centuries demonstrates the point. Hendrick shows how between the 1880s and 1920s the fears of socio-political élites regarding the economic, social and racial future of Britain were projected on to young people – young men in particular. Hendrick (*ibid*.: 97) argues that eugenics, for example, added a dimension of 'enormous significance' to the social problems highlighted by various inquiries in the early 20th century. In brief, the adolescent 'found itself strapped to a new image as guardian of the race' (*ibid*.: 96). Of course, guardianship of the British race was multi-faceted, but the focus was especially upon the future ability of adolescents to have and successfully rear children; biological and social reproduction were the key to the future of the British race and both were held to be threatened through the conjoining of two issues: ineffective families and the freedom from their biological family that earning a wage allowed to young men. Fabian reformer Sidney Webb, for instance, told the Edwardian Poor Law Commission that there should be a reduction in the wages of young men because such workers were 'indisciplined, precocious in evil, earning at 17 or 18 more wages than suffice to keep him, independent of home control and yet unsteadied by a man's responsibilities' (*ibid*.: 121). Muncie (2004) argues that for social commentators the alleged affluence of young workers raised concern over the potential of 'the family' to control its offspring. He notes the social reformer Reginald Bray who 'was convinced that the working-class family was devoid of discipline and supervision because parents were fearful of exercising their authority lest their sons leave and take their earnings with them' (*ibid*.: 73).

The problem for youth is that it carries the aspirations for society's future on its shoulders. The aim of government interventions, whether concerned with biological, economic or social efficiency, has been to produce citizens that are up to the job of carrying forward those aspirations. Pearson (1983) notes how differing ideological positions can be drawn upon in myth-making around the moral and social health of a nation. This was particularly the case in the 1980s and early 1990s when, although from disparate positions, the focus became young working-class men through what Scourfield and Drakeford (2002: 630) describe as a 'masculine deficit', 'the gap between what working-class young men expect out of life as men and their actual life chances'.

The problem with young men

We saw in the previous section that there has been a close association between the economic position of young working-class men and fears of their potential for disorder. This was most clearly articulated in the early decades of the 20th century when the concern was the employment of young men and the freedoms that it brought them. A concern with affluence also permeated later debates about post-Second World War youth sub-cultures (Pearson 1983; Muncie 2004). While concern about young men being free from the control of their parents continued into the 1980s and 1990s (Stewart and Stewart 1988), the main concern shifted to the issue of their *unemployment* and the so-called 'dependency culture' that was alleged to accompany it. As we have seen, unemployment among young people rose rapidly from the 1970s and peaked in the middle years of the 1980s. This represented the first instance of mass unemployment among young people in the post-Second World War period and was problematised because it was thought to be a threat to social order (Davies 1986; Brown 1997). Such arguments came from analysts and commentators of different ideological and political persuasions.

'Underclass', men and crime

Much has been written about the cultural 'underclass' thesis (see, for example, MacDonald 1997; Grover and Stewart 2002, ch. 5; MacDonald and Marsh 2005). We do not have space here to rehearse the deeply problematic nature of it (see, for instance, Walker 1990; Heath 1991; Bagguley and Mann 1992; Dean and Taylor-Gooby 1992;

Alcock 1993, ch. 12; Mann 1994; Slipman 1994; Lister 1996). However, despite the fact that the thesis has been criticised on empirical and theoretical grounds, it was nonetheless influential in policy-making (Jeffs 1997; Grover and Stewart 2002). One of its main influences was the way in which it put gender, most notably working-class men, upon the crime and social policy agendas in what Roseneil and Mann (1996) describe as a backlash against feminism and against many of the social changes from the 1970s that reduced women's economic and social dependence on men. This was particularly the case in concerns with the cultural 'underclass', with what was seen as the loss among working-class men of the breadwinner role, which, it was argued, was having an impact across a range of social and economic practices, including 'the culture of sex and violence ... high long-term male unemployment rates, the deterioration in academic performance of boys even in scientific subjects, possibly some loss of business confidence ... and arguably the formation of right wing nationalist movements across Europe' (Dench 1994, cited in Hearn 1998: 38). Charles Murray (1990: 22–23) – chief exponent of the cultural 'underclass' thesis – summed up the argument thus:

> work is more important than merely making a living, getting married and raising a family are more than a way to pass the time. Supporting a family is a central means for a man to prove to himself that he is a *'mensch'*. Men who do not support families find other ways to prove that they are men, which tend to take various destructive forms. As many have commented through the centuries, young men are essentially barbarians for whom marriage – meaning not just the wedding vows, but the act of taking responsibility for wife and children – is an indispensable civilising force. Young men who don't go to work, don't make good marriage material. Often they don't get married at all; when they do, they haven't the ability to fill their traditional role. In either case, too many of them remain barbarians.

In associating male youth with barbarism Murray's arguments have resonances with the now discredited work of American psychologist Granville Hall who, drawing upon Darwinian ideas and Haeckl's theory of recapitulation in the early 20th century, argued 'that each individual's passage from birth to maturity re-enacts the same purported stages as those of humanity in its passage to contemporary civilization' (Davis 1990: 60). Muncie (2004: 69) notes how this involved the stages of development, 'from early animal-like primitivism (childhood) through savagery (adolescence) to civilisation (adulthood)'. For Murray, young working-class males could only reach the civilised state of adulthood through marriage and the responsibilities associated with it. In this argument marriage is the 'civilising force' required if social stability is to be ensured (Grover and Stewart 2002).

Murray's explanation of the reason why young men were being cut adrift from the role of breadwinner related to the alleged incentives offered by welfare benefits and services for women to live and to raise children on their own. The unemployed working-class male was essentially redundant in Murray's analysis. He was no longer needed to provide for a family because of the provision of the state. This was problematic for Murray because it meant that such males were unlikely to experience the civilising process of marriage. They would remain, as he so colourfully argued, 'barbarians'. As such, they pose a problem for society because, with no role in 'the family', young working-class men also have no need to take paid employment since they have no dependants to provide for. This merely reinforces the image that young men are not marriageable prospects and encourages them to engage in illegal activities:

> Young men who are subsisting on crime or the dole are not likely to be trustworthy providers, which makes having a baby without a husband a more practical alternative. If a young man's girl friend doesn't need him to help support the baby, it makes less sense for him to plug away at a menial job and more sense to have some fun – which in turn makes hustling and crime more attractive, marriage less attractive. (Murray 1990: 48)

While their explanation is somewhat different to that of Murray's, the substance of the ethical socialists Dennis and Erdos's (1993: 106; see also Dennis 1997: ch. 15) argument is similar:

> Unemployment was indeed the key to the Tyneside riots of 1991. But not unemployment in the sense of the absence of opportunities to work as a paid employee in a drudging job (much less remunerative and exciting than crime).
>
> It was unemployment in the sense of the weakening or complete disappearance of the expectation that a young man should prepare himself for the larger employment to which a job is merely instrumental. This is his employment for a lifetime in a partnership of mutual support of a mature man and mature

woman. It is employment in a years' long commitment to nurturing and socializing until his child is in turn able to earn its own living and raise its own family.

The result of the exclusion of men from marriage was the rise of what Dennis and Erdos called 'incivility'. For Dennis and Erdos, the social disorder that engulfed Meadow Hall in 1991 was essentially the result of an erosion of moral responsibility, in particular, a responsibility of young men to their families, and an undermining of the importance of 'the family' by what Dennis and Erdos call the 'effective intelligentsia' (*ibid*.: 33). The mutuality of familial relationships has, in Dennis and Erdos's analysis, given way to materialistic and individualised notions of self-interest. The cultural environment in which 'the family' was able to thrive has been replaced by a cultural environment which is 'weakening ... the link between sex, procreation, child-care, child-rearing, and loyalty in the life-long provision on a non-commercial basis of mutual care within a common place of residence' (*ibid*: 107). In this process, they believe young men are being stripped of their traditional roles.

The idea of young working-class men being cast adrift from social and economic attachments is also reflected in the work of Morgan (1999) who argues that such men are no longer needed in the role of breadwinner because of deregulation in labour markets, the increasing participation of married women in the labour market, and an alleged favouring of lone mother-headed families over two-parent families in the tax/benefit system. According to Morgan the consequence of these three factors and the influence of 'anti-family social engineers [in] Ministerial Office' (Morgan 1999: 33) is a situation whereby young men no longer have any pre-defined role in society. This has led to criminality among young working-class men or, as she puts it, the creation of a 'warrior class', detached from the 'family man role' with its 'incentives for orderly and patient participation in the community' (*ibid*.: 143).

Structural accounts of the changing position of men

The view of young men being cut adrift from their traditional roles in society, however, is not just the province of 'underclass' theorists. While emphasising social, rather than individual antecedents, similar conclusions are reached by commentators from the Left. So, for example, the American sociologist William Julius Wilson (1987: 5) is concerned with 'how the liberal perspective might be refocused to challenge the now-dominant conservative views [represented by analysts such as Charles Murray] on the ghetto underclass'. Essentially Wilson's argument is that the increase in lone motherhood among young Black women was because of a decline in the pool of marriageable young Black men who, through high rates of unemployment, were most directly affected by economic restructuring in the USA from the 1970s. Wilson equates being 'marriageable' with being in paid employment.

Although not racially specific, similar arguments have been made in Britain. So, for example, Coote (1994: 2–3, original emphasis) notes that:

> while women have *added* the role of wage-earner to their traditional role of home-maker and carer, men have so far simply *lost* their traditional breadwinning role. Young men grow up fearing there will be no jobs for them, and lacking ... the means of realising their aspirations to become men.
>
> In communities where there are no jobs for men or women, the girls still have their rites of passage: they can claim adult status by becoming mothers ... Most young mothers make a good job of parenting, considering the odds stacked against them. When they fail to marry the fathers of their children, they may be making a realistic assessment of the available options. The boys who get them pregnant may appear to them to have very little else to offer.
>
> The young men must find other ways of growing up.

The alternative ways of growing up, Coote argues, are likely to involve offending as 'the best opportunity to prove their manhood' (*ibid*.: 4). In this sense, Coote seems to be suggesting that crime is a resource upon which young unemployed men draw in order to construct their masculine identity (cf. Messerschmidt 1993) in a period when working-class men have '*lost* their traditional breadwinning role'.

Campbell (1993) located the uprisings that occurred on social rented housing estates in 1991 as the consequence of the pursuit of Thatcherism that she argues 'doomed' the poor neighbourhoods in which she researched. These neighbourhoods were, Campbell notes (1993: xi), 'evacuated by British business and the economic discipline of the New Right left them unable to make a legitimate living'. In contrast to the 'underclass' argument that the problem for young unemployed working-class men was that they were not being civilised by marriage, Campbell argued that it was unemployment *per se* that was the problem. In this context, offending behaviour, such as joyriding, illicit drug use, ram raiding and burglary were understood as actions through which young working-class men in disadvantaged neighbourhoods could assert themselves as men; it was a *'masculine* response to an economic crisis' (*ibid*.: 303, original italics). In this sense, for Campbell it was not a crisis of masculinity that was the problem in poor neighbourhoods, but an extreme form of masculinity, premised upon violence and conflict as a means of problem solving. Placing the uprisings of 1991 in their wider context, Campbell (1993: 323) notes:

> In the Nineties young men were schooled in unprecedented displays of personal and public force ... The lads on the estates were not estranged from those cultural reference points ... The lads' problem was not that they were starved of male role models, it was that they were saturated with them. That was the problem with no name that set the estates on fire in 1991.

Such accounts of the changing fortunes of young men in working-class neighbourhoods, however, are problematic. Former Minister for Welfare Reform, Frank Field MP (1995: 10), for instance, described Wilson's approach as an 'American wheeze', preferring instead to locate increases in never-married lone mothers in the unemployment of young women, rather than young men (Grover and Stewart 2002). The use of the concept of masculinity in such debates is also problematic, for it does not engage with the observation that there are different forms of masculinity (Connell 1995). Moreover, Hearn (1998: 49) argues that such readings of the causes of offending become subsumed 'into the natural gloss of growing up', rather than taking seriously the gendered power of boys and young men into account. In this context, Hearn (1998) argues that young men are defined as being problematic because of their potential to reject patriarchy as a mode of domination, in favour of fratriarchy, a more 'troubling' masculinity for policy-makers. Remy (1990: 44–45) notes that fratriarchy:

> is a mode of male domination which is concerned with a quite different set of values from those of patriarchy. Although the *fratrist* can be expected to share all the common assumptions about matters such as the origin of life in the father, together with the whole ideology which springs from this, he is preoccupied with matters other than paternity and parenting,

raising children, providing for a wife and family, and acting as guardian of a moral code. Unlike patriarchy, fratriarchy is based simply on the self-interest of the association of men itself. It reflects the demand of a group of lads to have the 'freedom to do as they please, to have a good time'. Its character is summed up in the phrase 'causing a bit of bovver'.

The implication is that the fratrist is more problematic than the patriarch because the latter is less concerned with causing 'a bit bovver', at least in the public sphere, although, given the nature and extent of male on female domestic violence he may well be doing it in the private sphere. Hearn's observations, however, provide a means of understanding elements of the transitions between childhood and adulthood, for it suggests that in order to understand policy developments aimed at young men, we need to engage with the management of gendered power relations that this process involves.

Unfortunately, much of the literature (with perhaps the exception of Campbell 1993) discussed in this section does not engage with the issue of gendered power relations between young men and women, for despite the differing intellectual traditions framing the various explanations of why young working-class men are engaged in criminal and disorderly behaviour, the implications of the behavioural 'underclass' and more structural accounts are similar; that in order to address their disorderly and offending behaviour what such men require is to recapture that which they have lost; paid employment and, closely connected, patriarchal responsibilities. Such arguments are familiar in the criminology literature. In his excellent account of crime in market societies, Ian Taylor (1999) for instance, draws upon the work of Bob Connell (1995), to argue that 'the aggressive colonization of contemporary street space by young men' reflected a 'protest masculinity', rooted in the 'crisis of the mass manufacturing labour markets of the Fordist period [and which] has involved the demolition of the systems of socialization of young men (including those provided within the family of birth) into the disciplines of family life and the disciplines of working class life itself'. Downes (1998: 2) makes a similar point, although he uses the term 'crisis of masculinity' for 'youths with no foreseeable hope of gaining self-respect through regular well-paid work'.

Such analyses are both encouraging and problematic. They are encouraging because they recognise that crime is predominantly a male activity and because, rather than taking this for granted, they see it is as requiring an explanation. However, particularly in the case of Downes (1998), such analyses raise concern because of the way in which masculinity is conceptualised. The 'crisis of masculinity' thesis is arguably premised upon the idea that there is a single form of masculinity that young men learn, and that they engage in criminal activity either as an expression of some elements (for example, dominance and/or aggressiveness) of that masculinity, or because they are lacking certain aspects of it (for example, having a well-paid job). In this sense, crime is either the consequence of young men acting out aspects of masculinity or a replacement for those elements they do not have.

However, it is clear that there are many masculinities in contemporary society that are ordered by age, class, 'race' and sexuality (Connell 1995). Reflecting upon this, Messerschmidt (1993, 1997) points to how relationships between hegemonic (the form of masculinity that is idealised as dominant and desirable) and subordinated masculinities (those masculinities that do not match up to the hegemonic ideal) can help to explain how masculinities can be 'accomplished' by drawing upon crime as a resource when other resources, such as paid work or the breadwinner role, are lacking. In brief, crime can be drawn upon by men in attempts to mark the masculine off from the feminine. What this means, however, is that the idea of crime as contributing to the accomplishment of masculinity is as conservative as other approaches that take the crimes of men as reflecting learned or reactions to learned gendered expectations, for in both approaches it is patriarchal assumptions that structure the criminal actions of young men.

In this context, the rest of this chapter argues that the analysis that young men require paid work and (private) patriarchal responsibilities has come partly to structure social policy developments for young men. There are various ways of explaining this. Land (1999), for instance, focuses upon the emphasis upon human capital in policies such as the New Deal for Young People (NDYP) as reflecting a desire of New Labour to encourage the 'male breadwinner model', while Grover and Stewart (2002: 117) point to the disciplinary aspects of the NDYP as the mechanism through which New Labour hope 'to make young men better prospects as potential breadwinners'. Those two issues – human capital and discipline – are central to the following discussion that examines the ways in which, through social policy interventions, it was hoped that the offending and anti-social behaviour of young men could be addressed by helping to recapture what Scourfield and Drakeford (2002: 621) describe as 'privileges of masculinity'.

Men, crime and unemployment in policy

Downes (1998) argues that under Conservative governments of the 1980s crime became explained by reference to pre-Thatcherite change (the permissive society), resistance to the Thatcherite project (for instance, left-wing teachers and local authorities) and/or biological and psychological defects. Social explanations, Downes notes, became 'just excuses' (*ibid.*: 2). This is at odds with Brown's (1997) interpretation that youth unemployment was of concern, even to Thatcherite Conservatives. The approach taken in *Crime and Inequality* is that youth unemployment created a number of dilemmas for Conservative governments and, later, their New Labour successors which resulted in tensions in policy-making. For the Conservatives these included, at worst, the denial of the social causes of crime or, at best, little discussion of them, alongside the development of programmes and policies for unemployed youth that were partly aimed at tackling crime and social disorder. Finn (1987), for instance, notes how following uprisings in several of Britain's inner cities in July 1981 the Conservatives announced a £500 million package of measures that provided funds to honour a pledge of a guaranteed place on the *Youth Opportunities Programme* (YOP) and monies to fund the *Young Workers Scheme* (YWS).

Then, in the mid-1990s a senior civil servant told Grover and Stewart (2002: 111):

> The real main headache I can see is this quite large and growing group of young men between the ages of about 16 and 30 now, who have never worked and whose prospects of working are very poor ... they used to get married and settle down. They used to marry the young girls who are the ... single non-married women. The single non-married women for reasons which are not too difficult to know are not very keen to marry them, because they are better off on their own. Not just in cash terms, but because these people are pretty unmarriageable prospects. I mean, they have got criminal records. They get drunk. They beat you up. They do not produce money. So who would marry them? ... We are trying hard, the JSA among other things, to stop that cohort from perpetuating, but it is very difficult. It starts with the families, the broken homes ...

The acceptance of a version of the 'masculine deficit' thesis by policy-makers is clear, something that has been carried forward into

New Labour's policies. So, for instance, New Labour's White Paper on youth crime, *No More Excuses* (Secretary of State for the Home Department 1997) can be read as a document that individualises the causes of crime by reducing them to a number of 'risk factors' related to the experience of young people in their families and at school, and as a tool of responsibilisation through a focus upon parenting (see Chapter 4). However, the White Paper also argues that paid employment is linked in various ways to male youth crime. For instance, it problematises youth crime because of its potential to adversely affect the future of young men. Hence, it observes that 'allowing young people to drift into a life of crime undermines their welfare and denies them the opportunity to develop into fully contributing members of society' (*ibid.*: 2). Given that paid employment is the way in which the contribution of males is measured in contemporary society, the concern here is that youth offending will prevent young men contributing to society through their work, which is held to be central to their well-being, as well as to society's. Furthermore, *No More Excuses* argued that in the context of peer group and sibling pressure the problems facing young men were a lack of opportunities, particularly related to employment and partnering, that would help them to 'grow out' of offending behaviour (*ibid.*: para. 1.10).

By making such assertions the White Paper was drawing upon arguments that are familiar in criminology. One of the most consistent findings in criminological research has been that after a peak in the late teenage years the incidence of offending among young men decreases (Bottoms *et al.* 2004: Figure 1). This points to age being a significant factor in explaining offending behaviour. However, as Gadd and Farrall 2004) argue, ageing itself does not cause desistance from offending. In contrast, criminal careers research (for instance, Laub and Sampson 2001; Farrall 2002) suggests that: 'Male offenders typically cease to offend at about the same time they embark on the processes associated with family formation and (re)enter stable employment ... Both employment and family formation are events in the life-course that happen more frequently at certain ages than others' (Gadd and Farrall 2004: 124). Drawing upon the work of Laub and Sampson (2001), Maruna (2006: 121–122) suggest that the reasons for this relate to the 'social bonds developed in adulthood. Attachments in young adulthood (especially to a spouse or a career) provide an individual with "something to lose" by offending'.

In this context, it was perhaps understandable why it was noted in *No More Excuses* that one of the government-wide initiatives aimed at restoring 'hope and opportunity' as a means of tackling the causes of youth crime was the provision of 'real opportunities for jobs, training and leisure' (*ibid.*: para. 3.4). The NDYP was held to be central to this strategy, demonstrating what is held in New Labour's responsibilisation agenda to be the integrative capacity of paid employment (cf. Levitas 1996, 1998).

The connections made between a lack of paid work and crime have presented dilemmas for recent governments of both the Left and Right because both see the free market as the economic way forward. This means that neither has been willing directly to create jobs in order to facilitate increased paid employment for young men (and women). In contrast, it is argued that the most governments can hope to do is to foster macro-economic stability to enable the market to create jobs (HM Treasury 2006). In this context, the focus has been upon the supply-side, rather than attempts by governments to second-guess the demand for workers. This means the focus has been upon young unemployed men, their attitudes to paid employment, their work-related skills and the costs of hiring them for capitalist enterprises. In this sense, unemployment has ceased to be a social problem, but a problem of individual pathology; young men are held to be unemployed because they have the wrong (anti-work) attitude, wrong skills and/or are not willing (often argued to be because of the operation of the benefit system) to work for the wages available for entry-level jobs (cf. Grover 2007). Hence, over the past two decades or so there has been a search for policies aimed at preventing young men from becoming unemployed, and at getting those who are unemployed into paid work. These policies have focused upon young men themselves as being the problem, as a means – at least in part – of managing their disorderly and offending behaviour.

Not in education, employment or training (NEET)

According to Williamson (1997) the term NEET is a sanitised version of 'status 0' that was used by careers services to denote 16- and 17-year-olds who were not in paid work, training or education. Furlong's (2006) work, however, suggests the emergence of the term was linked to social security policy changes (the abolition of out-of-work benefits for 16- and 17-year-olds – discussed below) that meant, in an administrative sense, from the 'late 1980s youth unemployment ceased to exist in the UK'. He implies that NEET is a more politically palatable term to describe young unemployed people because the majority of NEET young people (83 per cent of males and 63 per cent of females) in Furlong's Scottish study were, indeed, 'out of work and looking for jobs'.

NEET is mostly used to refer 16–18-year-olds, and figures suggest that about 1:10 of such people are NEET (Social Exclusion Unit 1999; Convery 2002; OFSTED 2007). The problem with NEET young people for the government is that they are estimated to be financially very costly in the long term (Godfrey *et al.* 2002) because, it is argued, being NEET is associated with later social and labour market exclusion. As Furlong (2006: 554) suggests, the NEET categorisation has replaced 'a precisely defined category' (unemployment) with a 'heterogeneous category' that includes a range of socio-economic conditions and scenarios. Nevertheless, the overarching aim of the NEET agenda is clear: to get as many young people as possible into, or competing for, paid employment. In order to address the NEET phenomenon, New Labour have invested in two main policies: Connexions and the Education Maintenance Allowance.

Connexions

Connexions emerged as a policy from the government papers, *Bridging the Gap* (Social Exclusion Unit 1999) and *Learning to Succeed* (Secretary of State for Education and Employment 1999) as a mechanism to deliver, as Tony Blair said in 1999 (cited in Coles 2005: 10), 'the best start in life for every young person'. Its main role was to provide support and advice to all young people, although it was to focus upon the especially disadvantaged or disaffected; those 'at risk' of social exclusion because of particular circumstances they were facing in the transition to paid employment (MacDonald and Marsh 2001).

Evaluations suggest that services offered by Connexions, beyond generalist careers advice, are orientated towards such groups of young people, for example, those with learning disabilities or difficulties and, to a lesser degree, teenage mothers and young carers, illicit drug and harmful substance users, young offenders, young homeless people and young people leaving care (Dickinson 2001). There is some evidence that Connexions does have a positive impact upon the young people using its services. In interviews with young people, for instance, Hoggarth and Smith (2004) found that Connexions was helping to meet 'the transition needs of young people' (for example, arranging training and college placements) (para. 2.3.7); supporting personal development (such as encouraging feelings of self-esteem, worth and confidence) and helping to address the causes of the needs of young people. However, Hoggarth and Smith (*ibid.*: 13) also note that the positive impact of Connexions was 'by no means, as widespread or consistent as might be expected'. They explained this observation with reference to a range of marketing and administrative problems with it. However, for our purposes the most important reasons for the limited impact of Connexions relate to its focus upon the NEET 'problem', for its focus upon this introduces fundamental difficulties into a service that is supposed to be wide-ranging and holistic.

Hoggarth and Smith conceptualise Connexions as having 'hard' and 'soft' outcomes. 'Hard' outcomes relate to those that are easy to measure, while 'soft' outcomes are far more nebulous and more difficult to quantify, but equally important to the social and economic development of young people. 'Hard' outcomes – how Connexions's performance is measured – are essentially concerned with reducing the NEET population; between November 2002 and November 2004, for instance, Connexions's target was to reduce the NEET population by 10 per cent. Wylie (2004) notes that this focus upon the NEET target is too narrow to support young people successfully in multiple and complex transitions between childhood and adulthood, while Hoggarth and Smith (2004: para. 6.12.4.1) note that it 'can have counterproductive effects in loss of contact or a negative relation (for young people) to the service'. In brief, in the operation of Connexions there is a tension between, on the one hand, the need for it to demonstrate its role and importance in dealing with the NEET phenomenon and, on the other hand, the wide-ranging of needs of young people in transitions from childhood to adulthood (*ibid.*: para. 7.13.5).

Tensions have also been highlighted between the different priorities of the agencies that Connexions brought together. Ainley *et al.* (2002), for instance, note cases where Connexions personal advisers have been pushing schools for the reinstatement of excluded pupils, with the schools refusing as it would undermine their main measure of success: the number of pupils successfully passing GCSEs. In this sense, Connexions demonstrates some of the institutional difficulties with the idea of joined-up thinking and service delivery. While Connexions advisers are expected to work coherently across service boundaries, that coherence is undermined by the priorities of the various policy areas upon which their work impinges.

However, despite the problems with, and tensions structuring the work of, Connexions there is disquiet that under the *Youth Matters* agenda (Secretary of State for Education and Skills 2005) Connexions is to be devolved, along with its budget, to local authorities working through children's trusts, schools and colleges. For Coles (2005: 17) the danger is that the needs of young people will become neglected even further as they may become submerged 'beneath the voices of children, babies and families', and that any advocate role that Connexions plays in securing the rights of young people will be lost. In many ways, the *Youth Matters* Green Paper suggests a greater focus upon the transitions that young people face, and greater emphasis upon the role of parents in these processes. While this can be read as part of the responsibilisation of parents (see Chapter 4) that we are witnessing in contemporary society, it also introduces a new power dynamic to the situation, for the Green Paper makes it clear that information and guidance should be for both parents and young people. Parents, however, can contribute to the difficulties facing young people, rather than alleviate them, as Hoggarth and Smith (2004) demonstrate with some examples related to relationship breakdown.

The Education Maintenance Allowance

The idea of the Education Maintenance Allowance (EMA) is not new. Rice (1987) traces it to issues highlighted in a 1954 report by the Central Advisory Council on Education examining the factors influencing the decision to leave full-time education. While the report noted that the social attitudes and overcrowding in homes were important factors in shaping the decision to leave education, it also argued that a shortage of money 'affects the decision to leave in an appreciable number of cases, and the proportion of these is naturally highest among the children of semi-skilled and unskilled workers' (Ministry of Education 1954, cited in Rice 1987: 465–466). As a consequence of these findings, the 1956 Weaver Committee recommended the introduction of a means-tested EMA for children in full-time education beyond the compulsory school age. This recommendation was never introduced at a national level, although some local authorities, most notably the Inner London Education Authority, did operate a similar scheme (see the *Guardian*, 2 August 1984 on fears for its demise). However, in the context of rapidly increasing unemployment, there was a flurry of interest in EMAs in the 1980s (Gordon 1980; Dean 1982; Essen and Wedge 1982; Burghes and Stagles 1983; Rice 1987), although the then Conservative government protested at a lack of empirical justification for their introduction (Rice 1987). According to the *Guardian* (4 December 1985), however, a report by Labour Party educationalists in the mid 1980s recommended that all 'full time students aged 16–19 should be eligible for a £27-a-week education maintenance allowance'.

A decade later Labour was arguing that there was a 'strong case for a national income-related grant to support the poorest 16- and 17-year-olds who stay on in full time education and training' (Borrie 1994: 134). Such a scheme was introduced by New Labour, at first on a pilot basis, from 1999 and then nationally from 2004. The aim of the EMA is to increase participation rates of young people from lower income households in post-compulsory education and training. It also aims to increase the retention of young people in education at the end of year 11 and to increase the educational performance of young people by paying performance-related bonuses. In other words, it is a measure that, it is hoped, will keep poorer young people, young men in particular, in education and training for longer while improving their skills-related employability.

The evidence is inconsistent as to whether or not the EMA is successful at increasing participation. On the one hand, quantitative analysis of pilot and control areas suggests that it has increased the participation of young people in post-compulsory education (Middleton *et al.* 2005; Maguire and Rennison 2005), with a particular impact upon young people from socio-economic groups 2 (non-manual workers), 3 (skilled manual workers), 4 (semi-skilled and unskilled workers) and 5 (those not in paid work) (Middleton *et al.* 2003) and young men compared to young women (Middleton *et al.* 2005). In this sense, the quantitative evidence suggests that the EMA is impacting upon those social groups – working-class males – with whom there is most concern about joblessness and the social consequences of this.

However, more qualitative approaches suggest the EMA has a limited impact on decision-making concerning what course of action to take in the post-compulsory education because: 'Decisions about post-compulsory education had mostly been taken before the young people learned of the existence of EMA' (Legard *et al.* 2001: ii). While, of course, this may have changed following the national media coverage of EMA, it does point to a need to understand in depth the decision-making process in relation to post-compulsory education. More worryingly, however, is the impact of the EMA on NEET young people. As we have seen, EMA is one of the main social policies developed in order to tackle the NEET phenomenon, and while the statistical analysis suggests that it does prevent some young people entering the NEET category by encouraging them to remain in education, it is also the case that the EMA has little impact in attracting people back to education (Maguire and Rennison 2005). In other words, those people with whom the government should be most concerned – for example, people excluded from school – are little affected by the EMA. In fact, Maguire and Rennison's (2005, Table 5: 195) work demonstrates that in pilot areas of the EMA a higher proportion (48.8 per cent) of people who were NEET at 16 were also NEET two years later compared to those in control areas (45.5 per cent) and that a lower percentage were in full-time education in the EMA pilot areas (8.7 per cent) compared to the control areas (12.2 per cent).

Addressing the NEET phenomenon?

In many ways attempts to tackle the NEET 'problem' have been a failure, for it is still the case that about 10 per cent of 16- and 17-year-olds are not in education, employment or training. Hence, the announcement in the Green Paper, *Raising Expectations: staying in education and training post-16* (Secretary of State for Education and Skills 2007) that the government intends to criminalise young people outside of education and training by extending the age of compulsory participation in it to 18 by 2015. While it is argued in the Green Paper that this development will have macro- and micro-economic benefits and a number of social benefits (including reductions in offending and anti-social behaviour – see Feinstein 2002 for discussion of such arguments), it is also clear that the proposals in the Green Paper are concerned with disciplining the 10 per cent of young people – those deemed to have 'lower aspirations' and those 'who would have most to gain from longer participation and higher attainment' (then Secretary of State for Education and Skills, Alan Johnson MP, House of Commons Debates 2007) – into partaking in formal education and/or training. This is demonstrated by the fact that the extension of participation in education and training is to be backed by 'tough penalties' (the *Guardian*, 23 March 2007). The Green Paper proposes that these penalities should include an Attendance Order (requiring that a young person should undertake a particular form of education or training, where this will take place and when), fixed notice penalties, fines and community sentences.

Whether the introduction of compulsion will help to tackle the NEET phenomenon is difficult to say. However, Steve Sinnott, General Secretary of the National Union of Teachers, was reported as warning that: 'Criminalising young people is no way to ensure committed involvement. It will only serve to alienate and undermine any desire disaffected young people feel towards continuing their education' (*ibid.*). What Sinnott is pointing to is a tension between the analysis of the Green Paper and the tools proposed to deal with the issues raised by the analysis. In brief, if non-participation in education and training is caused by low aspirations (and it is not clear this is the case – non-participation in government employment schemes, for instance, can be driven by aspirations beyond what such schemes are often able to deliver to young people), it is difficult to see how criminalising young people will increase their aspirations. In contrast, such a move will stigmatise them as being problematic and outside of the norm.

Furthermore, policies to tackle NEET young people, whether Connexions, the EMA or extending the age for compulsory education/ training, are structured through a recurring theme of this book: they decontextualise phenomena, such as education and training, from their structural framework. The underlying principle of tackling the NEET issue is an economic instrumentalism; that engaging young people in education and training will improve their chances of gaining paid work. However, the focus is upon young people and, therefore, little attention is paid to the demand for labour, even if it is better educated. In some areas, most notably those traditionally associated with heavy industries, primary production and manufacturing, there is a lack of employment vacancies and where they do exist it is likely that they require few formal qualifications (Felstead *et al.* 2002). It is at this level – the numbers of jobs available and their nature – where the problem lies for many of Britain's young people, rather than the qualifications that they may or may not have.

Tackling the unemployment of young men

The previous section focused upon developments aimed at increasing the human capital of younger people and children in the hope of increasing their chances of gaining employment once they have ceased to be in education. However, as the policies aimed at reducing the NEET phenomenon seem so far to have only a limited impact, it is clear that in many instances young people will be unemployed after finishing their education. For the past two decades there has been a range of social policy developments aimed at increasing the employment of young men in particular. These have focused upon three strategies: financial incentives to take paid work; training; and the coercion of young people into paid work or training.

Financial incentives to take paid work

We saw in Chapter 2 that the wages of young people have fallen behind average increases over the past two decades or so. While it might be argued that this is the consequence of economic change that increasingly places a premium upon training, skills and lifelong learning (cf. Barclay 1995, HM Treasury 1997b), it is also because of the influence of the idea that by the 1980s young people were too expensive to employ (Wells 1983). As Mizen (2004) notes, the evidential base for this claim was never strong, but it did dovetail with several strands of Thatcherite thought, most notably a desire to free labour markets from institutional interventions and constraints that were held to increase labour costs. In this context, it was to become clear that the Conservatives had radical plans for young unemployed people from their very first years in government. For example, in a paper written by the Central Policy Review Staff (CPRS) in 1981 (and leaked in 1983) it was suggested that social security benefits for young people should be reduced; that young people should be removed from the remit of wages councils (bodies that then set minimum wages in industries that were notorious for paying low wages) and that employers should be paid a subsidy by the government in order to reduce the wages of young people (Finn 1987). The aim of all three of these policies was to place downward pressure on the wages of young people, and all were eventually introduced (Grover and Stewart 2002; Mizen 2004).

From 1982, for example, the *Young Workers Scheme* (YWS) paid employers a subsidy if they took on a young person under the age of 18 who was in their first year of work and paid them a low wage. In 1983 the YWS became the *New Workers Scheme* (NWS) when the qualifying age was extended to 21. The NWS lasted until 1988 and affected some 289,000 young people (Bradley 1995). In 1988 employees under the age of 21 were removed from the jurisdiction of the Wages Councils. Both of these measures were designed to reduce the costs of employing young workers. This was thought to have at least two advantages. First, it was hoped that such measures would reduce the wage expectations of young people across their life course; starting on lower wages would mean they would expect to earn less over their working life (Grover and Stewart 2002). Second, and more important for our purposes, it was hoped that by reducing the costs of employing young people, more of them would be employed by capitalist enterprises. While such a move may have impoverished young people, it was hoped more of them would move into paid work, thereby reducing their potential for disorder.

In line with this policy of making young people cheaper to employ, Conservative governments also focused upon the *out-of-work benefit* of young unemployed people. They believed that such benefits were too high, increasing the numbers of unemployed young people, and the length of time they remained unemployed. Hence, there were concerted efforts to reduce the amount of out-of-work benefits young people were entitled to claim. In 1985, for example, there was a media panic that was partly government-fuelled about the alleged emergence of Britain's 'Costa Del Doles' (seaside resorts where it was argued that young unemployed people were living the high life in boarding houses paid for through social security benefits). Board and lodge payments were then abolished for young people (for discussion see Stewart, Lee and Stewart 1986). In an even more draconian move the 1986 Social Security Act withdrew benefits, except in tightly drawn circumstances, from 16- and 17-year-old unemployed people and reduced the levels of benefits that 18–24-year-olds could claim by abolishing the distinction between householders and non-householders and replacing it with age-related benefit levels.

While there is little doubt that such measures were part of the government's drive to reduce the costs of employing young people, it is also the case that they were located in the historical concerns (outlined at the beginning of this chapter) about the importance of families in the disciplining of their young people. Hence, it was argued that the board and lodge payments and householder/non-householder distinction in Supplementary Benefit needed to be abolished because they encouraged people to leave home when they were too young (cf. Tony Newton, then Minister for Social Security, House of Commons Debates 1985, col. 780), thereby removing them from the control of their birth families. Stewart and Stewart (1988) argue that the aim of such changes in social security policy in the latter part of the 1980s was to extend the period that young people were dependent upon their parents. Such concerns continued into the 1990s with the introduction of the *Single Room Rent* (SRR).

The SRR restricts the amount of HB people under the age of 25 living in private rented accommodation can claim to a figure that the local rent officer considers reasonable for one-room accommodation with the use of a shared kitchen, toilet and, more recently, a living room. Even if young people are not in such accommodation the SRR is applied anyway. Kemp and Rugg (1998) demonstrate how the SRR causes hardship for young people both in seeking accommodation and in paying for it once they have found it. In the late 1990s it was estimated that in London the median shortfall between HB and the rent paid by young people was £15 to £20 per week (London Research Centre 1999, cited in Kemp and Rugg 2001). If landlords and ladies are not willing to reduce rents this shortfall has to be made up from the benefit payments of young people which, as we saw in Chapter 1, are already below the poverty line. More recent evidence suggests that because of the SRR, private landlords are less willing to offer accommodation to young people, leading to homelessness or to their being offered housing on difficult-to-live-on estates:

> The restrictions that the SRR places on young claimants' ability to access private rented housing is preventing many from finding any private rented sector accommodation within their means. This, combined with the widely reported reluctance of many landlords to let to young people, appears to have resulted in a situation where many young people enter informal lettings or end up using 'friends' floors' or (in those parts of the country with low demand for council housing) are being offered public housing on the more problematic run-down estates. (Harvey and Houston 2005: 1)

The aim of these developments in social security policy was to ensure that young men would have little incentive to become, or to remain, unemployed and/or to ensure that they did not leave home at too young an age. However, their introduction has impoverished young men, particularly those who do not live with their birth families. While this may not be consistent with what we know about the material antecedents of offending and anti-social behaviour, it is consistent with neo-liberal economic orthodoxy that suggests that little can be done to create jobs except to ensure that the 'right' macro-economic framework is in position. The developments discussed in this and the following sections aim to encourage 'the market' to create jobs by ensuring that young men are as cheap to employ as is politically acceptable and that they have a basic work discipline required by employers.

Youth training and New Deals

The government stopped 16- and 17-year-olds from claiming IS in 1998 because it argued it could guarantee them a place on the already existing *Youth Training Scheme* (YTS). Finn (1987) demonstrates how the central aim of the YTS was to make young people more employable by, first (and consistent with the observations made above), reducing their wages. So, for example, it was argued that the YTS would 'bring about a change in the attitudes of young people to the value of training and acceptance of relatively lower wages for trainees' (Secretary of State for Employment *et al.* 1981: 13). Second, the YTS helped constitute a cheap and expendable form of labour. The then government boasted, for instance, that employers now had 'the opportunity to take on young men and women, train them and let them work for you almost entirely at our expense, and then decide whether or not to employ them' (quoted in Davies 1986: 59; Finn 1987: 162). Young people were aware of the use of the YTS in such manner, with complaints from them that it was not the same as having a 'real' job and often delivered little training (Baqi 1987; Finn 1987; Lee *et al.* 1990).

With changes in government priorities for training, the YTS was replaced in 1990 by *Youth Training* (YT). Bradley (1995) argues that into the 1990s the concern became Britain's relative poor performance in training compared to its competitors. The suggestion is that the government became genuinely concerned with the training of young people, with the aim of YT to 'encourage young people to acquire broad-based skills, to acquire a minimum of NVQ level 2 qualifications and thereby to increase the quantity and quality of intermediate skills in the workforce' (*ibid.*: 6). However, concern with youth wages was not lost as those on YT continued to be paid a low training allowance rather than a wage.

When New Labour was elected in 1997 its flagship policy, outlined in principle in the lead-up to the election, was the NDYP. Its introduction was framed by a discourse that suggested that young people did not work because they were lazy (see Grover and Stewart 2002: 53–54) and, because of this, those who are held not to be fully and cooperatively engaged with it face *benefit sanctions* for up to 26 weeks. Hence, the NDYP can also be understood as part of the regime aimed at pressuring young men into paid employment.

Coercing young men into paid work

Finn (1998) argues that changes in social security policy from the late 1980s can be understood as the emergence of a stricter benefit regime (SBR). The SBR was a combination of 'sticks' and 'carrots' in order to cajole unemployed people into paid work. The most important element of the SBR – the JSA – was introduced in 1996. While it was introduced for all unemployed people, it had a particular resonance for young men because they are, as we have seen, disproportionately unemployed. The JSA does not allow claimants to refuse work because of the hours and conditions being offered. Unemployed people who do place restrictions on the types of work they are willing to do face having their JSA sanctioned. Young people are disproportionately sanctioned under the JSA regime (Peters and Joyce 2006).

However, with the introduction of the NDYP, young people became the subject of the sanction regimes of two policies, for after six months they are subject to both the JSA and NDYP. This authoritarian approach has been declared a success. According to the government it 'has virtually ended long-term unemployment' among young people (Department for Work and Pensions 2003a: para. 8). However, such claims are problematic. First, while it is the case that the number of long-term unemployed young people is now lower than it was in the mid-1980s, it continues disproportionately to affect young people (see Chapter 2). Second, the NDYP seems little different to other programmes, such as YTS and YT in that it 'churns' young unemployed people between unemployment and casualised employment (Sunley *et al.* 2001). So, for example, by February 2006 just over 700,000 young men had been through the NDYP, representing just shy of a million individual starts on it.[1] These figures indicate that in the decade after the introduction of the NDYP 700,000 young men (aged 18–24 years) have been unemployed for at least six months. However, many of these young men will have been unemployed for considerably longer periods, for while 700,000 young men went through the NDYP in its first decade, there were over 990,000 spells of time that individual young men spent on it in the same period. As MacDonald and Marsh (2005: 108) observe, paid employment, even in the most depressed areas, has not disappeared completely for young people, for those in their study 'who were able and willing to look for employment had found it at some point'. The problem is that the work young people in such areas do find is often casualised, low paid and particularly unpleasant (see, for example, MacDonald and Marsh's [2005] analysis of their respondents' work in the local turkey processing factory).

Second, of the 700,000 young men who have been through the NDYP less than half (45.8 per cent) actually left it to enter paid work. One fifth (19.8 per cent) of leavers went on to claim unemployment and disability-related benefits, and, even more worryingly, a quarter (24.8 per cent of leavers) had unknown destinations. While it has been argued that the a majority of such leavers leave the NDYP for paid employment, the evidence is not convincing, particularly in regard to such leavers getting a stable job (Hales and Collins 1999). Quite what these young men are doing and how they are surviving financially is currently unknown, for the government's focus, as we saw above, has been NEET young people aged 16 to 18, rather than older NEET people.

This observation is worrying because the NDYP represents *the* mechanism that the government hopes will reintegrate young unemployed men back into mainstream society. It appears though that a significant proportion of young men are excluding themselves from it. The reasons for this are linked to its structure and operation. Most notably, the NDYP is often unable to meet their aspirations. The evidence, for instance, suggests that NDYP conscripts would prefer the employment option to any of the others. However, there is mismatch between this aspiration and the reality, for the smallest proportion (19 per cent of 'option' starts to September 2002) of NDYP conscripts were engaged in the employment option. The highest proportion (40 per cent) of conscripts had been involved in the education/training option, while a fifth (22 per cent) had been in the voluntary sector and another fifth (20 per cent) the environmental task force (Department for Work and Pensions 2002: 1).

This pattern of option participation is problematic because the sanction regime is closely related to the 'options' that NDYP conscripts are on. Figures (TUC 2002) show that while the employment option carries a lower proportion of sanctions than might be expected, the other three 'options' have higher than expected proportions of sanctions. Bivand (2002), for example, found that nearly a quarter of those on the environmental task force option had been punished, compared to 10 per cent in the voluntary sector, 9 per cent in full-time education and 4 per cent of those in a job with an employer. Bivand (*ibid.*) concluded that the NDYP was operating in a way in which the most excluded young unemployed people were the most likely to endure sanctions. These findings suggest that benefit sanctions are likely to reflect the amount of choice young people have and their enthusiasm for their 'option'. Young people's preference for the work-based route is reflected in the lower proportion of sanctions applied to those involved in it, but this is the option they are least likely to be on.

It is also the case that the work option is the one that is most likely to result in unsubsidised employment (a 'real' job) and that remaining in the 'gateway period' is a more effective way of securing unsubsidised employment than engaging with the other three options

(Dorsett 2001, 2006; Lissenburgh 2004). In other words, in terms of gaining employment, a young person is better off being unemployed in the 'gateway' than in engaging with the 'options' other than the work-based one. These observations support Jeffs and Spence's (2000) contention that the main role of the NDYP is to manage (i.e. reduce) the work expectations of young people to make them more in tune with local labour market conditions. They also expose the fundamental problem with the NDYP: it is only likely to be successful in getting young people into paid employment where there are jobs available for them to do. However, by its very nature it is likely to have most conscripts where there are few employment opportunities because of the state of local labour markets (Peck 1999; Sunley *et al.* 2001). Despite the economic argument that the NDYP is likely to increase the number of jobs in the economy (explained in Grover and Stewart 2002), it has not managed to do this on any great scale (National Audit Office 2002).

The combination of the lack of 'real' jobs accessible through the NDYP and its sanction regime is leading young people to exclude themselves from it. Concerns about this possibility were raised by young people in its early years (Bentley *et al.* 1999), while in their study of young people in Teesside MacDonald and Marsh (2005: 100) found that many felt that the NDYP was 'just another government scheme' that was not worth engaging with because it was unlikely to result in 'rewarding employment'. Karla *et al.* (2001) found that some young people took any work available in order to avoid the NDYP, while one young man told Hoogvelt and France (2000: 119): 'I didn't want to go on New Deal so I signed off because I think I have something better in the pipeline'; and another said, 'I don't think New Deal will be any good. I can do better on my own.' In this sense, it seems the NDYP is meeting the 'primary political aim to reduce the unemployment count – not by making young adults more "employable", but by operating in ways which alienate potential and actual recruits and thus further energise their search for jobs' (MacDonald and Marsh 2005: 100). Indeed, for many young people who remain within the remit of the NDYP it has merely replaced what one of Craine's (1997: 140) respondents described as the 'Black Magic Roundabout'; 'runnin' round in circles an' gettin' nowhere … like YOPs an' all that other shit.' In this sense, for many young people the NDYP has become the new revolving door to unemployment.

Conclusion

Concern with the anti-social and criminal potential of young men is not new. In recent years though there has been a particular concern with their destructive potential. From various perspectives the explanation for this is argued to relate to the problems faced by young working-class men in gaining paid work and – closely related – in taking private patriarchal responsibility for a wife and dependent children. The aim of various policies over recent decades has been to increase the participation of young men in paid work. If offending among young men is understood from a social control theory perspective the attractiveness of such policies can be understood, for the aim has been to give young men a vested interest in society's institutions through paid work and, in the longer term, though providing for a partner and children.

However, the chosen approach to achieve this is problematic because, first, it is inherently conservative, being dependent upon the (re)construction of private patriarchy and its attendant gender power relations; second, it decontextualises the unemployment of young men from its economic antecedents; and, third, it is premised upon an authoritarianism that has the potential to impoverish young men and/ or forces them into low-paid employment. In contrast to giving young men a 'stake' in society such an approach is likely to exacerbate their exclusion and to exacerbate the poor material conditions that frame offending and anti-social behaviour. It is instructive, for instance, that in their longitudinal study of the NDYP in Sheffield, Hoogvelt and France (2000: 121) found that after 18 months nearly half (16 of the 35) of the cohort that were disengaged from it 'were either in prison, on probation or waiting to go to court – all of them after incidents that had occurred since we had first interviewed them, and all but four of these were a record of burglary or other property offences'.

Note

1 Calculated using the Department for Work and Pensions's online Tabulation Tool (http://www.dwp.gov.uk/iad/workingage.asp).

Chapter 4

Parenting and anti-social behaviour

Introduction

This chapter is concerned with relationships between parenting and anti-social behaviour, and with the criminal justice and social policy interventions that have been introduced by the state in an attempt to manage those relationships. The chapter locates these issues in an historically enduring concern with poor working-class families and within more recent manifestations of those concerns in the particular brand of communitarianism – what is described as 'Anglicanised communitarianism' – that structures the thought of New Labour and that emphasises the moral agency of individuals no matter what their material circumstances are like.

The chapter examines the On Track Programme and Parenting Orders and, in the case of social policy interventions, developments in education and housing policy that increasingly wed access to services aimed at meeting particular sets of needs to the behaviour of individuals and their parents' (and in some cases their partners') ability to control that behaviour. The chapter argues that interventions as they are currently configured not only decontextualise parenting from its material context, thereby structuring it as a problem of poor people, rather than a problem of their marginalised status, but also that they have a particularly problematic impact upon poor women, whose material circumstances are threatened to a greater degree by such interventions than men's.

Families, anti-social behaviour and the 'parenting deficit'

Concern with relationships between parenting and what is now called anti-social behaviour did not emerge with the election of New Labour in 1997. Garrett (2006), for example, argues that in many ways New Labour attempted to pre-empt the Conservatives – who through the 1991 Criminal Justice Act increased the powers of courts aimed at ensuring that parents took care of, and exercised control over, their children (Drakeford 1996) while the 1996 Housing Act introduced a range of actions that could be taken against those argued to be anti-social tenants (and their dependants and visitors) of social landlords (Burney 2002) – on law and order issues. However, concerns with relationships between 'problem families' and anti-social behaviour have a far longer history than political spats between New Labour and the Conservatives in the 1990s. Pearson (1983: 214), for instance, highlights an enduring argument pointing to the 'perpetual decline of the family' in explanations of street violence and disorder.

It is little surprise then that by the 1960s juvenile delinquency had become firmly associated with the 'problem family', the 'working class residuum' who were thought not to have adjusted well to post-Second World War social and economic reorganisation (Clarke 1980: 92). What this meant was that the causes of juvenile delinquency and offending were defined as being the consequence of the socio-cultural failings of working-class families. It has been observed that even in the 1969 Children and Young Persons Act, often described as the epitome of welfarist concerns with the delinquent, 'primacy was accorded to individual factors, rather than structural factors such as poverty or poor housing' (Brown 1998: 60).

It is the notion of the 'problem family' – the 'urban poor ... who were, it was maintained, indolent, feckless, dirty and a drain on the resources of the post-war welfare state' – that as Prime Minister, Tony Blair 'worked hard to excavate ... and to relocate ... within twenty-first-century ASBO [Anti-Social Behaviour Order] politics' (Garrett 2007: 849). It is clear that the anti-social behaviour agenda, in particular its relationships to parenting, is seen as something that is class-specific. Despite claims, for example, that concerns with parenting are more or less classless,[1] it is the case that the concern is with the parenting skills of a particular section of the working class. The 'problem family', as noted above, is part of the poor working class. Reflecting this, anti-social behaviour is seen as something that poor working-class children and young people do and from the very start ASBOs were associated with poorer people and neighbourhoods

(Burney 2002). They were, Burney notes, the consequence of a 'rising volume of complaints of un-neighbourly and predatory behaviour, mainly from poor council estates in areas of high unemployment'. In this sense, it was the 'council estate (or more frequently the so-called "sink estate") which was to become the theatre in which the performance and regulation of "anti social behaviour" was to be enacted' (Garrett 2007: 842).

That said, it is not the case that anti-social behaviour and measures to control it are concerned only with residential areas. Bannister *et al.* (2006: 920) argue that zero tolerance of anti-social behaviour conjoins with the physical restructuring of urban spaces in the construction of what they describe as the 'respectable city'. In this regard, they argue that there is an economic imperative in the tackling of anti-social behaviour. The aim is to make city centres more 'respectable' by dealing with those who, according to Bauman (2004), can be considered to be poor and excluded because of their inability to consume. The aesthetics of consumption cannot be disturbed by images of urban blight and decay and by those who have been marginalised through global economic processes. Hence, Bannister *et al.* (2006: 925) argue that we are witnessing the 'purification of space both commercially and residentially'. Central to this process has been focus upon relationships between the skills of financially poor parents and anti-social behaviour.

Muncie (1999: 240) notes that the 1980s was a decade in which Conservative governments popularised the idea that parents were 'colluding with or even encouraging misbehaviour ... as the inevitable result of a 1960s permissive culture'. Through then Prime Minister Margaret Thatcher's call in the 1980s for a return to 'Victorian values' so as to 're-establish a sense of "discipline", "decency", "morality" and "responsibility"' (Goldson and Jamieson 2002: 85) and in the 1990s Prime Minister, John Major's (ill-fated) attempt to return Britain 'back to basics', responsibility for the delinquency of the young was increasingly placed upon parents and especially upon mothers (Drakeford 1996).

However, it was not until the election of New Labour in 1997 that criminal justice policy began to focus more closely upon the nature of parenting in explaining and preventing delinquency among young people. A powerful combination of the politics of criminal justice, a desire for 'evidence-based' policy-making and the influence of a particularly prescriptive and authoritarian brand of communitarianism created the conditions in which the focus for explaining delinquency became the so-called 'parenting deficit'.

While, as we saw in the previous section, the idea of a parenting deficit may not be new, it received a new lease of life through the work of Amitai Etzioni (1993), a communitarian thinker who is acknowledged as being one of the main influences on the thought of New Labour (Heron and Dwyer 1999). Etzioni (1993) starts from a critique of the individualism that was celebrated and encouraged in the 1980s. As Geoff Mulgan (1993: 1), former head of the Prime Minister's Strategy Unit under Tony Blair and an adviser to then Chancellor of the Exchequer Gordon Brown, says of the origins of Etzioni's work:

> Overindividualist societies seemed to lose out on personal responsibility and the everyday morals and mutual respect that make it possible to live in densely packed cities and nations. As societies seemed to fall apart many began to fear that the cult of choice was not only a symptom, but also a cause of fragmentation.

According to Mulgan (*ibid.*) the 'communitarian movement is the most developed response to this unease' and Etzioni 'is the undisputed intellectual leader of this movement' (*ibid.*: 2). For Etzioni (1993: 6) having children is a 'moral act' that intertwines the individual and 'community' through various rights and responsibilities, although his focus is mainly on the responsibilities of parents. 'Making a child', he argues:

> obligates the community to the parents. But it also obligates the parents to the community. For we all live with the consequences of children who are not brought up properly whether bad economic conditions or self-centred parents are to blame. Juvenile delinquents do more than break their parents' hearts, and drug abusers do more than give their parents grief. They mug the elderly, hold up stores and petrol stations and prey on innocent children returning from school. They grow to be useless, or worse, as employees, and they can drain taxpayers' resources and patience. In contrast, well brought up children are more than a joy to their families; they are (oddly, it is necessary to reiterate this) a foundation of proud and successful communities. Therefore, parents have a moral responsibility to the community to invest themselves in the proper upbringing of their children, and communities – to enable parents to so dedicate themselves. (*ibid.*)

Etzioni's analysis of producing and socialising children demonstrates some of the central elements of communitarian thought – for instance, concern with duty and obligation to one's family, neighbourhood and wider society – more generally.

The central argument of Etzioni's brand of communitarianism is that individualism does not lead, as neo-liberal economists and philosophers suggested, to social harmony. In contrast, the pursuit of self-interest tends towards social disintegration. Grover (2005a) notes that there is little controversial about such an analysis; it was a point made by many during the years of Thatcherism and Reaganomics. Etzioni's analysis becomes more controversial when he comes to examine the importance of social obligations to contemporary Western societies. Social obligations are crucial to such societies, he argues, because it is they that maintain 'social order and enhances the communities in which [people] live' (Deacon 2002: 64). Following on, it is equally crucial that such obligations are re-captured. This requires a rebalancing of rights and responsibilities to emphasise responsibilities individuals have to themselves, their families and society. It is only through accepting these responsibilities that individuals accept their social obligations to others. It is at this juncture that Etzioni's arguments are most controversial, for he believes that, if required, obligations should be enforced by the 'community'. Not only does this provide a link to right-wing 'underclass' theorists (Deacon 2002), it also helps to explain the increasing incursion of New Labour into the realm of parenting: it is held to be good for society.

Deacon (2000, 2002) argues that in New Labour's thought Etzioni's particularly moralistic and authoritarian brand of communitarianism combines with its preferred version of socialism – ethical or Christian socialism. Central to ethical socialism is the idea of 'personal responsibility under virtually all social circumstances. People act under favourable and unfavourable conditions but remain responsible moral agents' (Halsey 1993: x). According to ethical socialism, no matter what the socio-economic situation of the individual is they can always act in a responsible manner. It is this view of the responsible moral agent that Deacon (2000) argues conjoins with the idea of 'duty' in the Etzioni brand of communitarianism to produce an 'Anglicanised communitarianism'. The implication for parenting is that no matter what their socio-economic situation, parents should always be able to socialise their children to be useful and productive members of society. Because parents should always be able to act as responsible moral actors, the reason why they do not can be explained by a lack of knowledge (they do not know how to behave responsibly) or because they are wilfully neglecting their responsibilities (they cannot be bothered to behave responsibly). In either case they can, with the right tuition, be taught how to raise their children without the state having to address the material condition in which they raise those children.

Parenting and anti-social behaviour

For many years it was argued that 'the family' was or should be a sanctuary from the interventions of the state. While this has never quite been the case – the state has for many years been willing to intervene in those working-class families where the children were deemed to be a social problem or 'at risk' of harm – recently, parenting has become one of the most visible areas of state concern, with, for example, its being deemed central to tackling a whole host of socio-economic phenomena, from child poverty to anti-social behaviour (Respect Task Force 2006). The Respect Task Force holds that although parenting is 'primarily the business of parents and the Government does not want to interfere with that principle ... where parents are unwilling, or unable to meet their responsibilities we must ensure that they are challenged and supported to do so' (*ibid.*: 17; see also Blair 2005). Here the Respect Task Force is referring to what in other areas of intervention is referred to by New Labour as 'progressive universalism'; some services that every parent, or at least those meeting their responsibilities, can access through voluntary parent support programmes being delivered, for instance, in Children's Centres and more closely targeted services for the 'small minority of parents who refuse to take responsibility for their children's poor behaviour' (Respect Task Force 2006: 18). The 'problem family' is once again marked as being different to other families and, as such, is in need of enforced interventions. The main concern in the parenting agenda, therefore, is those parents who are deemed to be wilfully neglecting their children's behaviour. These concerns have been expressed in a number of criminal justice and social policy areas, to which we now turn.

Parenting, anti-social behaviour and criminal justice policy

It is within criminal justice policy that we see the greatest focus upon the so-called 'parenting deficit'. So, for example, as part of the

Crime Reduction Programme New Labour introduced On Track, 'an ambitious programme ... [setting] down new parameters for social crime prevention' (France *et al.* 2004: 75) targeted at 4–12-year-olds and their families in 24 high-deprivation, low-income areas within England and Wales (Armstrong *et al.* 2005). While the locally delivered interventions of the programme demonstrate that there is some recognition of relationships between poor material circumstance and offending and anti-social behaviour (Hine (2005) for instance, notes 'compensatory activities' available to some On Track participants), the main focus of the programme is upon various aspects of parenting.

The On Track programme was designed with, and measured by, reference to what the literature suggests the risk and protective factors are in terms of young people's offending and anti-social behaviour (France *et al.* 2004; McKeown and Ghate 2004; Armstrong *et al.* 2005; Hine 2005). Hine argues (*ibid.*: 118) such an approach is based upon a number of 'problematic premises', for instance, that the risk factors predicting future offending and anti-social behaviour are well established and that the risk factors facing children can be easily identified and measured. The thrust of her argument can be related to the 'core interventions' offered by the On Track programme that focus upon parenting skills as the primary cause of offending and anti-social behaviour among children. However, as Hine (*ibid.*) notes, 'although there is broad agreement about the areas of risk, such as poor parenting practices, there is little agreement about their detail.'

The On Track programme is a relatively small policy and is geographically specific. In contrast, the main way in which financially poor parents have been engaged in the criminal justice system is through a legal enforcement of what are held to be their responsibilities towards their children. It has been possible since the 1991 Criminal Justice Act for the judiciary to hold parents responsible for the actions of their children. This Act made parents responsible for the fines of their children and allowed magistrates to 'bind over the parents of a child aged under 16 so as to take "proper care and exercise control" over the child' (Drakeford 1996: 245). If, as Edwards (1992, cited in Drakeford, *ibid.*: 246) argues, the 1991 Criminal Justice Act 'implicated parents in the criminality of their children', then the Parenting Order, introduced as part of the 1998 Crime and Disorder Act, 'is the logical continuation of ... Conservative initiatives to criminalize what is considered to be 'inadequate parenting"' (Muncie 1999: 241).

The rationale for the Parenting Order was set out in the White Paper, *No More Excuses* (Secretary of State for the Home Department 1997). In the preface then Home Secretary, Jack Straw MP outlined its purpose: 'nipping offending in the bud, to prevent crime from becoming a way of life for so many young people' (*ibid*.: 1). The main problem for youth justice, Straw argued, was that an 'excuse culture [had] developed. It excuses itself for its inefficiency, and too often excuses the young offenders before it, implying they cannot help their behaviour because of their social circumstances' (*ibid*.). Straw's comments highlight the influence of what we have seen is described as Anglicanised Communitarianism; people can always act as responsible moral agents and because of this their social circumstances cannot be used to condone their behaviour.

The aim of the proposals in the White Paper was to 'stop making excuses for children who offend', by reinforcing 'the responsibility of young offenders – and their parents – for their delinquent behaviour' (*ibid*.: paras. 4.1 and 4.2). To enforce the responsibility of parents the Parenting Order would be introduced 'to help support parents to control the behaviour of their children' (*ibid*.: para. 4.11). In this respect, Goldson and Jamieson (2002: 88) argue the Parenting Order is a good example of the double speak of New Labour in which 'punitive authoritarianism [is shrouded] under the cloak of benign-welfarism', for what starts out as a measure to 'help' and 'support' parents address the anti-social behaviour of their child(ren) quickly descends into an authoritarian measure that decontextualises the behaviour of children and their parents' ability to cope with it (discussed below).

It was soon to become apparent though that for New Labour the policies of the 1998 Crime and Disorder Act were not adequate to address anti-social behaviour. While the youth justice system was no longer accused of excusing the behaviour of young people, the theme of responsibility, particularly that of parents in socialising their children, structured the 2003 White Paper, *Respect and Responsibility – Taking a Stand Against Anti-Social Behaviour* (Secretary of State for the Home Department 2003). Framing his ideas in Wilson and Kelling's (1982) Broken Windows thesis, then Home Secretary David Blunkett (Jack Straw's successor) noted that: 'We must be much tougher about forcing people not to behave anti-socially' (Secretary of State for the Home Department 2003: 4). The 2003 White Paper was much broader than the youth focus of *No More Excuses*. In contrast, *Respect and Responsibility* outlined 'the need for a cultural shift from a society where too many people are living with the consequences of anti-social behaviour, to a society where we respect each other, our property and shared public space' (*ibid*.: 6). Therefore, it focused upon a broad range of anti-social behaviours said to be blighting both residential and commercial spaces. Our concern is parenting and in this regard *Respect and Responsibility* restated that: 'The responsibility [to recognise that anti-social behaviour is not acceptable] starts in the family, where parents are accountable for the actions of children and set the standards they come to live by' (*ibid.*: 3). In order to ensure families met these responsibilities the White Paper announced a raft of proposals for parents 'unwilling or unable to respond to support' (*ibid.*: 8), provided through parenting classes and the Sure Start initiative. Anti-social behaviour was once again reduced to a 'small number of families ... who cause the most noise, whose children do not attend school on a regular basis or, if they do, cause trouble' (*ibid.*: para. 2.19). The continued focus upon the 'problem family' was self-evident.

However, the premise of *Respect and Responsibility* was that even these, the most disruptive families, could be brought into the normative fold. The White Paper announced the government's intention to introduce further measures, including hazily defined 'intensive support'; the fostering of children in order 'to provide the best opportunity for a child to develop in a setting where they can have the necessary support to which they are entitled and to develop a clear sense of responsibility for their own behaviour' (*ibid.*: para. 2.23); the extension of the use of Parenting Orders by allowing Youth Offending Teams to apply for such orders 'where the parent is not taking active steps to prevent the child's behaviour, and it is clear that the behaviour will continue' (*ibid.*: para. 2.44); and the extension of the Parenting Order to include a residential order.

However, in what has been described as a 'war on yobs' (the *Guardian*, 13 October 2005), two years later the Respect Task Force was set up, publishing its *Action Plan* (Respect Task Force 2006) the following year. The *Respect Action Plan* extends the themes and ideas of *Respect and Responsibility*, in particular the need to encourage a 'modern culture of respect', central to which is passing on 'decent values and standards of behaviour to our children' (*ibid.*: 3). Hence, the focus upon the role of parenting continued, with it being noted that by 'addressing poor parenting at the earliest opportunity, we [the government] will address one of the key causes of anti-social behaviour and reduce its long term effects' (*ibid.*: 17). The action plan outlined a number of developments at both a local and national level to improve 'parenting provision' (*ibid.*: 18) and to improve the skills of staff working with families. However, it also noted how resources would be used to focus 'help on parents who most need it' (*ibid.*). Such parents include teenage parents. On the one hand, they will be given financial incentives to attend parenting classes (including entitlement to the EMA while they attend them); on the other hand, punitive measures for younger parents (aged 16 and 17) are to be toughened for those who do not attend learning-focused interviews with the Connexions service.

For 'irresponsible parents' (*ibid.*: 19) of all ages the Task Force outlined a new trigger of 'serious misbehaviour' so that a Parenting Order can be made before a child is excluded from school; an extension of the agencies able to engage parents in parenting contracts and request Parenting Orders, and a desire to build into pre-sentence reports and national standards for young offenders recommendations on parenting. For the 'problem families' (*ibid.*: 21), those 'often referred to as "neighbours from hell"' (*ibid.*) – and not just the merely 'irresponsible' – the Respect Task Force recommends the establishment of 'intensive family support schemes'. Quoting the Dundee Project – a voluntary, rather than compulsory, form of family support – as an example of good practice, such schemes will be premised on 'intensive, tailored actions, with supervision and clear sanctions' (*ibid.*: 22; for discussion see Jamieson 2005; Garrett 2007a, 2007b; Bannister *et al.* 2007). In addition, the Action Plan notes a need for a cross-government strategy on 'problem families' and, as is discussed below, 'sanctions for households evicted for anti-social behaviour who refuse help' (Respect Task Force 2006: 23).

Over the past decade or so there have been great strides to intervene in order to address what are perceived to be poor practices of parents whose children are engaged in offending and anti-social behaviour, and, increasingly, those children deemed to be at risk of it. Henricson *et al.* (2000: 325) note that the 'original thinking which led to the introduction of the parenting order arose from reviews carried out in the early 1990s'. These reviews include Utting *et al.* (1993) which clearly indicated various aspects of parenting as being among the most important factors which research has linked to children's aggression and later delinquency (Utting *et al.* 1993). Such research that focuses upon the risk of offending and anti-social behaviour is, however, problematic because of the analytical frameworks – often attachment theory or social learning theory – that are used to explain why particular parenting practices increase the risk of anti-social and offending behaviour. Essentially the argument is that both theories are too broad in their approach and tend to decontextualise child–adult relationships. So, for instance, Rutter and Giller (1983: 253, original italics) argue that social learning theory 'lacks specificity on just *how* antisocial behaviour is acquired and why there are such marked individual differences in behaviour'. Similarly, there are 'unresolved problems' in social learning theory which include explaining why 'antisocial behaviour diminishes so markedly in early adult life' (*ibid.*).

These observations point to a more damning critique of risk-based approaches in that the 'issue of causation is often alluded to, but in the spirit of developing vigorous scientific methods of analysis what emerges is a series of correlations rather than "proven" cause-effect relations' (Muncie 1999: 98). In policy terms, there is evidence of confusion between correlations and causes in New Labour's approach to managing anti-social behaviour through focusing upon parenting. So, for example, in *Respect and Responsibility* (Secretary of State for the Home Department 2003) it is noted in a section on the *causes* of anti-social behaviour that there are *correlates* between various aspects of parenting and a range of behaviours deemed anti-social (for instance, drug and alcohol misuse). Similar observations can be made of the *Respect Action Plan* (Respect Task Force 2006: 17). Furthermore, while Brown (1998: 27–28) points to epistemological problems with studies focusing upon relationships between 'risk' and youth crime, her arguments are equally applicable to those approaches that relate risk to parenting. She notes that studies linking risk and youth crime:

> contribute to the construction of youth-as-other rather than in any way providing a critique of the marginalisation and scapegoating of young people in society. Griffin, indeed, terms this kind of research 'victim blaming' ... 'Victim blaming', although an emotively charged term, does convey the sleight of hand in such research: adult researchers define 'the problem' (what is anti-social, what is 'delinquent', what is socially acceptable), relegate young people to a zone of exclusion where they represent 'the problem', and seek to explain why these young people stand 'outside' of society: without, of course, authenticating the voices of young people themselves.

The general thrust of Brown's argument is that risk-based approaches reproduce conservative views; in this case, of young people as being 'other' and threatening, without attempting to deconstruct their socio-economic marginalisation and their ideological construction as being a group that is inherently problematic. Similar arguments can be made of attempts to connect anti-social behaviour and/or offending with parenting in that they reproduce a conservative view of 'problem' families that are outside of the 'mainstream' and a threat to it.

Parenting, anti-social behaviour and social policy

While criminal justice interventions are perhaps the most clearly concerned with parenting, they are by no means the only interventions concerned with such issues. Indeed, relationships held to exist between parenting and anti-social behaviour clearly demonstrate how some social policies, at least in part, are increasingly concerned with criminal justice-type issues. Here we focus upon developments in education and housing policy to make the point.

Education

When elected in 1997, New Labour pronounced education to be its 'number one priority' (1997 Labour Party Manifesto, cited in Stedward 2000: 170). While education had been one of the main concerns of the Labour Party in the post-Second World War period (Stedward 2000), by 1997 it had taken on a particular significance for at least two reasons. First, framed by concerns since the 1960s with human capital (*ibid.*), education was seen as enabling 'individuals to obtain employment and stable income sources in a global market' (Kendall and Holloway 2001: 154). Second, and related, Kendall and Holloway (*ibid.*) argue that education was 'also seen as a way to break the cycle of dependency ... by addressing issues of social exclusion'. With such importance placed upon education as enabling people to find their niche in the global economy, it is perhaps not surprising that New Labour would be concerned with ensuring that parents took an active interest in the education of their offspring, most notably ensuring that they reach school and behave once they are there. In pursuit of these concerns the 1996 Education Act was amended to raise the maximum penalty for failing to send a child to school to a fine of £2,500 and three months' imprisonment, while the 2003 Anti-social Behaviour Act introduced parenting contracts and extended Parenting Orders by allowing Local Educational Authorities (LEAs) to apply for them in respect of the parents of pupils excluded on the grounds of discipline. Parenting Contracts are intended for use with those parents whose children have been excluded from school, or those who have failed to ensure their child(ren) attend school regularly. The contract is signed 'voluntarily' by the parent as an agreement to comply with its requirements. Failure to do so can result in a fixed penalty notice, prosecution (for attendance-related contracts) or a court-imposed Parenting Order (for exclusion-related contracts).

Payne (2003: 323) describes the developments of the 2003 Anti-social Behaviour Act as sharing the 'punitive philosophy which underpins much of government thinking'. Her observations are particularly pertinent given the further extension of Parenting Orders in the 2006 Education and Inspection Act which allows Parenting Orders to be sought in cases where the pupil has 'seriously misbehaved but has not been excluded' (Department for Education and Skills 2006a: 291); and which allows schools to apply for Parenting Orders. The Act also makes parents responsible for ensuring that excluded pupils are supervised during their expulsion. If necessary, their responsibilities will be enforced through the criminal justice system by a new offence, punishable by a fine, if 'the excluded pupil is present in a public place at any time during school hours on a school day' in the first five days of their expulsion (2006 Education and Inspection Act, Ch. 2, s. 103).

In summary, education is held to be one of the main factors in attempts to increase the opportunities of children to become productive members of society when they are adults. This process cannot be threatened by disruptive behaviour and, therefore, it is increasingly protected by the criminalisation of financially poor parents who are deemed to be taking inadequate interest in their children's education and future. Education, however, is only one area in which the state and such parents come into close contact over the behaviour of the latter's offspring. The other is housing.

Housing

Over the past two decades there have been two social policy developments – eviction and the sanctioning of HB – aimed at addressing anti-social behaviour.

Eviction and the 1996 Housing Act

'The first government proposals addressing the issue [of how social landlords should engage with anti-social behaviour] were contained in the Department of Environment consultation paper in 1995 entitled *Anti-Social Behaviour on Council Estates: Consultation Paper on Probationary Tenancies*' (Hunter and Nixon 2001: 91). This consultation paper, Haworth and Manzi (1999) argue, had a distinctly moral agenda because it increasingly aligned the tenancies of social housing tenants to their own behaviour and that of their family and visitors. The suggestion of probationary or introductory tenancy, they note (*ibid.*), for example, was to distinguish the 'deserving' from the 'undeserving' by withholding a secure tenancy for at least a year in order for the new tenant to prove that they could act pro-socially. The consultation document, for example, noted that:

> A secure tenancy is a valuable asset, providing a home for life. *In the Government's view, this has to be earned* ... A probationary tenancy, to be converted automatically into a secure tenancy on its satisfactory completion, would give a clear signal to new tenants that anti-social behaviour was unacceptable and could result in the loss of their home. (Department of the Environment 1995, cited in Haworth and Manzi 1999: 161, their emphasis)

Probationary or introductory tenancies were introduced in the 1996 Housing Act. In order to deal with those people whose anti-social behaviour develops later on into their tenancy, the 2003 Anti-Social Behaviour Act introduced legislation that 'enables social landlords to demote existing secure tenancies to 12-month "probationary" tenancies' (Flint and Nixon 2006: 949). The aim is to give tenants the opportunity to change their behaviour or, if they do not, to enable landlords to evict them more easily.

The 1996 Housing Act also extended the nuisance grounds for the possession of tenancies, which essentially meant that it became 'easier for landlords to gain possession' (Hunter and Nixon 2001: 92), and introduced measures that allowed local authorities to seek injunctions against non-tenants 'where the person against whom it was sought had committed or threatened violence' (*ibid.*). This legislation has since been extended so that both local authorities and registered social landlords are able to seek such injunctions 'whether or not violence was involved' (Nixon and Hunter 2004: 4).

Burney (2002: 479; see also Papps 1998) argues that the 1996 Housing Act introduced a 'formidable range of action against recalcitrant tenants'. This is reflected in the more theoretically informed work of Flint (2002) who argues that we should understand the development of policies such as the 1996 Housing Act as techniques of governance through the responsibilisation of populations inhabiting particular social spaces, most notably the tenants of local authorities and registered social landlords. In this sense, the legislation is concerned with managing the behaviour of poor people, for those people living in local authority and registered social landlord accommodation tend to be from lower income groups. This is a familiar theme in the use of housing as a deterrent to, and/or a punishment for, anti-social behaviour, and is also reflected in the desire to sanction HB, financial support to help meet the housing costs (though not necessarily all of them) of the poorest people.

Housing Benefit sanctions and anti-social behaviour
We saw in the previous section that for over a decade it has been possible, using administrative and legal means, to evict people for anti-social behaviour. However, it is also the case that since the year 2000 there has been a concern, framed by the rights and responsibilities of New Labour's Anglicanised Communitarianism, that if people want to have the right to receive financial support for their housing needs, then they should be expected to behave in a responsible manner. In developing ideas to promote a 'healthy private rented sector', for example, the Green Paper on housing, *Quality and Choice: a decent home for all* (Department for the Environment, Transport and Regions 2000: para. 5.46), argued that the rules governing the payment of HB 'could be adapted to encourage both tenants and landlords to behave responsibly'. In the case of tenants, while the Green Paper (*ibid.*: para. 5.47) noted that local authorities would need to be assured that the 'innocent families of unruly tenants did not suffer', it suggested that they 'could be given the powers to reduce HB for unruly tenants as an alternative, or as part of the process of pursuing an Anti-Social Behaviour Order'. In the case of landlords, it was suggested that the payment of HB of anti-social tenants directly to them would be declined (*ibid.*: para. 5.48). This suggestion, however, contradicted other concerns with individual responsibility and the structure of the private rented housing sector, which means that the use of the direct payment of HB to landlords will, for most claimants, stop in April 2008 (see Priemus and Kemp 2004; Stephens 2005). In contrast, apart from clauses in the 2004 Housing Act allowing the introduction of selective landlord registration schemes in areas deemed to be of low housing demand, and where an area is deemed to be experiencing a 'significant and persistent problem caused by anti-social behaviour (Part 3, Section 80 6(a)), little action is taken against landlords who do not engage with the behaviour of their tenants.

Hence, the main focus has been upon withdrawing HB from tenants said to be engaged in anti-social behaviour. The first attempt at getting such a Bill passed came not from the government, but from former Minister for Welfare Reform and MP for Birkenhead, Frank Field. Field introduced to parliament a Private Members' Bill[2] in 2002 and argued in parliament that it represented 'a demand from the poor to control the unacceptable behaviour of people whom they do not want in their midst – not because they are uncharitable or unforgiving, but because any scrap of reasonable life has become impossible for them' (Standing Committee B 2002, cols. 15–16). Field was suggesting that the move to withhold HB was driven by a concern with the quality of life of poorer people, but in letting populist concerns drive the agenda Field was actually reproducing what we have seen is a long-standing distinction between 'deserving' and 'undeserving', and 'respectable' and 'irresponsible' poor people.

Field's proposal for withholding the payment of HB reflected his wider concern that there has been a *'collapse of decent behaviour'* (Field 2003: 9, original italics) and that: 'Making welfare dependent on good behaviour should be part of a new citizenship contract' (*ibid.*: 109). Field was close to New Labour's thought on this issue and the government supported the Bill by suggesting amendments 'to make the proposals compatible with ... European human rights law' (the *Guardian*, 11 July 2002), although its commitment to the Bill was not particularly significant because it was unable to secure enough time to ensure its safe passage through parliament.

The sanctioning of HB because of anti-social behaviour, however, did not disappear from the political agenda and it was announced in the White Paper, *Respect and Responsibilities: taking a stand against anti-social behaviour* (Secretary of State for the Home Department 2003, para. 4.48) that there would be a consultation on 'whether to give local authorities an enabling power to withhold payments of HB to individual tenants where they believe this is the most effective way of tackling anti-social behaviour'. The consultation took place in the summer of 2003 and was framed through an unambiguous reference to Anglicanised Communitarianism, for it noted that the 'rights we gain from civil society – including the right to financial support when we need it – should be balanced by responsibilities to behave responsibly towards our fellow citizens' (Department for Work and Pensions 2003a: para. 1). The aim of the sanction was twofold – to act as a deterrent to anti-social behaviour; and – suggesting little faith in the idea of its acting as a deterrent – that it would be a means of penalising people for such behaviour (*ibid.*, para. 15). The government's preference was for an administrative sanction that would not involve the courts, but would involve cooperation between HB departments and local authority anti-social behaviour co-ordinators, and, as with the potential to evict tenants because of anti-social behaviour, would have covered the behaviour of all of those at a particular address, including the tenant, her/his family and any visitors.

The majority of the responses to the consultation were negative, with 75 per cent of respondents being against the proposals. Community Safety Partnerships, charities and public bodies, local authorities and registered social landlords were particularly opposed to the proposal, although tenants and members of the public were more evenly split (Department for Work and Pensions 2004a). While many of the respondents supported the need to deal effectively with anti-social behaviour, there were objections related to the principle of punishing poor people by making them even poorer and/or homeless by withdrawing HB, which, for some, was inherently discriminatory (see, for example, Chartered Institute of Housing 2003, partly reproduced as S. Lister 2004). Others argued that such a sanction would not deal with the causes of anti-social behaviour and would merely exacerbate the material circumstances that frame such behaviour (for instance, CPAG 2003), while still others suggested that such proposals would be counter-productive in the government's desire to tackle social exclusion and, as part of this agenda, to simplify the benefit system (Department for Work and Pensions 2004a). As a result of such concerns the proposals were dropped.

Explaining why this was the case, then Minister for Work and Pensions Chris Pond MP argued that the government wanted to see what the effects were of measures introduced in the 2003 Anti-Social Behaviour Act before introducing even more measures, although he warned that the government had not ruled out using HB sanctions in the future (Department for Work and Pensions 2004b). That future arrived two years later with the 2006 Welfare Reform Bill.

As part of the RESPECT agenda the 2006 Welfare Reform Bill indicated the introduction of legislation that would allow local authorities, initially in pilot areas only, to 'sanction housing benefit where a person has been evicted for anti-social behaviour and refuses to address their behaviour using the support and help offered to them' (Department for Work and Pensions 2006a: 1). This was a diluted version of earlier attempts to sanction HB. It was justified on the grounds that unless 'a clear signal' was sent 'to those evicted for anti-social behaviour that they are at the end of the line and cannot simply expect to move to another property and continue their bad behaviour at the expense of decent hard-working families', public confidence in the welfare system would be undermined (John Hutton MP, then Secretary of State for Work and Pensions, House of Commons Debates 2006a, col. 627). In this sense, the need to maintain support for welfare provision was being mediated through the RESPECT agenda and demonstrates how the receipt of benefits designed to meet particular needs (in this case for housing) is thought to have a potentially important role in changing the behaviour of individuals. The message is clear: change your ways or lose your home! Unusually in dealing with the anti-social behaviour of tenants, the sanctioning of HB will apply to private tenants, as well as to those of registered social landlords. The proposals are concerned with the potential displacement of anti-social behaviour, for sanctions should prevent people who are evicted because of anti-social behaviour from merely moving to a new address without having engaged with 'support' to challenge and address that behaviour. What is not clear, however, is what will happen to those people who, for whatever reason, do not accept the 'support' on offer and therefore cannot pay rent for a new accommodation.

Parenting, material context and gender

New Labour's extension of concerns relating parenting to anti-social and offending behaviour has prompted a growing academic literature. Critiques are varied, from those concerned with the detail of the anti-social behaviour/parenting agenda to more theoretically informed approaches concerned with governance in contemporary society. Here, however, the focus is upon two issues that are central to *Crime and Inequality*: the decontextualising of parenting and anti-social behaviour from their material basis; and a gendered concern with the operation of measures to tackle anti-social behaviour.

Anti-social behaviour and parenting: the material context

A contradiction lies at the heart of New Labour's attempts to deal with anti-social behaviour through focusing upon parenting. Barlow and Duncan (2000a: 29 neatly sum this up when they argue in relation to Parenting Orders that the 'emphasis [is] on solving *social* problems (here labelled "family problems") ... through intervention in *individual* behaviour (here parenting)'. Barlow and Duncan's point is supported by the work of Goldson and Jamieson (2002) who note the ways in which recent developments in criminal justice policy (and one might add social policies) are structured through the idea of a parenting deficit that strips parenting and parental responsibility from their material context. While government ministers and policy-makers may like to think that material circumstances have little bearing upon parenting, it is more realistic, as Utting (1995: 40) argues, to think that '[l]iving on a low income in a run-down neighbourhood does not make it impossible to be an affectionate, authoritative parent ... [but] it undeniably makes it more difficult'. Parenting cannot be divorced from material conditions, for even the most skilful of parents will find difficulties with exercising those skills where they are lacking the 'necessary life opportunities and facilities' (Rutter, cited in Utting 1995: 33).

This is reflected in the evidence that can rarely locate the wilfully neglectful parents that seem to absorb so much policy time and effort. What the research evidence does indicate is that poor parents do as much as they can to prevent their children from engaging in offending and anti-social behaviour, given the material context in which they are living (Goldson and Jamieson 2002). In addition, Goldson and Jamieson quote their research with parents who were attending parenting projects and who 'described their consistent, if frustrated, efforts to "control" their children' (*ibid.*: 93). There was little sense in which the parents that Goldson and Jamieson (2002) interviewed could be understood to be wilfully neglectful in their parental duties and responsibilities in the ways that develop-ments in criminal justice often imply. Indeed, they found (*ibid.*) that those people attending parenting classes often spoke about their experiences of them, not in relation to the skills that they were being furnished with, but with the escape that the classes presented from a life structured through marginalisation, isolation and multi-layered socio-economic deprivation. As Goldson and Jamieson (*ibid.*: 94) note:

> it is telling of such parents' circumstances and experience of struggle that a youth justice intervention can be conceived in terms of 'escape', 'release', 'relief', time to meet with people who 'want to know how you are and how you are feeling', an opportunity simply to 'meet different people', 'a break from routine', and even a 'social life'.

This is an informative observation of the focus upon parenting, for the experiences of parenting programmes of these parents say more about the isolation and marginalisation of poor parents in contemporary society than they do about how skilful or otherwise they are as parents.

Criminalising poor mothers

While Goldson and Jamieson's (2002) work is helpful in its insights into relationships between poverty and exclusion, parenting and youth justice, the authors privilege concerns with class over other social divisions. Hence, their writing of 'punishing parents' – a term that is gender-neutral – disguises the fact that policies aimed at tackling the perceived 'parenting deficit', or evicting people from their tenancies either directly through the 1996 Housing Act (and, in the future, more indirectly through the withholding of HB), impact more greatly upon women than they do men. Because responsibility for the socialisation of children is still marked as being a characteristic of the feminine in contemporary society, women bear the brunt of policies designed to punish those who are seen as failing parents. As Scourfield and Drakeford (2002: 627) note:

> the impact of policies that impose home–school agreements, fine the parents of truants or require the parents of children appearing before the courts to attend parenting class falls quite disproportionately upon mothers, not fathers.

Scourfield and Drakeford's argument is supported by the evaluation of parenting programmes (Ghate and Ramella 2002) which found that the vast majority (81 per cent) of parents taking part in such programmes were mothers. In holding parents responsible for the actions of their children, it is actually women who are being criminalised. This should not be surprising given the (overly) optimistic view of fathering upon which many of New Labour's social and criminal justice policies are premised (Scourfield and Drakeford 2002) and was reflected in 2002 when a lone mother with two dependent children to care for became the first person to be imprisoned for failing to ensure that they attended school regularly under amendments introduced by New Labour to the 1996 Education Act (the *Guardian*, 14 May 2002). Her jailing was welcomed by the then Secretary of State for Education, Estelle Morris MP, as being a sign that truancy was being taking seriously and the punishment was helping to address the 'nervous[ness] about talking about parental responsibility' (*ibid.*). However, the Secretary of State did not seem to recognise the irony of the fact that after the mother's imprisonment, her children, had their older sister not stepped in, would have been without supervision.[3]

Such concerns have also been found in relation to evictions because of anti-social behaviour. In many ways, the findings of Hunter and

Nixon (2001) are consistent with the themes highlighted by Goldson and Jamieson (2002); that parents (mothers in the case of Hunter and Nixon) feel that they do all they can in order to control the behaviour of their children (and partners), which is often the cause of eviction proceedings against them as tenants. However, Hunter and Nixon (2001) argue that in institutional and legal discourses constructions of neighbourhood nuisance conjoin with the behavioural 'underclass' thesis (Murray 1984, 1990, 1994) to help explain why lone mothers appear more often than would be expected in cases of the repossession of social housing due to problematic behaviour. In such cases, Hunter and Nixon (*ibid.*) demonstrate how, through discursive concerns with parenting and partnering, lone mothers are held responsible for the anti-social behaviour of their male children and partners. They note (*ibid.*: 404), for example, how the language used by judges in appeal proceedings concerning repossession 'reflects a view of single parents, which suggests that in the absence of a husband, they are "inadequate parents"'. The comments of one judge were particularly telling:

> I have to say that I found her protests are not persuasive. At a time when her son was getting into deeper trouble at the school, and his offending was deteriorating, and he was video'd … scrawling graffiti on the wall, her attention was elsewhere … [S]he conceived a child in the summer of 1997 (that baby is now five months old) and will have been at the very best, visibly pregnant to her son, who might be forgiven for thinking that her attention, if not her affection, was elsewhere. (*ibid.*)

While Hunter and Nixon (*ibid.*) note that the comments of this judge reflect more general concerns with lone mothers, they arguably also reflect an equally enduring view of poor working-class families as profligate. In brief, and consistent with historical concerns with a culturally defined 'underclass' (see Macnicol 1987; Welshman 2006), the concern of the judge was the fact that the lone mother was having yet another child when he held she could not adequately socialise those she already had.

In the context of the parenting skills of lone mothers, which in this case also seems to extend to their ability to control partners who were often violent, Hunter and Nixon (*ibid.*: 401) argue that eviction is being used in a particularly punitive manner:

Instead of seeking to develop remedial interventions to tackle the underlying causes of the nuisance behaviour, landlords' strategies emphasized the threat or actual loss of the home as a method to control behaviour. More specifically in terms of taking action against women-headed households, there was a failure by many landlords to take into account the tenant's ability to control the perpetrator's behaviour. Notwithstanding the fact that in the majority of cases involving women-headed households, the main perpetrator of the behaviour complained about was not the woman, women were still held to be responsible for the antisocial behaviour. (*ibid.*: 401)

It is clear from these examples that it is not possible to understand fully strategies for dealing with anti-social behaviour without recognising that they have particularly punitive gender implications. We have seen how it is women (mainly lone mothers) who are held accountable for the anti-social behaviour of their children and their male partners. Rather than attempting to explain why those who are actually engaged in the anti-social behaviour are doing so, the focus is upon why lone mothers do not prevent their children and partners from acting in such a manner. This is clearly problematic for a set of policies informed by the notion of rights and responsibilities, for the responsibility, even if lone mothers have done all they can to control the behaviour of the children and partners, is shouldered by the women. The (often teenage) children, and particularly adult male partners, are not held to be responsible for their behaviour, which is explained by the failings of the women to be caring and effective parents and partners; the 'cowardly and ineffectual wife or mother' as described by one judge (*ibid.*: 404).

Parenting, anti-social behaviour and state welfare

Garrett (2006) points out that, central to the remoralisation of poorer communities has been:

the evolution of a new type of welfare state in which 'welfare' was to become 'a hand-up not a hand-out' (Blair 1999: 13 and 17) and its provision was to become more and more conditional on behaviour and a willingness to become 'economically active' (see Blair 1999; Levitas 1996). The 'anti-social behaviour' construct was, moreover, to fulfil an emblematic role within this emerging paradigm.

We have seen in this chapter how measures to tackle anti-social behaviour are not only emblematic of the 'something for something' welfare state, but, through the punitive elements of housing and benefit policy, are constitutive of it. Rodger (2006: 124, original emphasis) argues that recent anti-social behaviour legislation has changed the emphasis of the welfare state 'from one geared to *social steering* through the incentives provided by welfare services and benefits to that of *social control* through the imposition of supervisory orders and the disincentives provided by the criminal justice legislation and the *withholding*, or threat of withholding, of welfare support'. While Rodger (*ibid.*) is careful to point to historical continuity with concerns related to social control, he nevertheless argues that there is a need in contemporary society to understand how policies relate to culture, for social policies, he argues, 'cannot change values orientations, at least not in the sense discussed by ... those who support the antisocial behaviour legislation'. The main problem Rodger sees is that policies being pursued by New Labour are narrowly focused upon human capital (for instance, the ability to parent 'adequately'). In contrast, he suggests that in order to address the issues facing what he calls 'post-employment neighbourhoods' (*ibid.*: 137), there needs to be a greater emphasis upon cultural capital. In this sense, the issues faced by such neighbourhoods will not be addressed through quick political fixes that focus upon the human capital of individuals, but require social policies that 'seek to shape the existence within which people live their routine lives' (*ibid.*: 124). This, he suggests, means there 'needs to be more welfare support not less' (*ibid.*: 138).

The policy path chosen by New Labour, however, does involve reduced welfare support for those who are deemed to be anti-social or unable to control the behaviour of children and partners. If, as we have seen, offending and anti-social behaviour are linked empirically and theoretically to inequality, then the efficacy of housing policy and benefit policy, through which tenants and their dependants can and will be made homeless, can be questioned not only in terms of social justice, but also in terms of criminal justice. A case highlighted in the *Guardian* (23 December 2003) makes the point. A lone mother and her son were evicted from their 'two-up, two-down home on the grounds of [the son's] unreasonable behaviour'. A month after their evictions they remained homeless and separated; she was sleeping on her father's sofa and her son was staying with friends (her son could not stay with her at her father's because her father was fearful of losing his own tenancy if the son stayed and acted anti-socially). While the homelessness charity *Shelter* noted that '[l]egally they have to be rehoused', the 'council has accepted that she is unintentionally homeless, but it says she is an unsuitable tenant and it will not rehouse her' (*ibid.*). In the meantime, and as the woman at the centre of the story noted:

> How am I meant to control him now when he's nine miles away? When I try to track him down and go down to see him, he's never there. I leave him his bus fare to get down, 'cause he's got no money to get down, so I see him maybe once or twice a week.

The situation of this women and her child is unsatisfactory from a social justice point of view and is contradictory from a criminal justice point of view. The emphasis upon parenting requires greater interaction between children and their parents, not their separation through homelessness or, as we have seen in the case of truancy, imprisonment. These contradictions are the consequence of the desire to enforce particular forms of behaviour without attempting to engage with the causes of anti-social behaviour. And it is a problem that is likely to increase in the future. In 2002, for example, the *Guardian* (*ibid.*) notes that over 2,200 evictions were the consequence of the operation of ASBOs. More recently, it was estimated that the withholding of HB from those who do not engage with local authorities to address anti-social behaviour will result, once the scheme goes nationwide, in 1,500 tenants per annum being evicted (Department for Work and Pensions 2006b). As we have seen, anti-social behaviour is often perpetrated by people other than the tenant and, therefore, the number of people affected by homelessness and the consequence of eviction will be far higher than 1,500.

Concerns have been raised about the state through (anti)social policies making people, particularly children, homeless, but while such concerns are acknowledged (for example, John Hutton MP, Secretary of State for Work and Pensions, House of Commons Debates 2006a: col. 630), it is clear that an essentially utilitarian argument that distinguishes between the 'deserving' and 'undeserving' is driving the agenda. In this scenario those who 'flout any proper standards of social behaviour' are contrasted to their neighbours who are expected 'through their taxes and income, to support their [those engaged in anti-social behaviour] lifestyle' (*ibid.*).

Conclusion

The focus upon relationships held to exist between parenting and anti-social behaviour is a reflection of wider issues regarding the relationship between individual families and the state. We have seen that New Labour's intellectual roots are grounded in a brand of communitarianism that demands responsibilities from all adults, no matter what material circumstances structure their lives or what other pressures they face. This introduces tensions across a range of state interventions, but particularly so in the case of parenting and anti-social behaviour because it is structured through ideas that are fundamentally contradictory (Grover 2005a). Most notably, as we have seen, the idea that social obligation and responsibility must, if necessary, be enforced means that the state has to have the wherewithal to punish the errant. It can do this through criminal justice sanctions (for instance, fines for not adhering to Parenting Orders and imprisonment for not ensuring children attend school and so forth). However, it is also the case that the state is increasingly using social policies aimed at relieving particular forms of need as a means of deterrent and/or punishment; eviction from social housing and the proposed withdrawal of HB are good examples of such developments. If people want the right to live in social housing or in private rented accommodation supported through state benefits then they, their families, partners and visitors must act in a pro-social manner. If not, they are in real danger of losing their homes. Such developments do little to tackle the antecedents of anti-social behaviour. In contrast, they merely marginalise further already marginalised people, thereby contributing to the material context of anti-social and offending behaviour.

Notes

1 Louise Casey, the 'Government Co-ordinator for Respect' (Jamieson 2005: 180), for example, is reported as believing that 'the state can have a role in the family, since for some parents – both middle class and deprived poor – parenting is either a mystery or beyond them' (the *Guardian*, 26 July 2006).
2 The Housing Benefit (Withholding of Payment) Bill.
3 The *Daily Mirror* (14 May 2002) reported that the older sister 'said no one from social services told her that her mother had been jailed or that her sisters needed caring for'.

Chapter 5

Women, crime and inequality

Introduction

This chapter focuses upon relationships between women, crime and inequality by examining, first, relationships between women and signifiers of inequality and, second, using the work of Carlen (1988) and Phoenix (1999) the evidence regarding the nature of the relationships between female offending and material circumstances. The chapter then changes focus to examine arguments that women, as lone mothers, are a source of concern with regard to crime and anti-social behaviour because of their alleged inabilities to furnish their male children in particular with the correct role models. The chapter argues that as with other groups – such as young men – deemed to be problematic, the solution to the problem that lone mothers are thought to pose to society is seen as paid employment. Hence, the chapter also critically examines the mechanisms through which the state has attempted to engineer greater levels of employment among lone mothers, although it concludes that the drive to get more lone mothers into paid work will exacerbate their relatively poor material circumstances that contextualise their offending.

Women and inequality

In Chapter 2 we examined evidence of the nature and level of inequality in contemporary society. The data discussed there was not gendered. However, when we introduce gender to the analysis what we find is that there are substantial inequities between men and women. This is indicated by the following:

- On average, women earn less then men do. The difference in hourly earnings between men and women is nearly a fifth (17.1 per cent) (Equal Opportunities Commission 2006: 19).

- Women are more likely to work part time compared to men (42 per cent and 9 per cent respectively) (*ibid.* 2006: 11). This relates to the point above, for the difference between the average hourly wage for female part-time workers compared to male full-time workers is, at 38.4 per cent, even greater than that for female full-time workers. This is because part-time employment is associated with low pay, demonstrated by the fact that female workers, especially those who work part time, are the main beneficiaries of increases in the NMW (Low Pay Commission 2003, 2005).

- Labour markets are segregated in such a way that women are concentrated in those sectors related to activities and attributes that, in Fraser's (1997) analysis, are coded as being feminine. While, for instance, women make up nearly one half (47 per cent) of all employed people, they constitute nearly four out of every five (79 per cent) people employed in the health and social work sectors, and three-quarters (73 per cent) of those working in education (Equal Opportunities Commission 2006: 21). Within these sectors women are concentrated in the most poorly paid sectors. So, for instance, it is estimated that 98–99 per cent of early years child care workers, who are particularly poorly paid, are female (Cameron *et al.* 2002);

- Women are more likely than men to live in household types that are likely to be workless. So, for example, while in spring 2006 nearly four in 10 lone mother households were workless, only 4.9 per cent of couple households were (National Statistics 2006c).

- Women with dependent children are particularly disadvantaged in labour markets. There is what the Equalities Reviews (2007) call an 'employment penalty' (the number of percentage points less likely it is that mothers with dependent children will be engaged in paid work compared to men), for example, of 49 for lone and 45 for partnered mothers with children under 11 years of age. As children get older the 'penalty' reduces, but a partnered mother with children over the age of 11 still faces a 'penalty' of 29 (*ibid.*, Figure 3.8: 63).

- Women are more likely than men to live in familial forms that are at the greatest risk of poverty. So, for example, in 2001/02 over half (53 per cent) of lone mother headed households were living in poverty[1] compared to a fifth (20 per cent) of couple households with dependent children (Flaherty *et al.* 2004, Figure 2.3: 40).

- Given the above observations, it is perhaps not surprising that women are concentrated in the lower quintiles of the income distribution. In 2001/02 over half (54 per cent), for example, were in the lowest two quintiles, compared to only a quarter (26 per cent) of men (*ibid.*, Table 6.1: 165).

From these observations it is possible to see that the inequities and poverty faced by women have two main causes: their position *vis-à-vis* paid employment and their relationship to men. There is a conjoining here of what Fraser (1997) describes as the political economic and cultural valuation structures. In this sense, the inequalities that women face compared to men are the consequence of the ways in which capitalism exploits women in different ways compared to men (for example, by employing them on a part-time basis, rather than full time as is the case with men) *and* of the fact that through the cultural valuation system those traits coded as feminine are interpreted as having little economic value.

Underpinning such arguments is the assumption that women are, or should be, dependent upon men because their role in families with dependent children is as carer, rather than as earner, despite the important contribution to the family income made by their wages in couple households (Bradshaw *et al.* 2003). Here, there is a further conjoining of the economic and cultural, for the assumption of female dependency has historically been used as an economic tool by both labour in its demands for a 'breadwinner wage' or 'family wage' (see Land 1980; Humphries and Rubery 1984; Seccombe 1986) and capitalism through gendered inequities in wage and employment structures (see Hunt 1975; Hakim 1995). While there is an argument that there has been a move away from the constitution of the 'breadwinner model', particularly through social policies (see Lewis 2002; Duncan *et al.* 2003; Bennett 2002), as Chapter 3 demonstrated, recent policy developments for young men are partly structured through a desire to reconstruct what is seen as an erosion of female dependency in working-class households.

There is a problem of social justice here for all women workers, but there is a particular problem for women who are not dependent on men, but whose earnings are nevertheless structured through such assumptions. Moreover, the social security system that we now have is an extension of the post-Second World War system that assumed female dependency. Indeed, it is arguable that recent developments in social security policy have consolidated the relatively poor position of women in couple households. In the case of unemployed couples, for instance, the partners of JSA claimants face the responsibility of searching for and taking part in work activation measures without having access to an independent benefit income. In other words, they have responsibilities but no rights (Rake 2001). Second, while the subsidisation of paid work might give women in couple households more opportunities to be the main wage earner, it is actually presented as something that can be used to subsidise female dependency upon men. Comments from the then Prime Minister (Blair 2004: 1) that the 'working tax credit enables half a million mothers to choose to stay at home' rather than go out to work demonstrates a conservative agenda, rather than any serious attempt to tackle gender inequality.

Given these observations that, on average, women are poorer than men in contemporary society, what is evidence of relationships between their poor material circumstances and crime?

Women, crime and poverty

Criminology in the late 20th century was described as the 'most masculine of all the social sciences, a speciality that wore six-shooters on its hips and strutted its machismo' (Rafter and Heidensohn 1995: 5). However, it was with the development of second wave feminism that critiques of the criminological enterprise demonstrated its sexist nature (for example, Heidensohn 1968; Klein 1973; Smart 1977). 'Malestream' criminology was criticised for constructing female criminality as being the consequence of a stereotyped femininity that acted to confirm:

the biologically determined inferior status of women not only in conventional society but also in the 'world' of crime and delinquency ... The majority of ... these studies [for instance, Lombroso and Ferrero 1895; Thomas 1967; Cowie *et al.* 1968] refer to women in terms of their biological impulses and hormonal balance or in terms of their domesticity, maternal instinct and passivity. (Smart 1977: xiii–xiv)

Alongside such critiques of the criminological enterprise, we see in the 1970s more sociologically informed analyses of female crime emerging. So, for instance, it was argued that increasing female offending and aggression therein reflected the emancipation or liberation of women (Adler 1975; Simon 1975), an argument that has more recently been made by the media with reference to the phenomenon of girl gangs (Chesney-Lind 1999). The emancipation thesis, however, was criticised as being empirically and chronologically inaccurate (Smart 1979; Hartnagel 1982; Box and Hale 1983) and because, ideologically, it offered 'a new guise for the same old double standard: the Angel in the House must not – for the sake of the social order – be allowed to "fall"' (Downes and Rock 1998: 312). In contrast to notions of emancipation, Downes and Rock (*ibid.*) argue that it was, in fact, economic marginalisation that best explained the 'modest convergence in property crime rates' (see Box and Hale 1983).

The focus upon relationships between economic marginalisation and crime was taken forward in Britain in Carlen's (1988) *Women, Crime and Poverty*. Using, as we have noted in Chapter 2, a social control theoretical framework, Carlen examined the lives of 39 female offenders. In some ways, Carlen's study reinforces the argument that relating offending to material circumstances can be problematic. So, for example, while 32 of the 39 women had been poor all their lives (according to Field's [1989] definition of poverty that focuses upon certain groups at risk of poverty), only 12 argued that their poverty was a cause of their offending. Some respondents, for instance, argued that they did not consider poverty to be a cause of their offending because they did not realise at the time exactly how poor they were and that they knew other people who were poor, but who did not offend. It was also argued by some that they drifted into crime without giving the causation much thought and that offending was the consequence of a desire for excitement.

In fact, Carlen argues that there were four prime constituents of the law-breaking of the women in her study. Poverty was one. The others were: being in residential care; addictions; and the quest for excitement. However, arguably, the last three factors are, in various ways, related to poverty. Spending time in local authority care, for instance, is an experience closely associated with having poor life chances and material circumstances in adulthood (Broad 1998; Biehal and Wade 1999; Frost *et al.* 1999; Fitzpatrick 2000). With reference to drug use, heroin in particular, Carlen outlines strong arguments relating addiction to the marginalised lives of the women she interviewed. In the lives, for example, of the eight women who were or had been addicted to it, heroin played a 'blanking off' role. It was this that had been its major attraction, for they had plenty to blank off. Six had either been on the run from their families or local authority care and/or living on the streets. Carlen argues that while poverty does not cause people to use heroin nor does that use cause them to commit crime (although there was a clear indication that once addicted women used crime to fund their use of it), she does argue that whether or not the women continued using it depended upon the incentives they had to come off and stay off it. In brief, they were unlikely to cease using illicit drugs as long as they needed cocooning from their social and economic circumstances. Some of the women also made connections between boredom and a lack of money, particularly in a society where consumerism could deliver the 'good life'. In this context, Carlen (1988: 100) argues that: 'With no money to spend, the spending of time in itself became a killer'.

While Carlen (1994) is critical of the privilege that she gave to gender over other concepts, most notably 'race', in *Women, Crime and Poverty*, it is nevertheless a book that is rich in observation and in many ways demonstrates the interconnectedness of deprivation and emotionality that Young (2003) writes of as being crucial to understanding offending, for her study shows that crime can be more than just a mechanism for material gain. The stories told by the women make it difficult to consider many of their offences as being rational responses to their material circumstances. Many of the women, for example, drifted into offending through the development of social networks with women who were engaged in offending behaviours (see also Carlen *et al.* 1985). Moreover, offending brought more than material reward. We have seen, it brought excitement, but it also reduced isolation through the development of social networks with other marginalised and law-breaking women.

However, while the women's lives were marked by poverty, a sense of powerlessness and often racial and patriarchal oppression, Carlen is keen to highlight that the women had not given up on life, despite incidents of self-harm and suicide attempts. The women's stories demonstrated a struggle 'to *make* ends meet, to *take* on inequity, to *make* their lives' (Carlen 1988: 110). This struggle, Carlen argues, involved resistance to traditional forms of capitalist and patriarchal control (the workplace and 'the family'); a resistance, despite the poverty of the women, to 'crap jobs' and/or dependence upon men. In this sense, the women refused what Carlen (*ibid.*: 13) describes as the 'class deal' and 'gender deal' whose exploitation is disguised by ideologies of consumerism, familialism and the 'good family'. That resistance was partly enacted through their law-breaking.

These themes were reflected in Phoenix's (1999) more recent study of women who were criminalised for their involvement in prostitution. She, for example, demonstrates how her 21 respondents' involvement in prostitution was framed by the poor work and income chances for women, particularly those considered to be 'unskilled' and those returning to paid work after bearing and caring for children, outlined at the beginning of this chapter. Phoenix highlights, for instance, the ways in which work in the formal economy was found not to be a guard against poverty for the women and how casualised, flexibilised employment – what Gray (1998) refers to as 'flexploitation' – offered little in the way of security or stability. Capitalism could not offer an adequate or stable income to the women and their children in Phoenix's study. And once engaged in prostitution, entry-level employment that governments are so keen that workless people, particularly lone mothers, take, became even less financially attractive. As Christine told Phoenix (1999: 73):

> This old friend of mine used to come into the card shop and see, like, and I ended up going with her again [that is, back to the beat]. It was the money. I was getting fifty pounds a week working in that card shop. I could earn that working the street for an hour!

However, Phoenix's respondents also spoke of relationships between dependency upon unreliable and inadequate social security benefits and prostitution. Gail, for example, was failed by the *social fund* which refused her application for beds, bedding and a cooker for a new flat that was arranged by a neighbourhood housing officer because of the violence she was facing in her relationship. She 'had been unable to pay for a baby-minder in order to get a legitimate job and had been told by a casual acquaintance that she could "get sorted" by becoming involved in prostitution' (*ibid.*: 83). Other women spoke of a desire to leave prostitution, but found it difficult to do so because of inadequate social security benefits. In this sense, Phoenix argues that the women 'discussed their engagement in prostitution as though it was nothing more and nothing less than a means of earning money without the "hassle of signing on"' (*ibid.*: 84) and that it demonstrated some of the ways in which the lives of her respondents were structured through gendered notions of dependency that we have seen are implicit in many aspects of social security provision. Hence, Phoenix argues that prostitution was for her sample of women a strategy of survival; for instance, in the case of Katrina, to 'earn enough money to support herself without recourse to crime and the possibility of imprisonment, to house herself, to avoid living on state welfare benefits or in poverty, and to provide herself with the financial basis to be independent and live the life she wanted' (*ibid.*). Prostitution though, brought more than access to money. It is also clear from Phoenix's respondents that prostitution brought social advantages. As in Carlen's (1988) study, she found it provided networks of support that reduced the isolation of other respondents in the context of sexist and racist discourses about the alleged threat to social stability of women with dependent children living outside of ethnocentric interpretations of the patriarchal family. Furthermore, the women had internalised the discursive construction of 'dependency' as being problematic, for they spoke of prostitution as a 'strategy to achieve their ardently desired independence' (*ibid.*: 99) from their birth families (or local authority care), from men and from inadequate and unreliable state benefits.

It would be wrong to suggest, however, that prostitution was the solution to the multiple and interconnected issues that framed and helped constitute the lives of Phoenix's respondents. She demonstrates a number of tensions structuring the lives of women. Most important for our purposes are those that relate to poverty and its relationships to dependency. In this context, Phoenix's work points to exploitative practices through which ponces (pimps) extracted from the women in her study as much money as they could and which often involved relationships in which the women became dependent on men who acted in various ways violently towards them. Hence, while the women spoke of prostitution as being a survival strategy to address their poverty, they could also find their engagement in it threatening their survival through the financial and physical exploitation of their ponces.

The work of Carlen and Phoenix is important, for it points to the ways in which what Carlen (1988) describes as the class and sex 'deals' act to constitute the offending of poor women. They demonstrate the limited choices facing poor women who have rejected dependency on men and low-paid employment for their financial well-being and/or who are unable or unwilling to fulfil discursive constructions of 'traditional' femininity. However, it is these two institutions – the patriarchal family and paid work – that, for the purposes of addressing crime, there is most emphasis upon. We saw in Chapter 3, for example, that one of the main ways of tackling offending among young men has been to get them into paid work as the route to re-establishing 'the family' in poorer neighbourhoods. It is also the case that low paid work is exactly the type of work that governments, in their drive to get poor women into employment, expect such women, particularly lone mothers, to do. It is to this issue that we now turn because this drive to get lone mothers into paid work is partly motivated by the alleged benefits this will have in terms of tackling offending and anti-social behaviour among their (male) children.

Breeding delinquents? Lone mothers and role models

Women who do not conform to stereotyped notions of femininity are often seen as a threat to the social order. Such ideas have a well-established history and are reflected in, and constituted by, social policies (for example, Thane 1978; Lewis 1984; Carabine 2001). However, concerns about relationships between acceptable forms of femininity and social order were to come to the fore in the 1980s and 1990s when, in a concerted effort to re-regulate the welfare state as being more conducive to global neo-liberalism (Grover and Stewart 2002), the role of lone motherhood was focused upon in relation to a host of social and economic problems, including the potential of lone mothers to raise delinquent children.

Family form, role models and crime

> We will uphold family life as the most secure means of bringing up our children. Families are the core of our society. They should teach right from wrong. They should be the first defence against anti-social behaviour. (Blair 1997, quoted in Goldson and Jamieson 2002: 87)

While this particular quote form Blair refers to families, it is clear from New Labour's consultation document, *Supporting Families* (Secretary of State for the Home Department 1998), that it actually favours marriage and the nuclear family. Barlow and Duncan (2000a) demonstrate how *Supporting Families* practically ignores family forms beyond marriage, for example, directly addressing cohabitation and lone motherhood in only three out of 49 paragraphs regarding familial form. For the most part, *Supporting Families* is concerned with devising administrative mechanisms that can ensure that New Labour are 'strengthening marriage'. Why the focus upon marriage?

Despite the fact that it is difficult to tease out relationships between family form and offending and anti-social behaviour (Burghes 1996), marriage is held to be the bedrock of stability for children and therefore for wider society. *Supporting Families* (Secretary of State for the Home Department 1998: para. 4.8) summarises this position:

> marriage does provide a strong foundation for stability for the care of children. It also sets out rights and responsibilities for all concerned. It remains the choice of the majority of people in Britain. For all these reasons, it makes sense to the Government to do what it can to strengthen marriage.

In contrast, social problems such as drug abuse and crime are held to be the 'indirect symptoms of problems in the family' (*ibid.*: para. 2). The focus upon the benefits of marriage and the problems alleged to be associated with the 'breakdown' of 'the family' has led to the claim by Campbell (the *Guardian*, 5 November 1998, cited in Barlow and Duncan 2000b: 131) that *Supporting Families* was the 'Government's Make 'em Marry Crusade'.

Borrowing from Gouldner (1971), Goldson and Jamieson (2002) argue that the intellectual basis of New Labour governments shares particular 'domain assumptions' with that of the Conservative governments of the 1980s and 1990s. They relate this to continuing concerns about the so-called parenting deficit (discussed in Chapter 4). It is also possible to point to shared domain assumptions in relation to the importance placed upon the nuclear family in socialising children to know and understand their responsibilities when they become adults. In particular our focus here is upon the importance placed upon role models in teaching children about what will be expected of them in the future.

Duncan and Edwards (1997) argue that the two most potent discourses constructing lone motherhood are lone motherhood as 'social threat' and lone motherhood as 'social problem'. In the former, lone mothers are seen as 'active agents' in the creation of a behavioural 'underclass', 'a developing class that has no stake in the social order, is alienated from it and hostile to it, and thus is the source of crime, deviancy and social breakdown' (*ibid.*: 56). In the case of the latter, 'it is social circumstances that are seen as placing both lone mothers and their children in economically and socially disadvantaged positions' (*ibid.*: 57). However, Duncan and Edwards (*ibid.*: 59) rightly recognise that the two discourses are not mutually exclusive in that, in the social problem discourse, 'the absence of fathers not only causes social disadvantages, but also results in social deviancy, crime and hooliganism' (*ibid*.). While such arguments are deeply problematic – we have seen, for instance, Campbell's (1993) argument that offending and anti-social behaviour among young men can partly be explained through a saturation of, rather than a lack of exposure to, male role models – it is clear the idea that male children, particularly those in lone mother headed families, need greater access to male role models has inflected popular and policy concerns with the changing nature of families. In brief, with increasing numbers of lone mother headed families in recent decades, the concern has become the impact that this may be having upon male children. The worry is that without an everyday 'father figure', male children will not learn what their roles in society will be when they are adults. Hence, there has been great emphasis upon exposing boys to positive male role models in a hope that this will benefit them when they are making the transition to adulthood, for the belief is that without the input of such role models young boys:

> don't naturally grow up to be responsible fathers and husbands. They don't naturally grow up knowing to get up every morning at the same time and go to work. They don't naturally grow up thinking that work is not just a way to make money, but a way to hold one's head high in the world. And most emphatically of all, little boys do not reach adolescence naturally wanting to refrain from sex. (Murray 1990: 10–11)

Scourfield and Drakeford (2002), for instance, highlight David Blunkett's concern when Secretary of State for Education with a lack of role models for boys in nursery and primary school teaching. This anxiety was expressed in New Labour's Green Paper on childcare, *Meeting the Childcare Challenge* (Secretary of State for Education and Employment *et al.* 1998: para. 2.1, emphasis added) where in the context of recruiting staff to work in childcare services it was noted that: 'Working with children tends to be seen as a predominantly female occupation. *Yet male carers have much to offer, including acting as positive role models for boys – especially from families where the father is absent.*' Moreover, a lack of positive role models is associated with 'dysfunctional' families and their role in causing anti-social behaviour (Secretary of State for the Home Department 2003: para. 2.9). In this sense, young men in particular are held to be in need of mentors for positive role models that will contrast to the 'negative impact of some peer groups and gangs' (*ibid*.: 30). In these examples the focus is upon the need for adult males to be role models for male children.

There are, however, some roles that, it is held, can be demonstrated to male children by their mothers. This can be most clearly and consistently observed in labour market and social security policy. The White Paper, for instance, introducing the Child Support Agency (Lord Chancellor *et al.* 1990: para 6.1) notes that if the period lone mothers spent on out-of-work benefits could be reduced 'then [their] children themselves are likely to gain a more positive attitude to paid work and independence'. This view was extended by New Labour, when both in opposition and in government. One-time Secretary of State for Social Security Harriet Harman MP was tireless in her efforts to a get a similar argument across. She argued when in opposition, for instance, that:

> The problem [of the low level of employment among lone mothers] is not just financial, with children being brought up on the breadline and the tax payer facing a growing benefits bill. There is a deeper problem of children being brought up without seeing the world of work, and growing up with the expectation that life is about receiving benefits rather than going out to work. (House of Commons Debates 1997: col. 941)

Following on from such arguments, and in a more general sense, it is argued that family-friendly employment practices are important because they are: '**Good for children** ... working parents can give their children a higher standard of living and provide role models for adult employment' (Secretary of State for the Home Department 1998: para. 3.19, original bold type). More specifically, it has been observed that policies such as the *New Deal for Lone Parents* (NDLP), introduced by New Labour in 1998, have been driven in part by attempts to manage such concerns (Lewis *et al.* 2000; Millar 2000); the children of lone mothers will understand that they will have to work when they are adults, rather than securing their income from other legitimate or illegitimate sources.

Getting lone mothers into paid work

Grover (2005b) argues that there have been three ways in which over the past two decades attempts have been made to get lone mothers into work: financial incentives; increased pressure; and attempts to address low numbers of childcare places and their high cost. These three policy areas are interconnected and mutually dependent. As the recent government-commissioned report, *Reducing dependency, increasing opportunity: options for the future of welfare to work* (Freud 2007), highlights, it makes little sense to put pressure on lone mothers to work and, it might be added, provide financial incentives for them to take paid work, if childcare is not available.

The immediate origins of policies in these three areas lay in Conservative policies of the late 1980s and early 1990s (*Family Credit, Parent Plus* and the *Out of School Childcare Initiative*). However, since New Labour's election in 1997 the development of these policies has been rapid and, although they may be closely interconnected, we shall take them individually for analytical purposes.

Financial incentives: 'making work pay'

We saw in Chapter 2 that the 'making work pay' strategy is concerned with ensuring that there is a financial incentive to take paid work and that it has two elements – the NMW and tax credits. Both of these are particularly important to lone mothers because, generally speaking, they are more likely to work part time and to have low wages compared to 'the persistently employed' (Evans *et al.* 2004: 2). Second, while couple families may also claim in-work tax credits providing their wages are low enough, such benefits have been found to be particularly useful in facilitating paid work among lone mothers (Gregg and Harkness 2003; Francesconi and Van der Klaauw 2004; Brewer and Browne 2006). These findings are reflected in the proportion of tax credit recipients who are lone mothers. Over four in 10 (42.6 per cent) of tax credit recipients in work are lone mothers, and reflecting their relatively poor employment position, over half (53.9 per cent) of those receiving higher amounts are lone mothers[2] (extrapolated from National Statistics 2006d: Table 2.2).

There are different elements to tax credits: for children (child tax credit), adults (working tax credit) and for childcare costs (paid as part of working tax credit). The child tax credit is paid to all people with a low enough income – their employment status is immaterial. However, it, along with working tax credit, is withdrawn if income rises on the gaining of employment. While tax credits remain the main way in which New Labour provides the financial incentive to take paid work, the 2003 Pre-Budget Report (HM Treasury 2003) announced the introduction of what was to become known as the *In-Work Credit* and which provides an additional £40 per week (£60 per week in London) to lone mothers who after being in receipt of out-of-work benefits for at least a year have found a job. The In-Work Credit is payable for a year in a number of areas of Britain which either had 'relatively poor outcomes for lone parents on benefit and relatively high proportions of lone parents in the population' and where it is thought 'work incentives might be particularly poor' (Brewer *et al.* 2007: para. 2.1.1). The (albeit limited) evidence suggests that it is having little impact upon those lone mothers who are the least job-ready (*ibid.*).

Pressure to take paid work

From the 1970s to the 1990s social security policy for lone mothers was framed by the ideas of the Finer Report (Department of Health and Social Security 1974) that lone mothers should have a choice of whether to claim out-of-work benefits or go to work 'because the general view was that mothers (married or lone) should put the care of their children before paid employment' (Millar 2000: 335). From the 1990s, however, with increasing numbers of lone mother headed families, their cost, together with discursive concerns about their effect upon the fabric of society outlined above, led to attempts to 'encourage' them into paid work by, first, providing advice and information through policies such as Parent Plus (that New Labour developed into the NDLP). After the NDLP was deemed to be failing to attract enough lone mothers, they were subject to increased compulsion to work through what is now called the 'work first' approach (see Blair writing in the *Daily Mail*, 10 February 1999).

While there is currently no formal pressure on lone mothers to seek paid work, they are nonetheless expected to engage with 'work first' interviews with Jobcentre Plus staff to initiate their claims and at regular intervals thereafter. The frequency of these interviews depends on the age of the youngest child of the lone mother. Non-attendance without 'good reason' results in a benefit sanction. Between April 2001 and December 2005 77,400 sanctions were applied against lone mothers for non-attendance at 'work first' interviews. While this means less than one in 20 interviews resulted in a sanction (House of Commons Debates 2006b: col. 943W), it confirms trends outlined in Chapter 3 that social policies can exacerbate the poverty of poor people, for data on such sanctions demonstrate that, on average, they deprive lone mothers of more than £10 per week (*ibid.*).

The sanctioning of lone mothers in this way is concerning for at least two reasons. First, there is evidence that suggests many lone mothers are not clear about the detail of the sanctioning regime and are sometimes unaware that they have been sanctioned, thinking instead that 'their benefit had simply been reduced as a result of a reassessment as opposed to a sanction' (Joyce and Whiting 2006: 19). Because of this, Joyce and Whiting (2006) argue it is difficult to examine the impacts of the sanction regime, particularly on the approaches to paid work of lone mothers. That said, they do demonstrate that the sanctions have an impact upon the financial position of lone mothers:

> Sanctioned lone parents highlighted the difficulties they faced managing on reduced income, especially paying utility bills and rent. Customers only had money for essentials and missed out on extras, such as socialising. Lone parents also reported being unable to buy treats for their children, provide pocket money or pay for school trips. (*ibid.*: 3)

In other words, and in contradistinction to New Labour's claims about tackling social exclusion, the sanctioning regime excludes lone mothers and their children from partaking in everyday activities that most people take for granted. In addition, Joyce and Whiting (*ibid.*) point to the impact that the financial hardship of sanctions caused in terms of worsening mental health, in particular, increased levels of stress related to managing on a reduced income.

Second, it is likely in the future that the nature and extent of sanctioning lone mothers will be greatly extended. In December 2006 then Secretary of State for Work and Pensions John Hutton MP (2006) ordered a review of welfare to work-welfare policies required to increase the employment rate in Britain to 80 per cent. This review, led by investment banker David Freud, reported in the following March (Freud 2007). Among other things, he recommended that in order to increase the proportion of lone mothers in paid work they should be subjected to the JSA regime, whereby they will have to sign on as being available and actively seeking paid work every fortnight once their youngest child reaches the age of 12 (currently it is 16). However, because Freud argued that this age could be reduced as childcare becomes more available from 2010 (discussed below), it was speculated in the press (the *Guardian*, 12 February 2006; *The Independent*, 6 March 2007) that this would, over time, be reduced to the age of three.[3] In response to the report Gordon Brown MP (then Chancellor of the Exchequer, now Prime Minister) was reported as saying: 'This starts a new phase of welfare reform which I will champion.' In future the out-of-work benefit income for lone mothers is likely to be more precarious as sanctions under the JSA sanction regime are far more common[4] than they are under the 'work first' approach.

The challenge of childcare

On being elected in 1997 the National Childcare Strategy (Secretary of State for Education and Employment *et al.* 1998) became one of New Labour's 'flagship policies' (Daycare Trust 1998). This was followed by an interdepartmental review of childcare (Department for Education and Skills *et al.* 2002) and a 10-year childcare strategy (HM Treasury *et al.* 2004). The aim of these various reviews and strategies has been to increase the availability and affordability of childcare. The 10-year strategy, for instance, has the 'goal of 20 hours a week of free high quality care for 38 weeks for all 3 and 4 year olds with ... a first step of 15 hours a week for 38 weeks a year reaching all children by 2010' and 'an out of school childcare place for all children aged 3–14 between the hours of 8 a.m. to 6 p.m. each weekday by 2010' (HM Treasury *et al.* 2004: 1).

There has also been a particular focus upon disadvantaged neighbourhoods. The *Neighbourhood Nurseries Initiative* (NNI), for instance, sought to fulfil the 'Government's ambition ... for every lone parent living in a disadvantaged area to have a childcare place when they enter work' (Department for Education and Skills 2001: 1) by creating 45,000 childcare places in 900 nurseries in the most deprived 20 per cent of wards. It has now been enveloped by the Sure Start *Children's Centres* programme which aims to offer parents, particularly those in disadvantaged areas, access to various services related to the educational, care and health needs of children aged 0–5 years, but, as importantly from the government's perspective, it also places an emphasis upon paid employment for parents through the provision of basic skills training, and through close connections to personal advisers of *Jobcentre Plus*.

Between 1997 and 2006 there was a net increase in 644,000 registered childcare places, accounted for by large increases in the number of places provided by private-sector day nurseries, and out-of-school and holiday schemes (Daycare Trust 2006). Daycare Trust estimates that by 2006 there was one registered childcare place for every three children, an advance on the one childcare place for every six children in 1997 (Secretary of State for Education and Employment *et al.* 1998). There should be further gains in the number of childcare places if the 10-year childcare strategy is able to develop wraparound for all children between the age of three and 14. Indeed, as we have seen, plans for increasing the participation of lone mothers in paid work through the Freud proposals are reliant upon this happening.

The problem for the government is the sustainability of childcare, particularly in poorer areas. As we have seen, there is financial assistance towards the cost of childcare available through the tax credit system and from 2004 this was made more generous. However, even people who claim tax credit support have to find at least 20 per cent of the cost of the childcare they use, a proportion that may be prohibitive for many parents. Moreover, as Smith *et al.* (2005: 10) note, the NNI was structured through a 'delicate balance in charging fees parents [can] afford while maintaining income sufficient for nurseries' sustainability'. In earlier work McCalla *et al.* (2001: 72) questioned whether the private sector could resolve the childcare problems of poorer neighbourhoods, for the 'assumption remains unchallenged that with a little pump-priming, the market, in all its diversity, can be manipulated to meet government targets for childcare places'. Only the longer term will tell, although there is some evidence to suggest that the NNI has helped, at least partly, to facilitate the employment of lone mothers and other low-income families (Bell and La Valle 2005).

Lone mothers and paid work: rationalities and consistencies

The government has set a target of having 70 per cent of lone mothers in paid work by 2010. In some senses, success can be pointed to. In recent years the proportion of lone mothers in paid work has increased; from 41 per cent in 1992 to 56.5 per cent in spring 2006.[5] The increase in the proportion of lone mothers in paid work is reflected in the proportion of workless working age lone mother headed households that fell from over half (53.9 per cent) in spring 1992 to about four in ten (39.4 per cent) in Spring 2006 (National Statistics 2006c: Table 1(ii)). However, because of the increase in the number of lone mother headed households over this period, in absolute terms the number of workless working age lone mother headed households was higher in spring 2006 (699,000) than in spring 2002 (619,000). What these figures and other evidence suggest is that it is very unlikely that the target of 70 per cent of lone mothers being in paid employment by 2010 will be met (see evidence of Paul Gregg in Work and Pensions Committee 2007: 63).

The explanation for this is that the policy of providing increasingly large 'sticks' to force and 'carrots' to entice lone mothers into paid work is bereft of meaning for many of them. This is because of the way in which the motivation of lone mothers to take paid work is conceptualised. The focus upon financial incentives, the provision of childcare, and increasing mandatory requirements to force engagement with labour markets assumes that claimants are rational economic actors; that on being presented with the 'carrot' of higher incomes and help towards childcare costs, and the 'stick' of sanctions to beat them into work, they will oblige and take work that is available. However, in the case of lone mothers it is argued that this line of thinking is structured through a 'rationality mistake' (Barlow *et al.* 2002); the concept of the rational economic actor is flawed because the attitude of lone mothers to paid work cannot be divorced from the ways in which they conceptualise lone motherhood and its relationship to paid work. In this sense, Edwards and Duncan (1996; also Duncan and Edwards 1999) argue that we should consider the decision to take paid work by lone mothers as being structured by 'gendered moral rationalities' rather than economic rationalities. What this means in practice is that some lone mothers see paid work as being an important part of mothering, while others do not.

This is visible in research examining non-participation among lone mothers in the NDLP. One of the main reasons for non-participation is that 'caring for their child(ren) was of paramount importance to participants and was often viewed as a full-time job which took priority over all other factors' (Brown and Joyce 2007: 2). It is, of course, this attitude that it is hoped recent and future policies will change in order for lone parents to be able to demonstrate the 'correct' role model to their children.

For those lone mothers who do not see paid work as being part of 'good' mothering, the development of incentives and punishments is unlikely to impact very greatly. This is worrying because if, as we have noted, in future lone mothers are to be subjected to the JSA regime, they will be subject to a policy that does not allow people to refuse employment for economic reasons (wage levels, conditions and so forth), let alone moral considerations. The future for lone mothers looks like one where, no matter what the attitude of individual lone mothers is to paid work, they will be expected to do it and, if they refuse, they will be punished through financial sanctions.

The location of employment-related decisions in gendered moral rationalities, rather than economic rationalities, also points us to what appears to be an inconsistency in thinking about relationships between paid work and 'good' parenting. If lone mothers are at work how can they be expected to be fully involved in the parenting of their children? This problem, as we saw in Chapter 4, is also of great concern to New Labour governments in the tackling of offending and anti-social behaviour.

Barlow *et al.* (2000: 74) suggest that this inconsistency explains New Labour's support for the nuclear family:

> On the one hand there is a supposed parenting deficit, but on the other hand all adults below pensionable age have the ascribed duty to take on paid work. Traditional marriage, with two-parent married families, seems to offer the best way of dealing with the contradiction, for this is the family form that best facilitates the combination of parenting with paid work.

However, it is also the case that there have been attempts to alleviate these tensions through social policy interventions to address what is described as the problem of latchkey kids. First, provided employers are cooperative – and they are not always (cf. Lakey *et al.* 2002) – the tax-benefit system is designed to enable lone mothers to balance work with paid employment. This is reflected in the fact that they need only work 16 hours per week in order to claim in-work benefits. Tony Newton MP (the then Secretary of State for Social Security), for example, told Parliament (House of Commons Debates 1990a: col. 731) that reducing the number of hours people had to work in order to claim *Family Credit* from 24 to 16 was a measure that would increase:

> the scope [of FC] but in a way likely to be of particular importance to lone parents. We shall make it possible to claim this benefit when working only for 16 hours weekly, instead of the present 24. That should make it much easier for parents to combine work with their responsibilities for their children.

In other words, setting a relatively low (16 hours) threshold for claiming in-work support would mean that lone mothers could balance the two issues – paid employment and the care of their children – thought to be important in preventing offending and anti-social behaviour among their children. Not only would the male children of lone mothers recognise the importance of paid employment, through having a role model in such employment, but also they would not be at risk of engaging in offending behaviour because of the absence of the one parent they lived with.

Second, as we have seen, there is a focus upon increasing the availability of childcare, most recently wraparound childcare supplied in, but not necessarily by, schools. This strand of policy involves the commodification of parenting through paid workers being responsible for the caring and socialisation of the children attending. For the state, such childcare also offers the advantage of socialising children in an environment away from parents who through the recent focus upon parenting are often seen as failing to raise their children adequately (see Chapter 4). Blair (2004: 3–4) hinted at such issues when in a speech about the 10-year childcare strategy he argued that, first, he wanted 'an end to latch key kids' and, second, that wraparound childcare 'was not about children being abandoned in schools for ten hours a day, all year round. It's about providing a service that engages children, helping them to flourish through sports, play, music while meeting the needs of working parents.' In this sense, the 10-year childcare strategy has multiple roles: freeing parents to work, but in doing so helping to manage potential problems with the behaviour of their children by providing them with an environment in which they can develop rather than – as is the impression often given – flounder as a result of being raised by adults with poor parenting skills.

Lone mothers and policy: reproducing the material context of offending?

There is a tension between, on the one hand, the material basis of women's offending and policies aimed at getting lone mothers into paid work. In brief, the desire to get lone mothers into employment is likely to consolidate their, and women's more generally, relatively poor position in the labour market and their poverty compared to men. There are several reasons for this. First, the drive to get lone mothers into paid work arguably institutionalises the double burden – social reproduction and economic production – that structures the lives of women with dependent children. This has benefits for both capitalism and patriarchy; the former benefits by paying women less for their labour compared to men and by having little responsibility for the social reproduction of future generations of labour, while patriarchy benefits because men are excused from engaging with the socialisation of their children. In this sense, men are freed to pursue those activities in life – especially full-time paid work – marked as being masculine and rewarded as being far more valuable than social reproduction that continues to be marked as being feminine and which, because of this, impacts significantly upon the ability of women to undertake paid work on the same terms as men.

Second, the aim of the strategy is to encourage women to take up low-paid, entry-level employment. However, this type of initial employment may prevent women from moving into better paid employment in the way that New Labour's ideas about the meritocratic nature of labour markets might suggest they would be able to. In a report for the Cabinet Office, for example, Atkinson and Williams (2003) note that 'low skill, low status jobs ... provide little or no basis for substantial advancement through the labour market'. This observation relates to 'low skill, low status jobs' generally. However, there is some evidence that suggests that given the current and future configurations of policies aimed at getting lone mothers into paid work, their position is particularly precarious. Not only do lone mothers leave paid work at twice the rate of non-lone mothers (Evans *et al.* 2004), the payment of in-work benefits has the effect of helping to trap lone parents in low-paid work. Bryson *et al.* (1997: 1), for example, found that FC (the predecessor of New Labour's in-work tax credits) 'encouraged lone mothers to stick in low paid jobs for long periods, so that they fell further behind in their earnings'. Reflecting upon such evidence Bryson (1998) demonstrates 'disturbing evidence that some lone parents may have used FC to take up jobs below their full potential, finding later that they have the wrong work experience to move upwards' (in Gray 2001: 195). More recent research is not much more encouraging, finding that those lone mothers receiving the maximum amount of *Working Families Tax Credit* had lower wage growth than similar non-recipients (Lydon and Walker 2005).

The point here is, as the Work and Pensions Committee (2007: para. 92) was told by Lisa Harker, author of *Delivering on Child Poverty: what would it take?* (Harker 2006), 'Finding the right job for the right person is worth it and it pays off in the long run.' The problem is that future policies which, as we have seen, will include the transfer of lone mothers to the JSA regime, are likely to have the opposite effect, for they are concerned with getting people into any work, rather than that which is the 'right job for the right person'. New Labour has shown some concern that people moving into employment from out-of-work benefits risk becoming stuck in low paid work. Hence, in October 2003 it introduced the Employment, Retention and Advancement (ERA) 'demonstration project' which aims to help certain benefit claimants, including lone mothers, to find, keep and move forward in their employment through a casework approach, as well as financial incentives to remain in work and to train. Whether such programmes can help people to improve their labour market position is not yet clear, although it is likely that what appears to be a rather individualistic approach, focusing upon employees, will need to be broadened to incorporate employers if it is likely to be successful (Johnson 2002). This may prove to be problematic as it has been observed that employers often attach low priority to reducing turnover through training in low-skilled jobs (Atkinson and Williams 2003). Of course, for the state the type of paid work that lone mothers enter is immaterial. The role model argument conjoins with an economic one suggesting that what is important is the tackling of worklessness, rather than being too bothered about the type of work that lone mothers are doing.

Conclusion

This chapter has focused upon two related issues: relationships between the relatively poor material circumstances of women and their law-breaking, and the idea of lone mothers as a criminological threat because of an alleged inability to furnish their male children with the correct role models. While this latter idea has little empirical foundation, it is partly responsible for the drive to get more lone mothers into paid employment. In doing so, the focus is upon making women take even greater responsibility for their children and their children's behaviour. However, the desire to get lone mothers into paid work will do little to tackle the contextual factors of offending, and in many ways will exaggerate those that we have seen help frame the offending of poor women. The government's approach of increasingly authoritarian methods, premised upon benefit sanctions, will not ease the class and sex 'deals' that structure the lives of poor women, but will reflect and reproduce them.

Notes

1 Defined as 60 per cent of the median income after housing costs.
2 The figures exclude those receiving the Family Element or less only.
3 In the welfare Green Paper, *In-Work, Better Off* (Secretary of State for Work and Pensions 2007) the government argued that lone mothers would be expected to claim JSA when their youngest child was aged 12 from

2008 and, then, from 2010 when their youngest child was aged seven years.

4 For example, in the quarter ending November 2006 there were nearly as many (65,000) sanctions applied to JSA claimants as had been applied in nearly six years under the 'work first' regime for lone mothers (77,400) (National Statistics 2007; House of Commons Debates 2006b: col. 943W).

5 Figures from *More lone parents in work, but concern over high job exit rates*, University of Bath Press Release, 23 September 2004 and *Lone parent employment rate at 56.5 per cent*, http://www.statistics.gov.uk/cci/nugget. asp?id=409 (accessed 23 February 2007).

Chapter 6

Crime, inequality and ethnicity

Introduction

This chapter explores relationships between crime, inequality and ethnicity by, first, focusing upon the socio-economic position of BME people and, second, through focusing upon the position of BME people in relation to the criminal justice system. The chapter is primarily concerned with the position of black and Asian people in Britain. This is because it is people from these minority ethnic groups who are seen as being particularly problematic in terms of crime and disorder in contemporary society. There is a particular focus upon the urban uprisings that took place in Brixton, London in 1981 and in former mill towns and cities of northern England in 2001.

The chapter examines how the material conditions of these BME people have been treated in responses at a central government level to the two episodes of disorder and argues that a concern with cultural forms and practices (multiculturalism in the case of the 1981 uprising and integrationism in the case of the 2001 uprisings) has taken precedence over a concern with the socio-economic disadvantages that contextualise the offending and disorderly behaviour of BME people. However, the chapter also analyses attempts to integrate BME people in contemporary society by getting them into paid work through those policy mechanisms, such as the new deals, that are designed to get people of all ethnicities into employment. It is from such approaches that the main problem with the contemporary strategy of tackling the disadvantages faced by BME people emerges. This problem is a lack of engagement with the racism faced by BME people. The chapter concludes that developments in policy are, at best, likely to consolidate, and at worst to exaggerate, the poor material conditions of BME.

Inequality and ethnicity

Employment

BME people are less likely to be in paid work compared to white people. So, for instance, the employment rate for white people aged 18–49 is approximately 80 per cent, compared to about 55 per cent for BME people of the same age (Freud 2007, Figure 19: 39). An employment gap also exists when comparing white and BME lone mothers; white lone mothers have an employment rate of about 53 per cent, compared to approximately 25 per cent of BME lone mothers (*ibid.*). However, such figures disguise differences between minority ethnic groups. In 2004, for instance, while the employment rate of white people was 77 per cent, it was 67 per cent for Black Caribbean people, 58 per cent for Black African people and even lower for Bangladeshi (46 per cent) and Pakistani (40 per cent) people. People of Black African, Bangladeshi and Pakistani heritage, therefore, are particularly disadvantaged in terms of paid employment.

Unemployment

Perhaps unsurprisingly given the above figures, BME people are more likely to be unemployed compared to white people. Blackaby *et al.* (1998, 1999, 2002), for example, demonstrate that over the past three decades unemployment has disproportionately been endured by BME people. More recent figures demonstrate that such differences in unemployment rates persist. In 2001/02, for instance, five per cent of white males aged 16–64 were unemployed. However, the unemployment rate for Bangladeshi males was four times that rate at 20 per cent, while for Pakistani males (16 per cent), Black Caribbean (14 per cent) and Black African (15 per cent) males it was three times the rate for white males. As we saw in Chapter 3, unemployment falls disproportionately upon the young. This is the case for young white males, but is particularly so for young BME males. In 2001/02, for example, while 12 per cent of young white males were unemployed, nearly a third of Black African (31 per cent), Pakistani (28 per cent) and Black Caribbean (27 per cent) young men were also unemployed. In terms of unemployment, Bangladeshi men were the most disadvantaged with an unemployment rate of 41 per cent.[1]

Employment segregation

When BME people are in paid work, they tend to be concentrated in sectors associated with low pay. In 2001, for example, nearly half (46 per cent) of Bangladeshi men worked in restaurants and kitchens. The majority of these men (84 per cent) worked in the lowest paid occupations – cooks, waiters and kitchen assistants – of this area of economic activity. The remaining 16 per cent were restaurant managers, although the proportion of Bangladeshi men who were employed as such had fallen by about half between 1991 and 2001 (Blackwell and Guinea-Martin 2005, Table 9: 510). Black Caribbean men are concentrated in low-grade service sector occupations, such as sales assistants, security guards and van drivers. However, while nearly six per cent of Black African men are in better paid work as software professionals and medical practitioners, more than twice that figure are employed as security guards, sales assistants and cleaners.

Wages

BME people are more likely to be in low-paid employment compared to white people. In 2004, for instance, while the median hourly wage for white males was £9.31, it was lower for Asian (except Indian males who were paid a median of £9.56 per hour) and black men. Pakistani and Bangladeshi men were paid the least, some two-thirds (£6.25 per hour) of the white median, while black males were paid three-quarters of the white median. For females the figures are somewhat different. We saw in the previous chapter that women are, on average, paid less than men. However, if ethnicity is taken into account black and Indian women earn more (£8.27 and £7.60 respectively) than the median hourly wage earned by white women (£7.06 per hour) and the median hourly wage earned by black (£7.00) and Pakistani and Bangladeshi men (£6.25 per hour) (all figures from Low Pay Commission 2005, Tables 4.6 and 4.7).

Poverty

BME people are more likely to be living in poor households compared to white people. In 2005/06 18 per cent of white people lived in households in the bottom fifth of incomes. However, for Pakistani and Bangladeshi people the figure at 61 per cent was over three times this figure and was double it for Black non-Caribbean people (34 per cent) and Black Caribbean people (43 per cent) (Department for Work and Pensions 2007, Table 3.1, figures are after housing costs). These figures remained fairly constant over the preceding five years (Department for Work and Pensions 2003b). Child poverty rates are particularly high for the children of BME families. Platt (2007), for example, shows a child poverty rate of 25 per cent for the white population, 37 per cent for Black Caribbean; 55.7 per cent for Black African people; 60 per cent for Pakistani people; and a staggering 72 per cent for Bangladeshi people.

In summary, Black and Asian people, especially Bangladeshi and Pakistani people, face the socio-economic disadvantages that many white people do, but more acutely. They are less likely to be in paid work than white people and in low-paid work when they are employed. As a consequence, they are far more likely to be living in poverty compared to white people.

Connecting inequality, crime and ethnicity

There can be little doubt that inequality is an important contextual factor in explaining the offending of BME groups. However, it is a complex picture. So, for instance, while we have seen that Pakistani and Bangladeshi people are among the poorest in British society, they do not have the highest rates of offending. In fact, self-report studies suggest that while black and white respondents have a similar level of offending, those of Indian, Pakistani and Bangladeshi heritage have lower rates of offending (Graham and Bowling 1995; Flood-Page et al. 2000). Graham and Bowling (1995), for example, found in their sample of 2,500 young people, 44 per cent of white and 43 per cent of black respondents said that they had committed an offence, while 30 per cent of Indian, 28 per cent of Pakistani and 13 per cent of Bangladeshi young people admitted to offending. While other self-report surveys have found different proportions willing to admit to offending, the trends have been similar; Asian young people report a lower rate of offending compared to white and black youngsters, despite the fact that, on average, they are likely to be poorer.

However, the similarity in offending rates between black and white people and the lower rates of offending for Asian people are not reflected in the proportion of BME and white people in the criminal

Table 6.1 The general and prison populations by ethnicity (per cent)

	General population	Prison population (British nationals only)	Prison population (incl. foreign nationals)
Asian or Asian British	4.0	4.7	6.5
Black or Black British	2.0	10.6	15.1
White	92.1	81.7	74.2

Notes: Figures may not add up to 100 per cent due to rounding.
Figures for the general population are taken from the 2001 census.
Figures for the prison population are for the fourth quarter of 2005.

Sources: Home Office (nd); National Statistics, http://www.statistics.gov.uk/cci/nugget.asp?id=273 (accessed 21 May 2007).

justice system. Table 6.1, for example, compares the ethnicity of the general population with that of the prison population. It shows that black people are particularly overrepresented in British prisons. The proportion of black people among the prison population is approximately five times the size of the proportion of black people in the general population. If *all* prisoners (including foreign nationals) are considered, this figure increases to nearly eight times. While the proportion of the prison population that is recorded as Asian or Asian British is similar for Asian people in the general population when British nationals only are considered, they are overrepresented by more than a half when all prisoners are considered.

However, when we disaggregate the ethnicity of the prison population by gender we can see that the proportion of the prison population that is black is even greater than the figures in Table 6.1 suggest. Hence, while about 1 per cent of the British population are black males and about 1 per cent black females, Table 6.2 demonstrates that they appear in the prison population at 10 times these proportions for British nationals only, and 15 and 20 times respectively if all those people imprisoned are considered.

These observations raise a number of important issues. First, they raise questions about understandings of relationships between offending and inequality. This is because while we have seen that BME people are, on average, poorer and more excluded than white people, it is not the poorest and most excluded BME groups that make up the largest proportion of the BME prison population. In

Table 6.2 Prison population by ethnicity and gender (per cent)

	Prison population (British nationals only)		Prison population (incl. foreign nationals)	
	Male	Female	Male	Female
Asian or Asian British	4.8	1.7	6.8	2.4
Black or Black British	10.7	10.2	14.9	20.7
White	81.6	83.0	74.5	70.2

Notes: Figures may not add up to 100 per cent due to rounding.
Figures are for the fourth quarter of 2005.
Source: Home Office (nd)

contrast, those groups that are the poorest and most excluded – Bangladeshi and Pakistani people – account for a smaller proportion of the prison population compared to black and black British people. What this suggests is that while poverty and exclusion are something that is common to the experiences of many black and Asian people, the former are criminalised to a greater extent than the latter. While increasingly there is concern about the potential criminality of 'Asian gangs' and 'extremists' (Phillips and Bowling 2007) and Asian people have for many years been constructed as being devious and dishonest (Bowling and Phillips 2002), it is black people, especially young African Caribbean males, who are defined as being *the* crime problem facing Britain (Gilroy 1987a, 1987b; Bowling and Phillips 2002) as recent concerns with violence involving guns and knives, which is often described in terms of 'black on black' crime, testifies. In brief, it is a combination of the poor material circumstances of black people and their criminalisation that helps us to understand why such people make up the prison population at a far higher proportion than their numbers in the general population. We have already discussed the evidence of the former, and in the case of the latter we can point to policing practices, especially the exercise of 'stop and search' powers which are disproportionately used against young black people, males in particular (for example, Gordon 1993; Institute of Race Relations 1987; Spencer and Hough 2000; Metropolitan Police Association 2004). In 2003/04, for instance, 14 per 1,000 of the white population were stopped and searched by the police compared to 93 per 1,000 of the black population and 29 per 1,000 of the Asian population (Statewatch 2005). In brief, black people are nearly seven times more likely to be stopped and searched by the police compared to the white population, and Asian people are over twice as likely.

The recent association of Asian people with disorder and 'ethnic extremism', however, is likely to have increased the number of stop and searches of Asian people, who are increasingly policed by racial profile (Kundnani 2004). The racialised nature of the use of stop and search powers means they have been a source of tension between the police and BME people. As former Labour MP Bernie Grant argued:

> nothing has been more damaging to the relationship between the police and black community than the ill-judged use of stop and search powers. For young black men in particular, the humiliating experience of being repeatedly stopped and searched is a fact of life ... It is hardly surprising that those on the receiving end of this treatment should develop hostile attitudes towards the police. The right to walk the streets is a fundamental one, and one that is quite rightly jealously guarded. (NACRO 1997, cited in Bowling and Phillips 2002: 138–139)

The racialised use of stop and search was one of the longer term contexts of an uprising in Brixton in the spring of 1981.

Uprising in Brixton: ethnicity and the need for multiculturalism

Britain has rarely been the peaceful place that it is often portrayed as. It has a history of unrest through which concerns about social and economic injustice have been expressed (Thompson 1963). With the increase in immigration after the Second World War, episodes of unrest were increasingly racialised. From the 1958 Notting Hill 'race riots' through the uprisings in Brixton of 1981 and in former mill towns and cities of northern England in 2001, collective expressions of dissatisfaction with the existing social order have included a conjoining of discriminatory criminal justice (especially policing) practices and socio-economic disadvantage.

Benyon (1984a: 3) argues that '1981 will surely long be remembered as the year of riots'. The first of these 'riots' (hereafter described as uprisings) occurred over the weekend of 12–14 April in Brixton, south London. Following the uprising Lord Scarman was asked by the then Home Secretary, William Whitelaw MP, to 'inquire urgently into the serious disorder' (Scarman 1981: para. 1.1). However, by the time he reported in November 1981 (Scarman 1981) he was able to make some observations of uprisings that had also occurred in Southall, Toxteth and Moss Side and in various urban areas of the West Midlands through the summer of 1981.

In his report Scarman argued that the Brixton uprising was due to a combination of factors, most notably the nature of policing and the material circumstances of black people living there. Scarman (1981: para. 4.97) argued that 'the police must carry some responsibility for the outbreak of disorder'. However, that responsibility only extended to poor practice (a breakdown in police–community relations), 'a failure to adjust policies and methods to meet the needs of policing in a multi-racial society' (*ibid.*) and 'harassment, and racial prejudice among junior officers' (*ibid.*). Scarman was firm in his rejection of institutional racism in the Metropolitan Police as being an explanation for the contribution that policing had made to the uprising. Essentially, he argued that there were a few racist 'bad apples' in a non-racist barrel. Britain would have to wait nearly another two decades, following the murder of a young black man, Stephen Lawrence, and an incompetent police investigation of his death, for such an admission of institutional racism in the police (MacPherson 1999; for discussion see Lea 2000; McLaughlin and Murji 1999).

The denial of institutional racism in the Metropolitan Police was to prove to be the most controversial aspect of Scarman's report. In it, police operations, such as 'Swamp 81',[2] that were premised upon connecting black people and black cultures to street crime (cf. Gilroy 1987a, 1987b) were held to be legitimate modes of policing, although he argued that in hindsight 'Swamp 81' was a 'serious mistake, given the tension which existed between the police and the local community in the early months of the year' (Scarman 1981: para. 4.76). In other words, the 'swamping' of areas where BME people lived was acceptable if 'community relations' were good, although, given the evidence to the Scarman Inquiry, it was obvious that such methods of policing actually contributed to the erosion of 'community relations'. In this context, Scarman was criticised for not understanding and not arguing that policing was one example of state racism that also encompasses other areas of public policy, most notably immigration policy (see, for example, Behrens 1982; Unsworth 1982). Unsworth (1982) was particularly critical, highlighting the broader context of the Brixton uprising in changing class and 'race' relationships in the early years of Thatcherism.

While the main focus of Scarman's report related to policing, he also argued that there were social policy changes that were required in order to improve the material conditions of people living in areas such as Brixton. Scarman (1981) was right when he argued that the material conditions black people faced in Brixton were essentially a more acute version of those that white people faced. He highlighted education, unemployment, especially among young black people, and housing as being particularly problematic. This view was certainly against the *public* discourse of those with political power at the time who preferred to locate the causes of the uprising in a criminogenic pathology of those engaged in it. Then Prime Minister Margaret Thatcher, for example, 'refused to accept that poverty was a cause of the disorders ... [and implied] that anyone who suggested a cause for the riots was in some way seeking to excuse them' (Benyon 1984a: 5). Hence, Scarman's analysis of the importance of the material context of the Brixton uprising was welcomed by many analysts (for example, Unsworth 1982; Benyon 1984b; Roberts 1984; Taylor 1984).

However, the influence of the Scarman Report was perhaps most widely felt in its implications for 'race relations', in particular its impact upon multiculturalism. Kundnani (2002: 68) argues that the 'multiculturalist formula of "celebrating difference" ... [was] a response to the riots of the early 1980s'. However, he goes on to note (*ibid.*) how multiculturalism was 'always a double-edged sword' and that following the Brixton uprising multiculturalism 'changed from a line of defence to a mode of control' (*ibid.*):

> Multiculturalism now [after the Brixton uprising] meant taking black culture off the streets – where it had been politicised and turned into rebellion against the state – and putting it in the council chamber, in the classroom and on the television, managed and reified. Black culture was thus turned from a living movement into an object of passive contemplation, something to be 'celebrated' rather than acted on.

In this context, Sivanandan (2006: 3) argues that the response to the Brixton uprising and the Scarman Report was 'pouring money into ethnic projects and strengthening ethnic cultures'. As a strategy to address the concerns of black people this was problematic because of its failure to engage with racism (Sivanandan 2006).

For Sivanadan (*ibid.*) it is multicultural society rather then multiculturalism that requires defence. This is perhaps fortuitous, for Kundnani (2002) argues that since the beginning of the 21st century multiculturalism in Britain has been in 'crisis' because of least three reasons. These are, first, the perseverance of the parents of Stephen Lawrence that eventually led to an admission of institutional racism in the Metropolitan Police (MacPherson 1999) means that the 'terms of the debate could be changed from cultural recognition to state racism' (*ibid.*: 69). Second, Kundnani argues that New Labour's immigration policy, which among other things has introduced policies that financially impoverish asylum seekers and, for unsuccessful asylum applicants, can then remove their children because of familial poverty (for example, Sales 2002, 2007; Cunningham and Tomlinson 2005; Cunningham and Cunningham 2007), is not compatible with multiculturalism. Third, Kundnani (2002: 270) argues that particularly among Asian people 'culture is no longer a cage within which opposition can be effectively contained'. This point relates to changing discourses around Asian people and culture:

> Bangladeshi and Pakistani communities, especially, remain mired in poverty. And the rebelliousness normally associated with white and Afro-Caribbean youths has infused working class Asians. Their old image of passivity has given way to one of aggression and criminality (*ibid.*: 70).

This construction of young Asian people was, Kundnani (*ibid.*) argues, confirmed by the violent protest in former mill towns and cities in the North of England, to which we now turn.

Uprisings in former mill towns: the need for integration

In the summer of 2001, uprisings were witnessed in Bradford, Burnley and Oldham.[3] In these cases it was young Asian men, mainly of Pakistani and Bangladeshi heritage, who were engaged in violent protest. Following the uprisings the local authorities responsible for the three areas set up investigations into their causes (Clarke 2001; Ouseley 2001; Ritchie 2001). The three reports came to differing conclusions. The Bradford review focused upon relationships between white and Asian people, arguing for a more ethnically tolerant city in a multicultural sense (Ouseley 2001). The material conditions of Bradford's white and Asian working class was little discussed. In the 50-page report, for example, unemployment was mentioned only once, deprivation twice and social exclusion three times. In the case of Burnley the role of 'race' and racism were almost completely ignored. Here, the focus was upon the poverty and exclusion of people from all ethnic groups and the criminality of white and Asian gangs (Clarke 2001). The report concerning Oldham (Ritchie 2001) was different still, emphasising the conjoining of material deprivation and racism (white on Asian and Asian on white).

However, our main concern is with the reaction at a national level. Following the uprisings the Home Office appointed Ted Cantle to lead a review into *'the issues that need to be addressed in developing confident, active communities and social cohesion'* (Cantle 2001: para. 1.1, original italics). It is generally accepted that while the socio-economic marginalisation of young Asian people was acknowledged in the Cantle Report, the greatest explanatory weight was given to arguments that cultural difference, 'Asian criminality' and self-segregation among Asian people and families were the causes of the uprisings, for example, Kundnani 2001; Kalra 2002; Alexander 2004; Burnett 2004; Phillips 2005. The first paragraph of the Cantle Report's executive summary (Cantle 2001: para. 2.1), neatly highlights what was held by the review team to be the most pressing issue:

> Whilst the physical segregation of housing estates and inner city areas came as no surprise, the team was particularly struck by the depth of polarisation of our towns and cities. The extent to which these physical divisions were compounded by so many other aspects of our daily lives, was very evident. Separate educational arrangements, community and voluntary bodies, employment, places of worship, language, social and cultural networks, means that many communities operate on the basis of a series of parallel lives. These lives often do not seem to touch at any point, let alone overlap and promote any meaningful interchanges.

In this context, it was argued that there was little idea of what it meant to be a citizen in contemporary Britain where 'many still look backwards to some supposedly halcyon days of a mono-cultural society, or alternatively look to their country of origin for some form of identity' (*ibid.*: para. 2.6). In brief, the conclusions of the Cantle Report were yet another factor pointing to what we have seen Kundnani (2002) argues to be the 'death of multiculturalism', for its main thrust was that multiculturalism had failed to bring ethnic groups closer together in Britain. In contrast, it had led to their separation; their living and leading 'parallel lives'. Hence, what the Cantle Report argued Britain required was policies that would encourage a shared sense of what it is to be British, an approach that has framed the government's 'race relations' agenda since 2001. The focus is now upon 'community cohesion' rather than cultural diversity.

This shift is worrying on a number of grounds, but most notably the emphasis upon 'Britishness' as being the core of 'community cohesion' policy ignores the importance of the material context of ethnic difference. While, for instance, the Cantle Report does make recommendations regarding regeneration and employment, they are too broad to be of any real use and arguably underestimate the disadvantages, outlined at the beginning of this chapter, faced by Asian people and people from other minority ethnic groups. On this point, the local studies of the uprisings in Burnley (Clarke 2001) and Oldham (Ritchie 2001) are far more informative, for they highlight the extent and depth of material deprivation of both working-class Asian and white people.

Hudson *et al.* (2007: 109) argue that 'social cohesion must also be underpinned by the amelioration of material poverty and disadvantage'. In their research in 'multi-ethnic neighbourhoods' in London and Manchester (Policy Studies Institute 2007: 1) they found that struggles related to material resources, particularly housing and employment, were a major source of tension between BME and white people, and between both BME and white people and newly arriving immigrants in the areas in which they lived. Their findings have resonance with explanations of racist offending (Smith *et al.* 2002; Ray and Smith 2004; Ray *et al.* 2004).

In contrast to focusing upon the material context of the uprisings in Bradford, Burnley and Oldham, the Cantle Report's main concern was with establishing what might be understood to be the unifying features of 'Britishness' and in this respect it had a distinctly New Labour flavour, for it was framed by reference to rights and responsibilities, with a far greater emphasis upon the latter. While it was not clear in the report what rights would be afforded to BME people, and little discussion of this occurred after the report's publication (Kundnani 2004), the report was clear that they should be balanced with responsibilities (Cantle 2001: para. 6.1). The responsibility of individuals, the Cantle Report argued, could most clearly be expressed in a 'statement of allegiance' to 'Britishness':

> A meaningful concept of 'citizenship' needs establishing – and championing – which recognizes (in education programmes in particular) the contribution of all cultures to this Nation's [Britain's] development throughout its history, but establishes a clear primary loyalty to this Nation. This is, after all, the responsibility of citizenship and a clearer statement of allegiance ... should be considered. (*ibid.*: para. 5.1.15)

Loyalty to the nation is held in the Cantle report to be the greatest expression of responsibility and, premised upon communitarian ideals, citizenship is aligned with that responsibility (cf. Dwyer 2004).

Something akin to Cantle's 'statement of allegiance' was introduced as the 'citizenship oath' in the 2002 Nationality, Immigration and Asylum Act, whereby on registration of, or naturalisation as, a British citizen people have to 'swear by Almighty God that, on becoming a British citizen, I will be faithful and bear true allegiance to Her Majesty Queen Elizabeth the Second, Her Heirs and Successors according to law' (Schedule 5: para. 1, 2002 Nationality and Asylum Act).

The 'citizenship oath' is perhaps the most powerful symbol of the drive to integrationism that structures the 'community cohesion' approach to 'race relations'. Kundnani (2007: 26) notes, for instance, that while those on the right of politics in Britain have for many years thought 'cultural diversity ... a threat to national cohesion and security', after the uprisings of 2001 and the attacks in London in July 2005, it was criticised 'equally vigorously by liberals and by those on the centre left'. While he suggests that those on the left and right differ in their view of whether 'alien' populations can be assimilated, there seems, he argues, to be a political consensus that multiculturalism 'has encouraged [particularly] Muslims to separate themselves and live by their own values, resulting in extremism and, ultimately, the fostering of a mortal home-grown terrorist threat' (*ibid.*).

However, there is a misplaced assumption here that segregation is the consequence of an overemphasis upon diversity. In contrast, Kundnani (2002) argues that the ethnic segregation highlighted by Cantle and others was the consequence of industrial decline and its attendant material deprivations, institutional racism and 'white flight'. In relation to institutional racism, Kundnani points to such practices in housing policy in Bradford where from its 'large stock of council housing, just 2 per cent has been allocated to Asians' (Kundnani 2001: 107) and in Oldham where the local authority was 'found guilty of operating a segregationist housing policy following a Commission for Racial Equality investigation in the early 1990s' (*ibid.*). In addition, Kundnani (2002: 70–71) points to the fact that in 1999 Greater Manchester Police 'was declared institutionally racist by its own chief constable', although following the uprising in Oldham that declaration was lost to a focus upon Asian criminality and a concern with Asian gangs. This was despite the fact that during the uprisings young Asian people faced aggressive policing (Kundnani 2001; Burnett 2004) which has arguably worsened following the attacks in the USA in September 2001 and those in London in July 2005.

Burnett (2004) highlights the contradictory nature of the government's position in this regard. While social disorder and 'extremism' are held to be the responsibility of Asian people, who must be encouraged to take responsibility for the policing and integration of their young, such arguments were not extended to those engaged in the uprisings in 2001. Those involved in the uprisings were protecting their people and property from far right groups, because they felt that the police were unable or unwilling to do so. They were, in other words, acting as responsible citizens, something that they have had to do for many years and which has been the catalyst for previous uprisings involving Asian people, most notably that in Southall in 1981 (Scarman 1981: para. 2.25).

With regard to Kundnani's argument about 'white flight', we can point to a wider neglect of the role of white people in the uprisings. More specifically, the Cantle Report, and the 'community cohesion' agenda more broadly, is only concerned with BME people. Because 'community cohesion' has been reduced to a 'cultural problem' that can only be 'dealt with by focusing on issues of citizenship, nationality and belonging' (Burnett 2004: 7), it is BME who are held to be problematic; they are the threat to 'Britishness' and, therefore, it is they who have to demonstrate their allegiance to British values. This is problematic because it is not particularly clear what 'British values' are, although in a recent speech the then Prime Minister, Tony Blair MP (2006c: 2) argued that they included a 'belief in democracy, the rule of law, tolerance, equal treatment for all, respect for this country and its shared heritage', and reflecting such sentiments new British citizens must, in addition to the 'oath of allegiance', must also pledge:

> I will give my loyalty to the United Kingdom and respect its rights and freedoms. I will uphold its democratic values. I will observe its law faithfully and fulfil my duties and obligations as a British citizen. (Schedule 5: para. 1, 2002 Nationality and Asylum Act)

However, given individual racism and the recent activities of far right organisations, it is arguable that many white people do not hold some or all of these values (see, for instance, ETHNOS 2006). The problem here is that there is no question about the allegiance of the white majority to such definitions of 'Britishness' in the 'community cohesion' approach. As Burnett (2004) notes:

It is absurd to assume that the white youths heard [in the 2001 uprisings] singing such chants as 'If you all hate Pakis, clap your hands', and who later pleaded guilty to affray for their role in the violence in Oldham in 2001, will be expected to swear allegiance to England.

The 'community cohesion' approach, therefore, is premised upon the idea that it is only immigrants and those who have lived in the UK but never opted for a British passport who need to prove their allegiance to the Crown. Kundnani (2004: 108) argues that this 'has nothing to do with citizenship and everything to do with preserving the mythical idea of an essential – and therefore racialised – Britishness. Under the community doctrine, it is no longer possible to be black first and British second.' He also argues (2007) that the demand for allegiance to 'Britishness' goes further than just an application to 'new settlers', but is symbolic of a concern with the allegiance of British Muslims to 'Britishness'.

Uprising, culture and material conditions

In cultural terms the reactions to the uprisings in 1981 by young black men and in 2001 by young Asian men were very different. We have seen in the preceding sections that after the 1981 uprising the solution was thought to be in multiculturalism. However, the reaction to the 2001 uprisings has involved a drive towards assimilation, cohesion and integration in order to foster a greater and more coherent sense of 'Britishness'. By the early years of the 21st century 'higher doses of "culture"' (Kundnani 2002: 70), that were held to be the solution to the uprising of black people in the 1980s, were no longer seen as being palatable. Indeed, they were held to be the problem, for while black youths in the 1980s were held to be violently protesting 'because of a lack of culture (what was referred to as "ethnic disadvantage")' (ibid.), Asian youths were held to be protesting in 2001 because of an excess of culture; 'they were too Muslim, too traditional' (ibid.). In this sense, while the involvement of white people in the immediate causes of the uprisings in 2001 (the National Front and Combat 18, for instance) was held to be the actions of a minority of extremists, 'those members of Asian communities who had participated were seen as "normal" examples of a generation of discontent and representative of an audacious criminal community as a whole' (Burnett 2004: 6–7).

While we have examined the importance placed upon culture as both the solution and the cause of social unrest and 'extremism', we have also noted how there was recognition in 1981 and 2001 that material conditions were also important in explaining the violent protest of BME people. This was perhaps more visible in the Scarman Report on the Brixton uprising, but it was, nevertheless, a theme that was to emerge from the Cantle Report on the uprisings of 2001. Furthermore, the report from the Ministerial Group on Public Order and Community Cohesion (2001) identified as one of its key issues high levels of unemployment, particularly among young BME people. More recently, then Prime Minister Tony Blair MP (2006c), linking material conditions to what he described as 'extremism' in Muslim communities, argued that:

> I do not ... ignore the social and economic dimension to extremism. Deprivation is a bad thing in itself and it can create the conditions in which extreme ideologies of all kinds can flourish. But it cannot be permitted as an excuse.
>
> The best way to deal with this is to do what, for a decade now, we have done: systematically to tackle disadvantage. The causes usually have nothing to do with ethnicity – they are low educational achievement and poor skills. But many ethnic minorities have been the beneficiaries of the New Deal, the neighbourhood renewal strategy, the minimum wage, Sure Start and so on.

Blair's comments are instructive, for while 'extremism' as he calls it has been closely linked in recent years to Asian cultural and religious beliefs and practices, he is suggesting in the quote that at least in part the solution to it can be found in policies applicable to people of *all* ethnicities. In this sense, and consistent with the 'community cohesion' agenda, he is denying that racial discrimination has any role in the material conditions that we have seen in *Crime and Inequality* are an important contextual factor in explaining offending and disorderly behaviour. These observations have important implications for the likely impact of social policies designed to 'tackle disadvantage', for such policies that suggest the socio-economic position of Black and Asian people 'have nothing to do with ethnicity' are likely to reproduce the disadvantages faced by BME people. Here, we focus upon paid work, for, as we have seen in previous chapters, it is held to be the most important route to a cohesive and orderly society.

Ethnicity, social policy and paid employment

In 2001 the government commissioned a piece of work examining the position of BME people in labour markets. This found that while some BME people, particularly those people of Indian and Chinese heritage, were 'on average, doing well and often out-performing whites in schools and in the labour market', other minority ethnic groups, most notably Black Caribbean, Pakistani and Bangladeshi people, had 'significantly higher unemployment and lower earnings than whites' (Strategy Unit 2003: 4). This was held to be problematic in economic terms because it represented underexploited talent, but was also held to be socially problematic because of its 'potential threats to social cohesion'[4] (*ibid*.). Even in the case of those 'out-performing whites' there were held to be problems, for they 'are not doing as well as they should be, given their education and other characteristics' (*ibid*.).

In addition to setting up a cross-departmental organisation – what was to become the Ethnic Minority Employment Task Force (EMETF) – to coordinate increased participation in paid work by BME people, the Strategy Unit report argued that there were three areas that required policy interventions. First, it was argued that the relatively poor educational and skill levels of BME people needed to be tackled in order to increase their employability. Second, the Strategy Unit argued that further efforts were required in order to 'promote equal opportunities in the workplace' (*ibid*.: 5). Third, action was said to be required in order to connect BME people to paid employment, especially those living in deprived areas.

Education and skills

According to the EMETF (2004: 5) attempts to increase the education and skills of BME people 'have largely been implemented through the Department for Educations and Skills' ... Aiming High strategy'. The Aiming High strategy was outlined in a consultation document (Department for Education and Skills 2003) that sought views upon ways in which the government might improve the educational performance of BME children. It was argued in the consultation document that while the government recognised that socio-economic inequalities were an important factor in explaining differences in educational achievements between ethnic groups, tackling those inequalities would not be enough to address the educational disadvantages of certain BME pupils (Black Caribbean and Pakistani youngsters in particular). Therefore, the consultation sought views on processes and practices within schools and the educational system more generally that might disadvantage those pupils.

The Aiming High strategy, therefore, has essentially involved a focus upon the ways in which schools operate in relation to the educational needs of BME pupils. Leadership on, and knowledge of, issues facing specific BME groups was seen as being central to the Aiming High strategy (see, for example, Tikly *et al.* 2006 on the African Caribbean Achievement Project). In addition, New Labour introduced in 1998 the Ethnic Minority Achievement Grant (EMAG) as a replacement for funding under Section 11 of the 1966 Local Government Act that provided 'assistance to local authorities that had substantial numbers of minority ethnic pupils "whose language and customs differ from those of the local community"' (Tikly *et al.* 2005: 287). Tikley *et al.* (2005) argue that the EMAG can be understood as extending New Labour's concerns with social exclusion into the education system, although they also note how in this respect it is structured through a tension with 'an assimilationist tendency which has neglected effort to see minority ethnic achievement as an issue and has, at times, pandered to more nationalistic and xenophobic tendencies within society and government' (*ibid.*: 293). They also point to the fact that their research suggested that the EMAG did little for many – most notably Black Caribbean – BME pupils. This, they argue, was due to a continuation under the EMAG of the Section 11 practice of funding support for those students for whom English was not their first language. Hence, they argue, a possible explanation for the EMAG's more favourable effect in raising the performance of Bangladeshi and Pakistani pupils.

Table 6.3 demonstrates changes in a standard measure – the obtaining of five 'good' GCSEs (grades A*–C) – of educational performance. It shows that between 1988 and 2004 all the ethnic groups that are of concern to us saw substantial increases in the proportion of their young people getting 'good' grades at GCSE. In fact, if we take the proportion change, the BME groups outperformed the white group. According to the figures this was particularly the case for Bangladeshi youngsters, the proportion of whom gaining five or more GCSEs grade A*–C increased by nearly 270 per cent. This may demonstrate improving educational performance, or may be a reflection of the low numbers of Bangladeshi pupils gaining five GCSEs grade A*–C. The figures in the table are disturbing, particularly for black youngsters who were facing a larger gap between themselves and white youngsters, in 2004 compared to 1998 (9 percentage points in 1988 compared to 16 percentage points in 2004).

Table 6.3 Proportion of pupils gaining 5 or more GCSEs grade A*–C by ethnicity, 1988–2004

	1988	2004	Percentage change
Bangladeshi	13	48	269.2
Black	17	36	111.8
Pakistani	20	45	125.0
White	26	52	100.0

Sources: Gillbourn and Mirza (2000); Department for Education and Skills (2006b).

It is clear that the government's strategy still has a long way to go to address the disadvantage that BME pupils face in education. This is particularly the case for black youngsters who continue to be labelled as the educational 'problem', both in schools, from which they are disproportionately excluded (Gillbourn and Mirza 2000; Blair 2001; Tomlinson 2005), and in policy terms. However, the current strategy is criticised for doing little to address the educational disadvantage that in particular Black Caribbean youngsters face. The main reason for this is related to institutional racism in education. The Aiming High strategy was itself partly driven by the 2000 Race Relations (Amendment) Act that, in the context of the MacPherson Report (1999) on the murder of Stephen Lawrence, placed 'a positive duty on public bodies to promote race equality' (Tikly *et al.* 2005: 288). However, despite this there is concern that institutional racism is not taken seriously in education. Drawing upon Alibhai-Brown (1999), Tikly *et al.* (*ibid.*: 290), for example, note that New Labour governments have been more concerned with 'reversing social exclusion, rather than directly addressing racial inequalities'. In this context, for example, they point to the fact that while targets were introduced to cut the number of permanent exclusions from schools by one-third, there was no recognition of the disproportionate number of exclusions of BME pupils, most notably those of African Caribbean heritage. The consequence, they rightly argue, is that the position of African Caribbean pupils is proportionately unlikely to change.

Crozier's (2005) observations have resonance with the arguments of Tikly *et al.* (2005). Through interviews with the parents of young African Caribbean males she rejects pathological approaches (such as the argument that black pupils have an anti-school culture) to explaining underachievement among such young people, locating their poor educational achievement in institutional racism:

What has been argued here is that the downward spiral of underachievement does not start with the child himself/herself but that it is the pathological view of the black, or in this case African Caribbean child, that is so embedded within the school institution that conspires against his or her success. It is suggested that until institutional racism is taken seriously in schools then league tables, targets or other educational policies to raise standards will have limited impact on the experience of the black child. (*ibid.*: 569)

Workplace discrimination

In order to tackle workplace discrimination the EMETF pointed to developments in the Commission for Racial Equality's *Code of Practice on Racial Equality in Employment* that took effect from April 2006 and developments within Jobcentre Plus, such as the employment of Diversity Sector Relationship Managers (DSRMs) and Specialist Employment Advisers (SEAs).

The Code of Practice outlines the responsibilities of employers in relation to ensuring equality of opportunity in their workplaces. However, it is only a *Code of Practice* and, therefore, does not impose any legal obligations upon employers in relation to racial discrimination. While this arguably makes it a weak tool, there are more fundamental problems with such an approach that are particularly concerning, for it is premised upon the assumption that workplace discrimination against BME people can be tackled by tweaking the laws governing racial discrimination. This approach, however, misses the point that BME people are exploited by capitalism in different ways from white people. In this sense, racial discrimination is part of the fabric of capitalism and, therefore, is not something that can be abolished by tweaking the law governing its operation (Sivanandan 2001).

The employment of specialist staff in Jobcentre Plus is essentially concerned with spreading good practice to employers. DSRMs, for instance, are charged with working with the human resource departments of the 'top' 100 companies in the UK on their recruitment of BME people (Hudson *et al.* 2006), while SEAs work to 'encourage recruitment from ethnic minority groups and promote the business benefit of diversity' (*ibid.*). This role is particularly problematic, for it implies that the employment of BME people, or having a 'diverse' labour force is only justifiable to employers if there is a 'business benefit' to having such a labour force. The reverse of this, however, seems to be that if there is not a business case for it, diversity of workers should not be pursued. It is at such junctures that demands for social justice and their delivery through capitalism are at odds and there is little to suggest that having specialist workers in Jobcentre Plus attempting to persuade employers to take on BME workers will have much impact on the disadvantage BME people face in terms of employment.

Connecting BME people to labour markets: a new deal?

From the early years of the introduction of the New Deal programmes there was debate focusing upon whether they would be able to meet the employment and training needs of BME people. So, for example, by drawing upon evidence of previous government-sponsored employment and training schemes Ogbonna and Noon (1999) outlined several areas of potential concern with the NDYP. First, they argued that the participation of young BME people in the new deal could not be taken for granted. Poor rates of success, as was the case on the YTS, would, they suggested, encourage BME people to withdraw from the scheme altogether, or only to engage with it passively. Both quantitative and qualitative evidence supports this concern of Ogbonna and Noon (1999). Quantitative research demonstrates that the outcomes of the NDYP are poorer for BME people compared to white people. So, for instance, 45.2 per cent of white young people leave it to enter paid work. However, only a third (33.0 per cent) of young black people and 40.4 per cent of Asian young people leave the NDYP for paid work. The poorer outcomes for young unemployed BME people partly reflect the fact that when they enter the options stage of the NDYP they are concentrated in those options that are the least likely to lead to paid work. In particular, compared to white young people they are less likely to be on the subsidised employment option (Fieldhouse et al. 2002; Dorsett 2004), the option that we saw in Chapter 3 is most likely to lead to a 'proper job'.

The poorer outcomes, particularly in the gaining of paid work, for BME people are reflected in the proportions of people leaving the NDYP for unknown destinations. While about a fifth (21.5 per cent) of white young people leave for such destinations, black and Asian young people are more likely to leave for unknown destinations. In the case of young black people, they are nearly as likely to leave for unknown destinations (31.7 per cent) as they are to leave for paid work (33.0 per cent). At 31.0 per cent, young Asian people are as likely as black youngsters to leave the NDYP for unknown destinations.[5] These figures should be particularly concerning to the government because, as we saw in Chapter 3, while it is officially argued that people leaving the NDYP are actually taking up paid work, the evidence for this is not convincing.

In addition, qualitative longitudinal research with young people in Oldham also suggests that the NDYP is having the effect of discouraging young BME (mainly Asian people in the case of Oldham) from participating in it (Kalra *et al.* 2001; Kalra 2002; Fieldhouse *et al.* 2002). Hence, it was found that young people took paid work to avoid participation in the NDYP. This was often work that was undervalued and which the young people would, in other circumstances, avoid. As, for instance, one Bangladeshi male told Kalra *et al.* (2001: 70):

> The job that I am doing was offered to me about 3 months before I was told I was going onto New Deal ... At the time I didn't take it ... But when I realised that I would have to go onto New Deal I decided to ring the boss up at the takeaway and take the job straight away and luckily he said it was still available.

In this case, the NDYP operated as a recruiting sergeant for that sector of the economy that we saw at the beginning of the chapter employs nearly half of all Bangladeshi men and demonstrates the conservative potential of policies such as the NDYP.

Second, and linked to their first concern, Ogbonna and Noon (1999) argued that, as with conventional markets, the quasi-market upon which the NDYP was to be (and is) premised, was likely to discriminate against BME. They feared this because of evidence (Baqi 1987; De Sousa 1987; Verma and Darby 1987; Cross and Smith 1987; Cross *et al* 1988) that suggested previous labour market initiatives directed BME people into 'less rewarding programmes or [sent] them to placement organisations where they receive[d] no real training or job opportunities' (Ogbonna and Noon 1999: 170).

While conscripts of the NDYP do not identify racial discrimination among New Deal staff as being an issue, they do highlight discrimination among employers willing to take new deal participants. Dorsett (2004), for example, found that BME conscripts of the NDYP were put forward for job vacancies as frequently as white participants. Hence, their lower rate of participation in the employment option 'may be due to discriminatory employment practices' (*ibid.*: 7). Supporting such observations, Merriman-Johnson (2005: 3) found that: 'Some clients said they felt they were held back by others' negative perceptions of their ambition or worthiness and their culture or association with being "black"'. In many ways, these findings should not be surprising, for the aim of the NDYP is to get young people into work in existing labour markets that operate in ways that discriminate against BME people.

Third, Ogbonna and Noon (1999) feared that the sanctions of the NDYP would be applied disproportionately to young BME people, an issue that the Trades Union Congress raised with the Work and Pensions Committee (2002). Ogbonna and Noon's (1999) concern was derived from research that indicated that BME people faced particular problems in relation to the benefit sanction regime of the JSA (Vincent and Dobson 1997). There was, the TUC argued, little to suggest that the sanctioning regime of the NDYP would operate differently from this. Furthermore, the sanctions on the NDYP are more likely to be applied to those people in the option stage who are not in the employment option. So, for example, while 7 per cent of those participants on the employment option of the NDYP are sanctioned, nearly a quarter (23.4 per cent) of those on the education or training option – the option that BME people are concentrated on – are sanctioned. Hence, it is the case that the NDYP is not only underperforming in helping young BME people to gain paid work, it is likely that it is disproportionately impoverishing them while doing so.

Such concerns, particularly related to the performance of the New Deals in getting BME people into paid work are equally applicable to the NDLP which shows differences in outcome for BME lone mothers compared to white lone mothers. The immediate destination of half (50.1 per cent) of white lone mothers leaving the NDLP is paid employment, compared to just over a third of black (36.7 per cent) and Asian (36.1 per cent) lone mothers. Indeed, black and Asian lone mothers are more likely to leave the NDLP to claim IS (39.2 per cent of black leavers and 40.4 per cent of Asian leavers) than they are to enter paid work. About a third (30.1 per cent) of white lone mothers leave the NDLP to claim IS.[6]

Looking to the future, the trends that are already visible are likely to become more exaggerated. Most notably, there are likely to be more requirements upon BME people to find paid work. This was signalled in 2007 by then Minister for Welfare, Jim Murphy MP who, while acknowledging that BME people were socially and economically disadvantaged and that 'the causes of this disadvantage are complex', went on to argue that 40,000 BME people 'were being denied the opportunity to work because they do not have the language skills to get a job' (Murphy 2007: 6). For Murphy, the solution to this was to divert financial resources away from translation services to 'teaching [English] language to get a job' (*ibid.*), something that has recently been argued to have a wider application.[7] However, the refocusing of resources is, as with the other policies that we have examined in *Crime and Inequality*, framed by the rights and responsibilities agenda. Hence, it was widely reported that if people whose first language is not English did not take the opportunities to learn it, then they would 'face sanctions such as having their unemployment benefit cut' (the *Guardian*, 12 February 2007).

Also, in February 2007, as we saw in the previous chapter, the Freud Review (Freud 2007) on the future of work-welfare was published. In his report Freud described non-employed BME people, along with other social groups (for example, lone mothers), as 'hard to help'. The aim of the Freud Review was to outline options for future policies to get more people into paid work in pursuit of the government's target of having 80 per cent of the working age population in employment by 2020. The most important aspect of the Freud Report for our purposes was the recommendation, which is being vigorously pursued by the government, that there should be

> a bifurcation in the provision of work activation services between Jobcentre Plus that will service the claiming and job-readiness needs of able-bodied claimants in the first year in which they are workless and considered to be available for work, and private sector contractors who will take on the 'hard to help' cases thereafter. (Grover 2007: 58)

Privatisation is a means of introducing free market principles as the solution to social problems. While privatisation in other areas of social policy provides a warning of its possible impact on job placement services (see, for example, Ginsburg 2005 on the privatisation of social housing), the privatisation of such services has a number of particularly concerning implications for the employment of BME people. First, Grover (2007) argues that there will be an economic imperative for a conservative approach to placing people into paid work. In brief, the payment of fees to private enterprises for getting people into paid work will encourage the contracted companies to place people into those jobs and sectors of the economy where there is a proven record of employment for their particular ethnic groups. This means BME people are likely to be placed in those jobs and sectors of the economy where they are currently concentrated; those that, as we saw at the start of this chapter, are often highlighted by low pay. Second, Grover (2007) argues that the Freud analysis and proposals are limited by their focus only upon the economic position of 'hard to help' people. As we have seen, Fraser (1997, 2000) argues that it is a conjoining of the political economic and cultural valuation systems that explains the relatively poor socio-economic of many BME people. The Freud Review only focuses upon the political economic position of non-employed people. However, without cultural reordering, attempts to force BME people into paid employment through highly conditional benefits will merely reproduce the economic inequalities they face.

Connecting BME people to labour market: reaching out?

The various New Deals are, as we have seen, aimed at all ethnic groups. In this sense, they are premised upon the assumption that the needs of BME people are little different to the white majority. However, there is some recognition that BME people may also have additional needs. We saw this above in relation to attempts to reduce employer discrimination through the employment of DSRMs and SEAs in Jobcentre Plus. It is also visible in efforts to connect BME people to labour markets through the *Ethnic Minority Outreach* (EMO) and the *Ethnic Minority Flexible Fund* (EMFF). The EMO and flexible fund assume 'that support and advice on work and training does not always reach some ethnic groups' (Work and Pensions Committee 2005: para. 185). The EMO is delivered by private and voluntary organisations and provides a link between the services provided by Jobcentre Plus and non-employed BME. In contrast, the flexible fund can be drawn upon by Jobcentre Plus staff to 'create local solutions to tackling ethnic minority unemployment' (*ibid.*). Like many policies aimed at connecting non-employed people to labour markets, they tend to help those closest (i.e. those most likely to gain paid work anyway) to labour markets (see Barnes *et al.* 2005). The EMO is reported as having had a 'major impact increasing the ethnic minorities' awareness of employment and training opportunities, especially among Indian and Pakistani women' (Barnes *et al.* 2005: 1). However, given that only 3,000 jobs were gained through the EMO in a four-year period (2001–2004) (EMETF 2004), this particular policy arguably underestimates the employment disadvantages faced by BME people.

Conclusion

While this chapter has demonstrated some of the difficulties in teasing out relationships between crime and inequality, it has also shown that inequality is an important contextual factor in understanding offending and disorder among BME people. We have concentrated on spectacular events – urban uprisings in 1981 and 2001 – but the arguments are also applicable to more mundane episodes of offending and disorder. However, we have seen that in the case of BME the material context of offending has not been engaged with to any great extent. This is because of the overriding concern with cultural issues, in particular the cultures of BME people, and the extent to which it is thought that BME people have cultures that are threatening to what is thought to be an easily identifiable 'Britishness'. We saw, for example, that after the uprisings of 1981 by predominantly black people multiculturalism was seen as the solution; there should be an acceptance of the culture forms and practices of BME people. However, in the more recent focus upon 'community cohesion' multiculturalism was deemed to be deeply problematic, leading to ethnic segregation, mistrust between ethnic groups and 'extremism' in some BME groups.

In this context, it is difficult to see how policies currently being pursued will tackle the disadvantages faced by BME people. While there is some recognition that BME people face disadvantages because of individual and institutional racism, the main ways, at least at a central government level, of tackling these are through policies aimed at all ethnic groups. Those policies that are aimed specifically at BME people are often structured through the idea that BME cultures are problematic and are funded at such levels that, if funding is taken as a sign of commitment to addressing social problems, suggest concerns with BME disadvantage are not particularly high on the policy agenda. Furthermore, the role of the state in discriminating against BME people through developments in immigration and asylum policy and criminal justice policy and practice (most notably policing), said to be necessary in the 'war on terror', does little for 'community cohesion' and arguably reinforces mistrust and suspicion of some, most notably Asian, BME groups.

At a cultural level BME people are inextricably linked to crime and disorder and because of the interrelationships between the cultural and economic, this has impacts at the material level (cf. Fraser 1997 2000). Hence, there is a fundamental problem with the current approach of addressing the material inequalities facing BME, for they are premised on tackling inequalities related to the political-economic position of BME (for example, getting them into paid work). There is little recognition that BME are equally disadvantaged by the cultural valuation system through which BME people are associated with crime and disorder. In this sense, tweaking with the political economy position of BME people will not have a great deal of effect. In contrast, the cultural-valuation system that associates being black and, increasingly, being Asian with socio-economic problems, including crime and disorder, will have to be addressed if political economy developments are to have any discernible effect on the material context of BME offending and 'disorderly' behaviour.

Notes

1 All figures are from http://www.statistics.gov.uk/STATBASE/ssdatadet. asp?vlnk=6209 (accessed 11 June 2007).
2 'Swamp 81' was a police operation that involved plain-clothes officers policing areas of Lambeth that had high rates of burglary and street robbery. The use of stop and search powers was central to the operation and neither 'community' leaders, nor local beat officers were informed of the operation in advance. Scarman (1981) noted that evidence submitted to the inquiry suggested that the operation had increased tensions in Brixton in the week immediately before the uprising.
3 Unrest was also witnessed in Leeds and Stoke-on-Trent, but not to the same extent and intensity as that in Bradford, Burnley and Oldham.
4 Such arguments are observable across a number of areas. The relatively poor educational achievement of some BME groups, for example, is held to be problematic because it 'endangers social cohesion and leaves personal and economic potential unrealised' (Department for Education and Skills 2003: 4).
5 All figures calculated using the Department for Work and Pensions's Tabulation Tool and are cumulative figures to November 2006.
6 All figures calculated using the Department for Work and Pensions's Tabulation Tool and are cumulative figures to November 2006.
7 It was reported in the *Guardian* (11 June 2007) that then 'communities secretary' Ruth Kelly MP felt that translation 'has been used too frequently and sometimes without thought to the consequences' and the result of this was that people did 'not have the incentive to learn the language [English]'. Kelly was commenting on the forthcoming report from the Commission on Integration and Community Cohesion (2007) that recommended local authorities should not automatically provide translation or, indeed, interpretation services, but should think carefully about the provision of such services in the context of four factors: that, with the exception of translation for someone who is arrested, there is no legal requirement to translate material; that translation 'can never be a substitute for learning English' (*ibid*.: 167); that translation 'should be reduced except where it builds integration and cohesion' (*ibid*.: 168); and that translation 'should be considered in the context of communication to

all communities' (*ibid.*). Kelly's ideas were shared by the chairperson, Darra Singh of the Commission on Integration and Community Cohesion, who noted in the *Observer* (10 June 2007): 'It is important that we encourage newcomers to learn English, rather than make it easier for them to get by without.'

Chapter 7

Street homelessness and crime

Introduction

In this chapter we are concerned with one of the most vulnerable groups in contemporary society – street homeless people – and the crimes that are enacted upon them. In particular, the chapter focuses upon the victimisation of rough sleepers by the general public, the 'respectable'. It examines this phenomenon using the work of Ballintyne (1999) and more qualitative accounts of life on the streets (for example, Cassidy 1999; Wardhaugh 2000) and uses Young's (1999, 2002) idea of vindictiveness in the gaze downwards of relative deprivation to explain why street homeless people become the victims of the crimes of 'respectable' people. The chapter argues that the discursive construction of welfare 'dependency' and historical concerns that have connected street homelessness with crime and disorder provide an important context for explaining crime enacted upon them. The chapter then goes on to examine the social policy responses to rough sleeping, arguing that because they are constructed in a utilitarian discourse, they contribute to the construction of rough sleepers as a criminal threat to social order; a threat that needs to be contained.

However, first we must make some observations about definitions. Homelessness is notoriously difficult to define. Like many of the concepts discussed in *Crime and Inequality*, it is a social construct, constructed through theory (Neale 1997), policy (Hutson and Liddiard 1994; Pleace *et al.* 1997) and the definitions of homeless people themselves (Hutson and Liddiard 1994; Neale 1997). It is generally agreed that people sleeping rough on the streets are homeless. However, such a definition is very narrow. More contentious is whether other people – for example, those living in various forms of temporary accommodation and those living in accommodation unsuitable for their needs – should be considered as homeless. Hence, it is argued that it might be better to think of homelessness as being a continuum, from street homelessness to a broader range of circumstances 'that only some commentators would describe as homelessness' (Hutson and Liddiard 1994: 27). This is important for our purposes, for rough sleeping is often interspersed with periods of 'hidden homeless' (Paylor 1995; Pleace *et al.* 1997), such as staying in night shelters and hostels, and possibly with friends and relatives. The idea of street homelessness is problematic because of the conceptual differences between a 'home' and a 'house':

> A 'house' is generally taken to be synonymous with a dwelling, or a physical structure, whereas a 'home' is not. A 'home' implies a set of social relations, or a set of activities within a physical structure, whereas a 'house' does not. (Watson 1984, cited in Hutson and Liddiard 1994: 29)

The implication of such observations, Neale (1997) argues, is that it can be difficult to define some homeless people as 'homeless' because, although they might not have a house, they do live in a situation structured through social relationships and engage in activities that might imply a home. Hutson and Liddiard (1994), for example, found that some young people who were homeless according to their definition did not consider themselves to be homeless because of their social networks and the activities that they undertook within those networks.

In addition, there are legal definitions to consider. Under homelessness law, to be considered homeless it is not enough to be lacking accommodation. In contrast, the legislation distinguishes between priority and non-priority homeless people; those 'deserving' and 'undeserving' of rehousing. These distinctions are a policy inheritance from the utilitarian and liberal genesis of various aspects of Britain's welfare policies (Pleace 1998) and relate to the circumstances of people presenting themselves to local authorities as homeless. For people to be accepted as such, judgements are made about the circumstances by which they became homeless in order to establish whether applicants can be held responsible for their homelessness ('intentionally' homeless); whether applicants have a 'local connection' to the area in which they are presenting themselves (for example, whether they have previously lived or worked there) and whether, according to guidance, they can be considered to be a priority for rehousing. In this sense, homelessness is a social construction; the consequence of a range of decisions made by administrators in order to manage a scarce resource (housing) through moral categorisations (Pleace 2000). For our immediate purposes this is important because through the construction of priority groups for rehousing, one of the main distinctions made is between childless people and those with dependent children; having dependent children, alongside some measures of vulnerability (for instance, due to old age and/or some form of disability), are the main ways of securing priority. With a few exceptions,[1] those people who do not have dependent children, providing that they are not considered to be 'vulnerable', are not a priority for re-housing. Hence, when we examine street homelessness or rough sleeping we are, on the whole, dealing with single people and, perhaps more rarely, childless couples. Hence, it not unknown for the term 'single homeless' to be used as an alternative to 'street homeless' and 'rough sleeper'.

Street homelessness and crime

There are at least three ways in which street homelessness and crime are related. First, the perpetration of crime is an important factor in explaining why young people particularly, but not exclusively, become street homeless. Hendessi (1992), for example, found four in 10 of young homeless women had been sexually abused before their homelessness. Wardhaugh (2000: 93), notes that while young (aged 16 to 21) women 'had often become homeless following child abuse within the home ... slightly older (21-plus) were likely (also) to have suffered violence within partnerships'. Such findings are supported in the work of Pain and Francis (2004) who argue that gender is important to explaining street homelessness. In particular, they note that for women sexual abuse is an important factor in explaining street homelessness, whereas for young men it is physical abuse; for example, the young man 'who told his mother he had had underage gay sex, and she told his father, who beat him up and threw him out' (*ibid.*: 102).

Second, street homeless people offend. We saw in Chapter 2 that the role of absolute deprivation in explaining offending behaviour has been widely criticised. However, it is clear from research with street homeless people that some commit crime because they are in absolute need; they do not have enough money for food and/or accommodation (Cassidy 1999; Wardhaugh 2000; May *et al.* 2005). In this context, it has been argued (Cohen and Machalek 1988; Snow *et al.* 1989; Carlen 1996) that some street homeless people offend as a means of survival; 'to help make ends meet' (Pain and Francis 2004: 105). Indeed, in this sense, McCarthy and Hagan (1991) argue that street homeless can be considered to be a 'criminogenic situation'. The accounts of street homeless people also suggest that some of the environments which they may inhabit – for example, night shelters and hostels – are threatening places; where they are fearful of other homeless people stealing their belongings and fearful of the violence and illicit drugs use in them (see for example, Wardhaugh 2000; May *et al.* 2005).

Third, street homeless people are the victims of crime. This is the main focus of this chapter.

Rough sleepers as victims of the crimes of the 'respectable'

In an American context Wachholz (2005) argues that crimes against street homeless people can be understood as hate crimes. She makes such claims because of the way in which street homeless people are victimised because they are part of a particular social group characterised by its homelessness. Hence, such crimes might be understood as being 'motivated by hatred, bias or prejudice' (McLaughlin 2006: 194). However, Ray and Smith (2004: 685) warn that the motivation for offending is often more complex than 'consciously motivated "haters" who are strangers to their victims ... and who target the victim as a member of a hated social group'. Hence, I do not use the term 'hate crime' when describing crimes committed against street homeless people by the 'respectable'. However, as we shall see, Wachholz's (2005: 145) argument that crimes against homeless people 'function to establish spatial boundaries between the homeless and more privileged groups' is useful in understanding offending against street homeless people. In the meantime, we need to focus upon the crimes committed against such people.

The Institute for Public Policy Research's report *Unsafe Streets* (Ballintyne 1998) presents a shocking portrayal of the victimisation of rough sleepers who 'experience levels of personal victimisation that would not be tolerated across a wider community' (Ballintyne, quoted in BBC 1999: 1), an observation also made by Kipke *et al.* (1997) and

Pain and Francis (2004). In Ballintyne's study 120 rough sleepers were interviewed about the crimes of which they had been the victim. The majority (78 per cent) of respondents had been the victim of at least one crime in their latest period of street homelessness. Female rough sleepers were particularly vulnerable; 95 per cent had been the victim of crime compared to 75 per cent of men. Unsurprisingly, given their lack of material possessions, street homeless people were more likely to be victims of contact (personal), rather than property crime. Ballintyne found that 45 per cent of respondents had been the victim of an assault compared to 3.2 per cent in the general population; and 35 per cent had been the victim of wounding, compared to 1 per cent of individuals in the general population. In other words, street homeless people were up to 15 times more likely to be the victim of an assault and were 35 times more likely to be the victim of wounding compared to the housed population.

The findings of Ballintyne are echoed in more qualitative work with street homeless people that shows, as the following examples demonstrate, that they face routine verbal abuse and harassment, and that the threat of violence is ever-present:

> I mean you get the lager louts who go up to you and try to kick your head in. Then you get gangs of women walking around giving you lots of verbal abuse. I've been robbed a few times, yeah, mace sprayed on me once, somebody sprayed me with mace spray, took ten pound off me ... but it's mostly verbal abuse I get basically ... the last couple of days because of the heat I've been getting a lot more abuse, people tell me to eff off, you just gotta ignore it. But by the end of the day you're feeling pretty browned off, the fifteenth and twentieth time. (Brendan, *Big Issue* vendor, living in a squat in Manchester, in Wardhaugh 2000: 92)

> I've had untold amounts of fights. When you're begging people tend to get a bit shitty with you. You'll always get someone coming up to you and saying, 'Get a job, get a life.' As if it's that simple.
>
> When you're begging at night things do get a bit leery because there are usually a lot more drunks about. Believe it or not, they tend to give more trouble to the men than the women. I was with a guy a couple of weeks ago and we asked a group of men if they could spare us any change. One turned round, came back, and tried to stab my friend in the back of the head with a Coke can. ...

The thing is, you get used to it. At the end of the day people can think you're scum, say 'Get a life' or whatever, but you need enough money to live and buy clothes, food and do the things 'normal' people do. (Vanessa, sleeping in car parks, in Cassidy 1999: 36)

While Vanessa's account regarding the gendered nature of the victimisation of rough sleepers differs to that of Ballintyne's account which found a higher level of offending against female rough sleepers, both the quotes highlight some of the main findings in relation to the crimes perpetrated against street homeless people; that they are multiple and an everyday feature of the lives of people sleeping rough, especially for those who rely upon street life (for example, begging and *Big Issue* selling) to secure their (low) incomes.

The quotes also demonstrate that street homeless people have to manage a range of risks related to these ways of securing income (see also Fitzpatrick and Kennedy 2001; Wachholz 2005). They are also instructive because they point to other findings that emerged from the Ballintyne (1999) research, in particular, the level and nature of crime committed against rough sleepers by the general public. We have seen that it would be wrong to argue that street homeless people do not commit crime against each other; the testimony of rough sleepers suggests otherwise (Cassidy 1999). However, as the above quotes suggest, crimes against street homeless people are often perpetrated by the general public, or, as Wardhaugh (2000: 96) notes, the '"respectable" citizen'. In fact, Ballintyne (1999) found that, overall, street homeless people were more likely to be offended against by the 'respectable' than by other rough sleepers. Only in the category of robbery were street homeless people more likely to be offended against by other rough sleepers compared to the 'respectable' citizen. For offences such as verbal abuse and wounding, two-thirds (64 and 63 per cent respectively) were committed by the general public.

Street homeless people are seen as being part of the law and order 'problem' (Dean and Gale 1999). However, the evidence discussed here suggests that they are also very likely to be the victims of crimes, and challenges the binaries that are often constructed around who are thought to be the victims and who are thought to be the perpetrators of crime (cf. Pain and Francis 2004). Furthermore, because street homeless people are assigned the status of perpetrator, rather than victim, they are increasingly subjected to control strategies, such as the clearing of streets of rough sleepers, aimed at making the 'respectable' feel safer (see M. Davis 1990, 1999; Pain 2000). Not only do such strategies ignore the victimisation of street homeless people, they may well contribute to the disdain with which many 'respectable' people view street homeless people, and which arguably helps to explain why they commit offences against such a vulnerable group of people.

Vindictiveness, relative deprivation and the undeserving poor

We have seen that McCarthy and Hagan (1991) argue that street homelessness can be considered to be a 'criminogenic situation'. They use this term to explain the crimes committed by young street homeless people. However, it might equally be applied to the victimisation of homeless people in the context of routine activity theory that suggests crime is committed when three things – the offender, a suitable target and the lack of 'capable guardians' – come together at a particular moment. Street homeless people might be considered to be particularly vulnerable targets in this sense because of the geographies that they inhabit and the activities, such as begging, that they often engage in, and because if 'capable guardians' are around they may take little interest in what in happening to rough sleepers. The problem with such arguments though is that they 'blame the victim'; homeless people are victimised because they place themselves in danger by living on the streets. However, as we have seen, street homeless people rarely choose to sleep rough, although they do develop strategies to avoid the risk of being victimised, for example, sleeping in well-lit and well-populated (by other homeless people) areas, keeping dogs for protection and developing mechanisms and strategies to cope with aggression from the general public (Cassidy 1999; Wardhaugh 2000). As Ian told Wardhaugh (2000: 97):

> You know when something's gonna happen, the problem is if you're sat down you've got to try and stand up, but not run away unless you're sure you can get away. Just be ready to run as soon as you get the chance ... You know which ones are going to do it [threaten or use violence]. They're always the loudmouth groups of lads ... the worst are the young people that go on the streets with loadsa money ... then they drink too much and don't know what they're doing ... [If] you go to the sort of proper drinking pubs and people's coming out of there, they'll throw you money.

Avoiding particular demographic groups and particularly dangerous spaces was central to Ian's way of avoiding being the victim of verbal and/or physical abuse. Moreover, rational choice theories do not actually explain why it is that homeless people, as opposed to others using the street, become the target for abuse and harassment. This is an issue to which we now turn.

Relative deprivation and the downward gaze

In criminology the idea of relative deprivation has been used as an explanation of criminal activity since the mid 1960s. Despite its association with others, the idea is associated particularly with left realist criminologists (Young 2006). The pursuit of left realists in the 1980s was to devise an explanation of crime that was politically acceptable to the left that had traditionally seen crime as being rooted in structural factors. There were argued to be many problems with this line of thinking, the most important of which was the fact that despite the general increase in living standards of industrial countries over the post-war period, there had also been a rise in crime levels. In this sense, it was argued to be difficult to understand crime as being the consequence of absolute levels of deprivation, because, generally speaking, absolute deprivation was decreasing in the post-Second World War period (until the 1970s) when crime was actually increasing. From our perspective such an approach is also problematic because it cannot explain why people who are materially more secure might commit offences against some of the most vulnerable people in contemporary society.

In order to understand this phenomenon we need to discuss Young's (1999, 2002) ideas of how the concept of relative deprivation can be used to explain what he describes as a 'sociology of vindictiveness' in contemporary society. While earlier in his career Young (1992; also Lea and Young 1984) argued that relative deprivation involved a gaze upwards to what others have, we saw in Chapter 2 that more recently (Young 1999, 2002) he argues that it can also involve a gaze downwards: a 'dismay at the relative well-being of those who although below one in the social hierarchy are perceived as unfairly advantaged: they make too easy a living even if it is not as good as one's own' (Young 1999: 9). For Young, the gaze upwards and the gaze downwards explain different aspects of the crime 'problem'. The former helps to explain why people engage in criminal activity, and the latter the demand for punitive action to be taken against the criminal. It is the gaze downwards that is of more importance to us.

Young (2002: 480) argues that: 'relative deprivation downwards, a feeling that those who work little or not at all are getting an easy ride on your back and your taxes, is a widespread sentiment'. This view of those 'below' in the social hierarchy, Young argues, helps foster a sense of resentment that is characterised by disproportionality, scapegoating and stereotyping. In this sense, the group gazed down upon is seen as making a disproportionate, compared to its actual, contribution to the problems of society and its members are represented as the main players in the creation of social problems, including crime and disorder.

Young argues that it is a structurally constituted 'underclass' that is gazed down upon. This 'underclass' is created as a consequence of the shift from what he terms the 'inclusive' society, characterised by 'high employment, stable family structures, and consensual values underpinned by the safety net of the welfare state' (*ibid.*: 459) to 'exclusive', late-modern society characterised by 'structural unemployment, economic precariousness, a systematic cutting of welfare provisions' (*ibid.*). He suggests that the 'underclass's' characteristics of idleness, state dependency, hedonism and irresponsibility (highlighted by behaviours such as illicit drug use, teenage pregnancy and fecklessness) are those that the 'respectable' have to suppress if they want to maintain their lifestyle. To survive in late-modern society demands a great deal of effort, self-control and restraint; hours are long, wages are poor and high levels of commitment to paid work are expected. It is this experience of restraint and sacrifice, Young suggests, which turns displeasure with the 'underclass' into vindictiveness and leads to its demonisation.

Young makes it clear that the process of demonisation is not simply about envy; the lawyer does not want to be a junky and the successful businesswoman would not want to be a single mother receiving state benefits. However, the very existence of the 'underclass', Young argues, 'hits the weak spots of our character armour' (*ibid.*: 482). In this context, feelings of vindictiveness drive calls for the containment and authoritarian treatment of the 'underclass'. Hence, for Young the relative deprivation gaze downwards helps to explain the authoritarian response to crime and disorder; a response that is highlighted by increased incarceration, net widening, and, as we have seen in previous chapters, responsibilisation and remoralisation.

However, in addition to this role in calling for the containment and authoritarian treatment of the 'underclass', it is possible to argue that Young's conceptualisation of the relative deprivation gaze downwards can help to explain the abuse and harassment its members face, most notably street homeless people (although one could add other vulnerable groups of people such as asylum seekers and refugees), for it arguably provides an important insight into the economic and socio-political context in which crimes against such people take place.

Yar and Penna (2004) argue that the historical periodisations in Young's thesis are problematic. While Young (2004) defends his thesis from such claims, it is clear that some poor and excluded people, including street homeless people, have historically been concerning to elites because of their alleged economic and moral costs. Chambliss (1964), for instance, analyses the introduction of the 1349 law governing the relief of vagrancy. This law criminalised the giving of alms to 'valiant beggars', making such actions punishable by imprisonment. He (*ibid.*: 6) demonstrates how the concern was with the effect that the giving of alms allegedly had on the behaviour of labour, with it being argued that 'many valiant beggars, as long as they may live of begging, do refuse to labor, giving themselves to idleness and vice, and sometimes to theft and other abominations'. The donating of alms, therefore, was held to erode the character of the beggar. It was said to encourage beggars into idleness and other forms of morally distasteful behaviours. Chambliss (1964) explains the introduction of the 1349 Act with reference to the political economy of the time and in particular the effect of the Black Death of 1348, which 'decimated the labour force' (*ibid.*: 7) in a period when the economy was heavily dependent upon a cheap supply of labour. The idea here is that the relief of the beggar would merely exacerbate labour shortages and therefore increases wage costs by encouraging the relieved into idleness.

Wardhaugh (2000) demonstrates that over the following 500 years vagrants and beggars could be physically punished (whipped, branded and put to death) and, later, imprisoned. While the criminal law continued to be used to manage vagrancy, from the seventeenth century laws relating to the relief of indigence were also used. Efforts were made, for example, through the 1662 Law of Settlement and Removal to remove people needing poor relief to their original place of settlement. Today, continuity with this demand can be found in the 'local connection' requirement of contemporary homelessness legislation (cf. Lowe 1997). Later, Wardhaugh (2000: 38) argues, the development of workhouses provided a 'spatial means for controlling the poor and placeless'.

While historical concerns with those people thought to be a 'burden' in a variety of ways cannot be ignored, it is the case, as Young (1999,

2000) and others (for example, Jones and Novak 1999; Grover and Stewart 2002) argue, that in the latter decades of the twentieth century there was a newly invigorated concern with those considered to be burdensome. Jones and Novak (1999: 5), for example, note:

> At the end of the twentieth century when, particularly in Britain and the USA, the market economy has once again come to be celebrated as the most efficient, indeed the only possible, basis for economic and social life, it is no accident that there has been a return to harsh and brutalising depictions of those who are its greatest victims. With the collapse of communism, capitalism is triumphant, its ravages inflicted on a global scale. Holding the poor responsible for their own fate undermines the anger that poverty and inequality provoke while removing blame from the system that is responsible. Instead, the poor are seen as an expensive 'burden' on society, for whom the 'average taxpayer' supposedly has little, especially when depicted as welfare 'scroungers', homeless, criminals and drug addicts.

At the end of the twentieth century concerns with welfare 'scrounging' and its various manifestations, including street homelessness, had a discursive role around 'the need to remoralise the workless millions to ensure the continued vitalities of the work ethic and the preservation of law and order' (Golding and Middleton 1982: 109). The 'scrounger' discourse helped construct the view that the welfare state, particularly social security policy, was a cause of the social and economic dilemmas Britain was facing, because it was economically burdensome and encouraging moral degeneracy. Poor people were not seen as enduring the consequences of shifting capitalist social relations and, therefore, worthy of state support, but were defined as being morally inept and undeserving. As Lynda Lee-Potter wrote in the *Daily Mail*:

> The ordinary decent kindly majority of us know there are people who need help. We want them to have it. We only get resentful and bitter when we see it going to the able-bodied parasite malingerers. (quoted in Golding and Middleton 1982: 66)

With overall expenditure on social security increasing during the recession years of the 1980s, the idea that benefit-dependent people were morally compromised and economically costly was to gain greater credence through the concept of the behavioural 'underclass'

(Murray 1990, 1994). Poor people were increasingly seen as a surplus population who had little to contribute and were marginal to society (cf. Bauman 1987). While New Labour believes that the poorest have something – their labour – to offer contemporary society (although little is said about whether capital should employ it), the moral discourse that problematises worklessness and state 'dependency' has changed little (Grover and Stewart 2002; Grover 2007).

Alongside the alleged economic and moral effects of state dependency was a discourse that constructed the payment of taxation for welfare benefits and services as being synonymous with an unnecessarily interfering and inefficient state. Sir Keith Joseph (1976: 19) – the man who has the dubious honour of introducing former Conservative Prime Minister Margaret Thatcher to monetarism – argued, for example, that in order to revive Britain's economic fortunes it required a:

> reduction of the state sector and the essential encouragement of enterprise. We are over-governed, over-spent, over-taxed, over-borrowed and over-manned ... We must also have substantial cuts in tax and public spending and bold incentives to wealth creators, without whose renewed efforts we shall all grow poorer.

What we have here is a volatile mix of discourses concerned with the alleged economic and moral costs of worklessness and 'benefit dependency', and paying for them. Using Young's (1999, 2002) analytical framework, it is possible to argue that poor people, particularly street homeless people, in the relative deprivation gaze downwards become an example *par excellence* of those who in Young's terms are 'unfairly disadvantaged' and who unlike the 'respectable' are not constrained in their behaviour because they do not have to work for their income which is supplied by an undiscerning social security system. It is through such observations that we can develop an explanation for crimes against some of the most vulnerable people in British society by the 'respectable'.

Although street homeless people, particularly if they are begging, are notable by their passivity (Dean and Melrose 1999), they have become conflated in the political imagination with aggressive begging, street drinking and general disorder. The social and economic problems faced by homeless people and the problems from which they are often fleeing are lost in a concern with the alleged cost of such threatening and unproductive members of society (cf. Bagguley and Mann 1992). In this sense street homeless people have become defined as burdensome and viewed by many as having an easy life. This view is often fuelled by misinformed media stories of the riches that, for example, begging and *Big Issue* selling can bring (cf. Erskine and McIntosh 1999).

It is instructive that common-sense understandings of paid work are central to the verbal abuse and harassment that 'respectable' people mete out to rough sleepers. Fitzpatrick and Kennedy (2001: 561), for example, found that being told to 'get a job' was 'an almost daily occurrence' and that many of the street homeless people they interviewed 'were particularly distressed by this verbal abuse and taunting because they were unable to respond without being labelled as "aggressive beggars"'. In a North American context Wachholz (2005, drawing upon Wagner 1993) argues that references made to paid work in speech to street homeless people mean that when poor people are visible, such as when they are on the streets, it is their status *vis-à-vis* paid work that becomes the primary public concern and not the immediate situation (for example, hunger and ill-health) that street homeless people face. The situation is little different in Britain where relationships to paid work define the included and excluded, the responsible and irresponsible. Because street homeless people do not have to work in common-sense understandings of the word, and are a visible sign of the 'burden' and moral consequences of the welfare state, they become the target of the frustrations, the vindictiveness of 'respectable' people in the gaze downwards of relative deprivation. This is manifested not just in greater calls for the control of street homeless people, but also in their abuse and harassment.

Tackling rough sleeping

It is generally agreed that the number of street homeless people in Britain increased greatly over the 1980s. There is some debate as to the reasons why this was the case. May *et al.* (2005), for instance, argue that the 'crisis' of rough sleeping that occurred in the 1980s was the consequence of 'roll-back neoliberalism' that was structured on the twin pillars of the free market and minimalist state intervention. These, they argue, structured social policies that contributed to the increase in street homelessness. Such explanations of street homelessness, however, are criticised for ignoring the individual experiences, such as familial 'breakdown', child abuse and domestic violence, that often frame street homelessness. However, Pleace and Quilgars (2003, following Neale 1997) argue that both structural and more individualised approaches focusing upon the characteristics and experiences of street homeless people are theoretically weak because neither has a particularly clear causality (see also Pleace 1998, 2000). However, they also note (Pleace and Quilgars 2003: 192) that in the late 1980s and early 1990s the view that came to predominate was that 'homeless people were often individuals who were particularly vulnerable to the structural forces that were causing homelessness'. They point to the work of Dant and Deacon (1989), Niner (1989) and Thomas and Niner (1989) as examples.

Contextualising his ideas in the theorisation of 'risk', Pleace (2000: 584) argues that such thinking has been influential in policies to tackle rough sleeping since the election of New Labour in 1997, for they have attempted to 'equip homeless people with the necessary skills and resources to mean that subsequent exposure to ... structural forces [such as the casualisation of labour markets and declining stocks of affordable housing] will not mean a return to homelessness'. He argues (ibid.) that New Labour's extension of the Conservative's Rough Sleepers Initiative (RSI) is a good example of such a policy.

The RSI was introduced in 1990 to address street homelessness, first in London and later in a small number of other conurbations where it had been identified as a problem. May et al. (2005) argue that it enabled the Conservatives to deal with a politically damaging issue, especially in London where it was most damaging, but in a way that did not alter the marginalised position of single people in relation to homelessness legislation (Fitzpatrick, Kemp and Klinker 2000) and which did not address the structural causes of single homelessness, including the introduction of the right to buy council housing in the early 1980s, the shift from subsidising the building of social housing to the subsidising of market rents through HB, and the retrenchment of welfare benefits – especially for young people – that we have discussed in previous chapters (Hutson and Liddiard 1994; Malpass and Murie 1994; Carlen 1996; May et al. 2005; Mullins and Murie 2006). May et al. (2005) argue that the RSI represented an attempt to contain street homelessness by rendering it less visible, something that was backed up by an increase in the use by police of their powers under Britain's vagrancy laws to clear the streets of rough sleepers. They argue, however, that the overall effect of the RSI under Conservative administrations was not particularly significant. By the time New Labour was elected in 1997 it was estimated that there were still about 2,000 people living on the streets of central London (*ibid*.).

As we have seen, New Labour has been concerned with tackling social exclusion. Perhaps the most visible manifestation of social exclusion is rough sleeping so it was not surprising that with its election in 1997 there would be an increased emphasis and vigour placed upon tackling it. One of the first reports published by the Social Exclusion Unit (1998) focused upon the issue. In it then Prime Minister Tony Blair outlined the reasons why rough sleeping needed to be addressed:

> There are good reasons for aiming to end rough sleeping. It is bad for those who do it, as they are intensely vulnerable to crime, drugs and alcohol, and at high risk of serious illness, and premature death. And rough sleeping is bad for the rest of society. The presence of some rough sleepers on the streets will attract others – often young and vulnerable – to join them. Many people feel intimidated by rough sleepers, beggars and street drinkers, and rough sleeping can blight areas and damage business and tourism. (*ibid*.: 1)

For Blair there was a conjoining of social justice and political economy arguments for tackling rough sleeping. In the case of the former, there was a welfarist concern with the well-being of rough sleepers and with those young people who were allegedly attracted to a life of rough sleeping by observing existing street homeless people. There is no evidence to suggest that street homeless people are attracted to this way of life by the existence of other rough sleepers (Pleace 2000), but Blair's line of argument is familiar in social policy discourse. It is part of the utilitarian tradition that suggests that the socio-economic conditions of the poorest people are always attractive to the not quite so poor. In this context, Pleace (2000: 586) argues that Blair's comments 'raises the spectre of deviance' in the explanation of rough sleeping. It is also a line of argument that contradicts other parts of the Social Exclusion Unit (1998: 1) report that suggested only a small minority of 'rough sleepers do so by choice'.

The political economic concern with rough sleeping is related, for it is part of the long tradition that in the past has conceptualised vagrants and now rough sleepers as being economically and morally threatening. The linking of rough sleeping with behaviours such as begging and street drinking leads to the conclusion that it is the source of spatially specific 'blight', damaging to business and tourism. The implication is that those elements of the free market that are premised upon consumption are in need of protection from those people who are often excluded from it. If consumption is to thrive consumers must feel safe, a feeling thought to be undermined by the presence of rough sleepers (cf. Pain 2000). In this context, recent developments in modes of managing offending and anti-social behaviour, such as the rapid spread of closed-circuit television cameras (CCTV) and the use of ASBOs, can be understood to have such a role in protecting economically valuable areas (such as city centres and shopping centres) from those persons, including street homeless people, who are held to blight them (see Norris and Armstrong 1999; Coleman 2003, 2004; MacDonald 2006).

With the need to protect such areas from the 'blight' of rough sleepers, and in line with New Labour's 'rights and responsibilities' agenda, it was also argued in *Rough Sleeping* (Social Exclusion Unit 1998: para. 4.23) that:

> The Government has no present plans to ... make it an offence to sleep rough. But since the explicit intention of the policy is to deliver clear streets, the Government believes that the public will feel they have a right to expect hostel places to be taken up as more become available.

This line of argument was taken forward in the paper (Office of the Deputy Prime Minister 1999: 9–10) outlining the Homelessness Action Plan (HAP) (discussed below) which argued that 'rough sleepers themselves have a responsibility to come in' and that:

> Once we [the government] are satisfied that realistic alternatives are readily available, we and the public at large are entitled to expect those working on the streets to persuade people to take advantage of them. This includes the police, who sometimes have not been able to use their powers because of a lack of options to move rough sleepers on.

New Labour's approach to tackling rough sleeping is structured through responsibilities for rough sleepers (to take advantage of developing services) and for those people charged with enforcing those policies, including Contact and Assessment Teams (CATs) and the police. In particular, it was argued that CATs should 'take a robust, positive and discerning approach in persuading people to accept help' (*ibid.*: 7). While there is some comfort to be gained from the fact that rough sleepers were not further criminalised by the introduction of new laws, statistics recording prosecutions for begging under the 1824 Vagrancy Act do show an increase in the late 1990s and early years of the twenty-first century. So, for example, in 1997 1,919 people were found guilty or cautioned for begging. This had risen to 2,658 in 1998, 3,004 in 2000 and over 3,400 in 2002 (Office for Criminal Justice Reform 2005, Table 3.20). While the numbers fall thereafter, in 2004 a third (32.2 per cent) more people were cautioned or prosecuted for begging than in 1997 (*ibid.*). These figures suggest, as the government desired, that the development of social policies to tackle rough sleeping have been accompanied by the more rigorous enforcement of the 1824 Vagrancy Act.[2]

The Social Exclusion Unit's (1998), *Rough Sleeping* paper set a target for reducing the incidence of rough sleeping by two-thirds by 2002. The main way in which this was to be achieved was, initially, through an extension of the RSI and then from 1999 through the Homelessness Action Plan (HAP). *Rough Sleeping* argued that one of the main problems facing the successful tackling of street homelessness was a lack of co-ordination. To overcome this New Labour introduced the Rough Sleepers Unit (RSU) which was led by 'homeless czar' (the *Guardian*, 13 October 1999) Louise Casey who, as we saw in Chapter 4 now heads the Respect Task Force. She went to the RSU from her job as Deputy Director of the homelessness charity, Shelter.

Coming in from the Cold (Office of the Deputy Prime Minister 1999: 1) outlined the government's strategy that would be pursued under the HAP and that would provide the 'tools, and the funding' to tackle rough sleeping through 'a genuine partnership between central and local government, the voluntary sector, statutory bodies, businesses, community groups and rough sleepers'. The idea of 'partnership' working, however, is deeply problematic because of the power relations that structure it (Byrne 1999). In our case, the idea of 'partnership' working is arguably at odds with the 'robust' policies and practices that inform the work of the partnerships and that risk apportioning blame to rough sleepers for their homelessness (Fooks and Pantazis 1999). In other words, elements of authoritarianism in the tackling of rough sleeping undermine the idea of 'partnership' working.

'Partnership' working to tackle rough sleeping has also meant the delivery of central government targets by those services willing to engage with its interpretation of rough sleeping and its approach to tackling street homelessness. While there has been some resistance among service providers to the ways in which it was expected that the

HAP would be delivered (May *et al.* 2005), there is also evidence that some service providers whose philosophies and practices were not consistent with that of central and local government were excluded from funding opportunities from such 'partnerships' (*ibid.*). In some cases this exclusion has included the use of police cautions and the threat of ASBOs to force service providers, particularly 'soup runs', to close down, a situation that leaves street homeless people without food and increases the pressure upon them to offend (see Statewatch, nd.; Johnsen *et al.* 2005). Such moves should not be surprising given the proposals for change that would inform the HAP and which were outlined in *Coming in from the Cold* (Office of the Deputy Prime Minister 1999):

- the provision of more bedspaces in London with the 'right sort of help for those who need it most' (*ibid.*: 5);
- a more focused, targeted approach to work with street homeless people, one that would 'ensure that we are not, in seeking to help, reinforcing street lifestyles rather than providing opportunities to end them' (*ibid.*: 6);
- the provision of services to rough sleepers when they 'need them most' (ibid.: 7);
- the provision of services to the 'most in need' (*ibid.*), such as those street homeless with mental health issues and/or drug and/or alcohol addictions;
- ensuring a continuity of care, so 'there is a clear route from the streets to a settled lifestyle' (*ibid.*: 8);
- the provision of 'opportunities for meaningful occupation'; opportunities to help develop self-esteem and the skills 'needed to sustain a lifestyle away from the streets' (*ibid.*: 9), with the 'ultimate objective' being to secure paid employment;
- improve incentives to 'come inside, both by offering provision which meets people's specific needs and by refocusing services away from those that sustain a street lifestyle' (*ibid.*);
- measures to 'prevent rough sleeping, so that new people do not see the streets as the only option' (*ibid.*).

What we see in these eight proposals is an historical concern with delineating the 'deserving' from the 'undeserving'. The HAP was clear that with limited financial resources the focus would be on those rough sleepers who were deemed to be most in need and who, because of various factors, were the least able to help themselves. This distinction was to centre around the able-bodied ('undeserving') and those with mental health issues and/or addictions ('deserving'). Maintaining such distinctions should not be surprising, for they are consistent with distinctions that are reflected in and constituted by homelessness legislation in Britain. We have seen that the legislation casts out single, able-bodied homeless people as a low priority for rehousing by, or on behalf of, local authorities. In this context, it was argued in *Coming in from the Cold* (Office of the Deputy Prime Minister 1999: 3) that resources should 'help the most vulnerable and not ... provide a fast track into permanent housing for healthy and able individuals'. While this demonstrates a degree of joined-up thinking, it actually says more about the exclusionary nature of allocating housing to homeless people and families than it does about co-ordination between various agencies of welfare governance.

Second, the proposals were structured through a utilitarianism that suggests that people rationally choose rough sleeping over other possible 'lifestyles'. This was demonstrated through reference in *Coming in from the Cold* (Office of the Deputy Prime Minister 1999) to the provision of 'incentives' to discourage rough sleeping 'lifestyles', and the implicit view in the paper that the provision of some services for street homeless people encouraged their rough sleeping. Such views were made explicit in comments by Louise Casey when she was head of the RSU. Casey did not flinch from criticising the 'well meaning [but] misplaced' actions of those providing support for homeless people in the form of soup runs, and the provision of clothing and bedding supplies (the *Guardian*, 18 November 1999). In October 2000 her line of thinking was reflected in the government's *Change a Life* campaign aimed at discouraging the public from giving cash to people begging in the streets. A 'government official' was quoted as saying:

> We want to encourage people to volunteer or give gifts in kind [to beggars] or to charities rather than stopping to give cash ... They [beggars] may not be homeless at all. They may just be there to fund a drug habit. (the *Observer*, 8 October 2000)

During the same campaign Casey was quoted as saying that coinage given to beggars may 'go towards the fiver needed for the next heroin hit' (the *Guardian*, 6 November 2000). Although there is evidence that some beggars use money they are given to buy illicit drugs (Fitzpatrick and Kennedy 2001), not all beggars do so and Fitzpatrick and Kennedy (*ibid.*: 561) also found that there was a 'clear consensus' among their respondents (beggars, rough sleepers and *Big Issue* sellers) that 'begging income was driven by "need" not "greed"'. However, Casey's comments were part of the government's 'tough choice' approach to welfare policy that emphasised, as we have seen, the responsibilities of recipients as well as, if not more than, their rights. Casey puts herself forward as a 'radical' (the *Guardian*, 18 November 2000), but her radicalism is in a utilitarian tradition of stigmatising and disciplining the poor and vulnerable. The discourse on street homeless merely reinforces the image of the dangerous rough sleeper (illicit drug and alcohol abuser) that the general public is in need of protection from. Moreover, such discourses merely help feed resentment of those people who are seen as socially, economically and morally burdensome to society. In this sense, they contribute to what we have seen Young (1999, 2002) describes as vindictiveness and which we have argued is a factor in the explanation of offences committed against street homeless people by 'respectable' people.

The proposals in *Coming in from the Cold* were equally problematic because they did little to prevent the causes of street homelessness. While the last proposal noted above refers to the prevention of homelessness, it takes an individualistic approach by focusing upon groups 'at risk' of homelessness, such as young people leaving care and people being discharged from prison, rather than its structural causes in the economic and socio-political spheres. In this context, for instance, the proposals do little to tackle the lack of affordable housing and the erosion of benefit levels for the poorest people. In contrast, the focus is upon a restricted number of 'risk' groups and ensuring that they have support when attempting to secure housing. While, of course, this should be done, it is a rather limited approach to preventing rough sleeping.

At first glance the HAP seems to have been remarkably successful in reducing the numbers of rough sleepers. The target of reducing street homelessness by two-thirds was achieved in November 2001 (Randall and Browne 2002). Five years later (June 2006) it was estimated that 502 people were sleeping rough across England. This had fallen by nearly three-quarters from 1,850 in June 1998.[3] The rough sleeping population though is not consistent and because of this it is estimated that at least five times as many people as are recorded in daily counts, such as in the figures above, may sleep rough in any one year (Social Exclusion Unit 1998). This means that a minimum of 2,500 people in England were still sleeping rough in 2006. However, claims for the success or otherwise of the HAP that are based upon quantitative measures are problematic. Pleace *et al.* (1997) argue that street homeless people are difficult to count because, first, they are mobile (Vincent *et al.* 1995); second, they tend to spend time in temporary accommodation as well as time on the streets and, third, women and BME street homeless people are less likely to be known about because they are less likely than white males to use services for rough sleepers (Davies *et al.* 1996). Therefore, it is likely that the relatively low levels of rough sleeping that are currently being recorded are masking a more numerically problematic situation in many, particularly rural, areas (May *et al.* 2005). May *et al.* (*ibid.*: 720), for instance, found in their study of Bodmin, a market town in Cornwall, that the 'assertive approach taken by HAP funded Contact and Assessment Teams ... in nearby urban areas has led to a displacement of people sleeping rough [to the Bodmin area]'. In brief, May *et al.* (2005) found that the 'robust' approach to tackling street homelessness that the government demanded of its 'partners' was encouraging some street homeless people to move to areas where they could avoid HAP projects aimed at bringing them into the normative fold. In May *et al.'s* (2005) study those areas were also those where street homeless people were often not recorded as being rough sleepers because of the local geography and because the services provided there were outwith the HAP.

So far in this chapter we have focused upon the most visible manifestation of homelessness. However, as we have noted, there are other forms of homelessness – for example, squatting and 'sofa surfing' (staying with friends and relatives) – that are far less visible, but which nevertheless represent a precarious relationship to housing markets, and one which can result in rough sleeping (Cassidy 1999). In their study of Bristol, May *et al.* (2005) argue that the HAP has actually increased the level of this type of homelessness. This is because there is a fundamental and historically enduring problem with the HAP. We have seen that the HAP was really only concerned with those people who were thought to be 'genuinely' rough sleepers, reproducing in contemporary society historical concerns with separating the 'deserving' and the 'undeserving'. At a practical level May *et al.* (2005: 724) found that this meant that hostels designed to provide a temporary respite from rough sleeping 'began to resemble a new form of social "housing" for the addicted and the mentally ill'. Not only did this create poor conditions in often unsuitable accommodation, it meant that many rough sleepers without such conditions could not access emergency, or indeed, any accommodation, and, as a consequence, they often joined the 'hidden homeless'. While this may have reduced the number of street homeless people, it did little to address homelessness in a broader sense and to improve access to permanent accommodation.

In addition to these problems with the HAP, there are others that relate to policies developed to address street homelessness among particular groups of people. Grover *et al.* (2004; also Grover and Stewart 2004), for example, argue that the Children (Leaving Care) Act 2000 could lead to greater exclusion among 16- and 17-year-old care leavers than was the case under previous systems of support. This is because the Children (Leaving Care) Act 2000 withdrew the right of such young people to claim benefits and to present themselves to local authorities as homeless. Responsibility for the financial and housing needs of care leavers was transferred to social services departments. Grover *et al.*'s (2004) concern is that in order to access financial and housing support provided by social services departments, young care leavers must be in contact with a personal adviser. However, because the Children Leaving Care Act 2000 is structured through reference to the 'corporate parent' that is expected to mirror the reward and punishment regime of 'normal' families, as well as their rationing of finite resources that are there to meet their children's demands, young care leavers may become disillusioned with the new regime and disengage from it. If they do this and lose contact with their personal adviser, their access to financial and housing support will be lost completely and, rather than being socially included, as the Act intended, they will be further excluded.

The precarious relationship of ex-prisoners to housing has been widely highlighted (for example, Paylor 1992, 1995; Carlisle 1996, 1997; Barkley and Collett 2000; Rough Sleepers Unit 2000), and there have been some developments in attempting to address street homelessness among ex-prisoners. So, for example, applicants recently released from young offenders' institutions and prisons were made priority need groups in the 2002 Homelessness Act. However, homelessness among ex-prisoners remains a major problem. Drawing upon evidence from 500 Citizens Advice Bureaux, Hopwood Road *et al.* (2007) highlight several problems with prisoners keeping, and ex-prisoners accessing, housing. In the case of prisoners keeping their housing, Hopwood Road *et al.* (*ibid.*) point to the need for advice services for prisoners to help, for instance, in negotiation between them and their landlords/ladies. While Hopwood Road *et al.* have a vested interest in making such arguments (they are, after all, writing on behalf of an advice-giving organisation), other research has pointed to a lack of communication between offenders and their landlords/ladies when the former are in prison as contributing to homelessness on release (for example, Social Exclusion Unit 2002).

For ex-prisoners, street homelessness is argued to be related to failings in the discharge system and its relationship to social security benefits to which ex-prisoners are entitled if they are not employed. These observations highlight the low level of discharge grant that has been held at £46.75 for the past decade, and which is supposed to meet the needs of ex-prisoners for the first week after discharge, although it is lower than the weekly 'adult' rate of IS, and takes little account of the fact that it often takes much longer than a week for benefits to be sorted out by Jobcentre Plus (*ibid.*). What this means is that ex-prisoners often do not have enough money for food, let alone accommodation, after their discharge. In such situations, ex-prisoners often have recourse to the Social Fund that is supposed to meet the emergency and exceptional needs of poor people:

A CAB [Citizens Advice Bureau] in Berkshire reported that a recently released prisoner was told by Jobcentre Plus that it would take up to six weeks to process his claim for JSA. Although he had been given a discharge grant of £46 on release, the money had only lasted 10 days. When the client applied [to the Social Fund] for a crisis loan, Jobcentre Plus refused his application on the basis that they did not think he could repay it. (Hopwood Road *et al.* 2007: para. 5.12)

In this particular case, the main problem was with the administration of benefits; both the length of time it took to pay the JSA and the problem of the crisis loan application being turned down because the applicant was judged to be too poor to repay it. This is a familiar criticism of the Social Fund in the social policy literature (Becker and Silburn 1990; NACAB 1990; Peelo *et al.* 1992), but it has particular pertinence for those people attempting to re-establish themselves in the 'community' after a period of imprisonment.

A second problem relates to the difficulty faced by single people in proving that they are a priority need for housing:

A Somerset CAB client, a single man estranged from his young daughters, had tried to commit suicide prior to his sentence. He was arrested by the police due to an outstanding warrant and was imprisoned. On release he had no money and nowhere to stay. The client had to sleep in his car in temperatures

> below freezing and he was in a vulnerable state of mind. His homelessness application was refused, as he was not considered to be vulnerable. After having been turned away, the client admitted to stealing petrol to keep his car running, and then when the temperatures dropped even lower, he ripped a telephone off the wall in the police station so that he could have a bed for the night. Following the intervention of the CAB, the local authority's homeless persons unit agreed to help him if he provided details of his medical condition. (*ibid.*: para. 5.28)

Not only does this case demonstrate the difficulties facing single homeless people in securing 'priority need' for rehousing, it also suggests that not all local authorities are accepting ex-prisoners as being a priority need group. In this case, without the intervention of the CAB the ex-prisoner would have remained homeless and, therefore, vulnerable to further offending (cf. Social Exclusion Unit 2002).

Conclusion

This chapter has focused upon relationships between street homelessness and crime. It has demonstrated that street homeless people are particularly vulnerable to crime victimisation and that they are, generally speaking, more likely to be offended against by 'respectable' people, rather than other street homeless people. We have explored why this might be by focusing upon the discursive construction of street homeless people as being economically and morally burdensome and the ways in which this may feed feelings of vindictiveness in the downwards gaze of relative deprivation. We have seen that, historically and in contemporary society, policies that have been developed to tackle rough sleeping and homelessness reflect and help constitute the view that people sleeping rough are burdensome. The most recent attempts at tackling street homelessness, for example, through the RSI and the HAP are little different, for they, at least in part, hold street homeless people responsible for the situation in which they find themselves. The main problem with this approach is that it does not tackle the structural causes of homelessness that are linked to wider social and economic inequalities and their relationships to various social policies, most notably social security and housing policy. Because of this, it is unlikely that street homelessness has been as successfully tackled as we are told it has been. This means that street homeless people remain vulnerable to the vindictiveness of the 'respectable'.

Notes

1 The 2002 Homelessness Act introduced new 'priority need groups' for housing that included young single people who might be considered as 'at risk', including young people aged 16 or 17, except for those who are not eligible for such assistance (for instance, asylum seekers); those who have been in local authority care and are considered to be 'relevant children' under the terms of the 2002 Children (Leaving Care) Act, and those judged to be 'children in need'. Young people covered by these exclusions should receive support from Social Service Departments (http://england.shelter. or.uk/advice/advice-155.cfm, accessed 19 July 2007).

2 Begging is an offence under Section 3 of the 1824 Vagrancy Act. While begging should not be conflated with rough sleeping (cf. Dean 1999), Fitzpatrick and Kennedy (2000, 2001) demonstrate that the two are often closely associated in that the majority of rough sleepers beg.

3 *National Rough Sleeping Estimates 2006* (http://www.communities.gov.uk/index.asp?id=1150131, accessed 18 July 2007).

Chapter 8

Financial penalties: punishing poor people

Introduction

We have seen that the criminal justice system essentially processes, manages and contains poor people. In relation to punishment, and following the seminal work of Georg Rusche (1933) and his later collaboration with Otto Kirchheimer (1939), it is argued that this is particularly the case with imprisonment which, it is contended, removes the surplus population during times of the over-supply of labour and, through the principle of 'less eligibility' – in this case, the idea that the condition of the prisoner should always be worse than that of the 'law abiding' public – acts as a deterrent to offending and constrains penal reform (Hudson 2000). However, imprisonment is only ever used as a punishment for a minority of offenders processed by the courts. In contrast, the majority – 69 per cent in 2005 (Office for Criminal Justice Reform 2006, Table 1.2) – of those convicted in England and Wales are punished by fines. This may be surprising because there appears to be an inverse relationship between the amount of literature regarding particular punishments and their incidence. In other words, a great deal has been written about imprisonment, but far less has been written about fines. Shaw's (1989: 30) complaint that it is 'almost as if the everyday nature of the fine (and for that matter the relatively undistinguished nature of the crimes for which it is usually imposed) had discouraged the interest of academics and research workers' is equally applicable in the twenty-first century.

The focus on prison is understandable because of the potential impact that it has, as a 'total institution' (Goffman 1962), upon individuals and, if they have any, their families. However, we should not be distracted from the fact that the use of financial penalties, such as fines and the withdrawal of benefits from those people not fulfilling the conditions of their community punishments, raises a number of pertinent issues in a society as deeply unequal as Britain. This chapter discusses these issues in the context of the argument developed by Barbara Hudson (1995, 1998, 1999, 2000, 2003) that economic hardship should be treated as a mitigating factor when offenders are being sentenced.

Sentencing and economic inequalities

In recent years an argument has emerged which suggests that, if criminal justice is to be achieved, then the economic and social condition of offenders should be considered when sentence is being passed. Perhaps the best-known proponent of such ideas in Britain is Barbara Hudson (1995, 1998, 1999, 2000, 2003). Hudson's argument emerges from a critique of desert theory. While desert theory 'has various shades and hues' (Ashworth 2005: 85), its essence is that a sentence should be proportionate to the crime(s) being punished.

However, the problem with desert theory is that because the focus is upon a particular crime or crimes, and ensuring that the sentence is proportionate to it or them, it has difficulty in accommodating factors that shape offending behaviour (Hudson 1995). Hudson (2000) argues that legal perspectives, especially those informed by desert-based theories, are problematic because of their narrow foci and because of their treatment of offenders as moral actors. She notes, for example, that in such approaches:

> deprivation fails to meet the legal criteria for non-responsibility, excuse, or justification ... [and] any broadening of these categories to accommodate deprivation would treat the deprived as less than fully responsible moral agents, as morally and legally inferior to more economically advantaged citizens. (Hudson 2000: 190)

In particular, Hudson (1995: 99; see also Tonry 1996) argues that the problem with proportionality in desert-based theories of punishment is that 'in practice [it] risks giving insufficient attention to differences in situation'. In other words, and reflecting Hudson's desire that criminal justice should help to promote a more just society, she questions whether, despite its appeal to fairness, just deserts can ever be just in a society, like Britain, that is socially and economically so unequal. Hudson argues that there are at least three reasons for this. First is the issue of how 'serious crime' is defined. Her point here is that the majority of crimes 'selected for vigorous enforcement and punishment are those crimes which are characteristically associated with the poor; burglary, shoplifting, "street crime" in general' (*ibid.*: 66), while, for example, white collar crime is neglected (see Hudson 2000).

The second reason relates to the social and economic status of those who administer justice. Hudson (1995) argues that the white, middle-aged and middle-class people who administer justice 'have little understanding of the circumstances of the younger, working- or non-working class, disproportionately black people who are its recipients'. In this sense, the notion of 'equal treatment' upon which just deserts is premised is a 'treatment appropriate for male, white legal subjects' (*ibid.*: 66).

Third is the issue of whether those people who receive unequal shares of society's resources should be equally obliged to live by its rules and be punished if they do not. In this regard, we first need to make a distinction between punishments premised upon consequentialist ideas – punishment that takes view to potential future offending – and retributive ideas that look to the past. Hudson (1995) rejects the mainstream argument that excluded people are more likely to benefit from punishments underpinned by desert – a retributive idea – than they would from those underpinned by consequentialist ideas (for example, deterrence). In this context, Hudson (1995: 67) points to the argument that those sentencing rationales premised upon considering possible future offending are more likely to disadvantage poor and minority ethnic people because 'most schemes whose prime aim is to prevent reoffending would include factors such as poor employment record and perhaps ethnicity as indicating likely future offending'.

Furthermore, Hudson rejects more radical ideas (for example, Tonry 1994) that risk making a distinction between the deserving and undeserving poor. Hudson's (1995: 68) criticism of Tonry (1994) is that his approach is based upon a normative assumption of respectability and, therefore, offenders would be 'vulnerable to disparate punishments depending on their abilities to construct a "sympathetic self", and we have enough information from research ...

to know that factors such as unemployment, domestic arrangements, demeanour are constructed differently for black defendants, women defendants, or residents of certain estates'.

In contrast to these mainstream and more radical ideas, Hudson argues that there should be a defence of 'economic duress' in those cases where the 'perpetrator has no income at all, or has no access to or control over their supposed income' (Hudson 1995: 71). She notes examples that include 16- and 17-year-olds who, as we have seen in previous chapters, do not have entitlement to social security benefits, except in tightly drawn circumstances, young homeless people who may engage in begging and/or squatting in order to survive, women whose 'menfolk do not give them any money' (ibid.: 71); and people leaving penal or residential institutions who, while having to secure food and shelter immediately, receive benefits in arrears.

Hudson argues that economic duress should be admissible as a '"relevant criterion" in establishing blameworthiness' (1998: 244) because of the constraint that poverty places upon choice. Drawing upon Groves and Frank (1986), Hudson suggests that it is only in the law that meaningful choice is seen in absolute terms. In everyday life it is a matter of degree:

> the millionaire and the ghetto-dweller might have the same number of choices available to them, but the millionaire's choices would be such as to enable them to achieve goods (money, shelter, social status, leisure activity) that are socially valued legitimately, whereas such opportunities would be severely restricted for the ghetto-dweller. (Hudson 1998: 244)

Following on, and borrowing from Garland (1997), Hudson argues that in this context the law conflates freedom and agency. Her argument is that, while agency – the capacity for action – is something universal to all human beings, freedom is concerned with the capacity to choose a particular course of action without external constraint. In this sense, freedom to choose a particular course of action is a matter of degree; agency can only operate within the potential range of 'unconstrained choice' (ibid.: 197). For Hudson, the agency of poor people to act in particular ways is constrained by their material circumstances, a fact that should be taken into account when sentence is being passed in courts.

However, her thesis is criticised. While Hutton (1999), for example, argues that it is quite legitimate for sentencers to take into account the wider circumstances of those upon whom they are passing sentence, he notes that sentencers are already able to do this through the discretion that the law affords them. Essentially, he argues that Hudson's conceptualisation of responsibility and its relationship to culpability is incompatible with liberal criminal law which is underpinned by ideas of individual responsibility and equality before the law. In this context, Hutton (*ibid.*: 576) argues, the law 'achieves the "cunning trick" by, on the one hand, rhetorically promising to treat individuals equally by pursuing consistency in sentencing, and on the other hand, allowing variations in culpability at the level of the offender'. Variations in culpability are, Hutton (*ibid.*) argues, recognised as long as they do not challenge the notion of individual responsibility.

Following on from these observations, Hutton (*ibid.*: 577) argues that what Hudson (1995) conceptualises as a 'social theory of culpability' should actually be thought of as a 'social theory of responsibility', for it shifts responsibility for offending from the individual to the group because of the material and social circumstances that are faced by particular groups. For Hutton (1999) this perverts the basis of liberal law, for it shifts responsibility from the individual to the group 'because of certain social circumstances which have disproportionately affected this group'. The implication of this is that individuals will no longer be treated equally before the law, but will be treated in a manner reflecting their group membership. Not only does this undermine one of the central tenets of the law, but, Hutton argues, it is deeply problematic on a practical level:

> How are the constraints to be identified, how are they to be measured, what disciplines will be accepted by the court as providing expert evidence on which the court can base a decision? What sort of calculus will be required to reflect properly the relative effect of these factors on culpability? How do we deal with the almost limitless possibility of combinations of factors? (*ibid.*: 578)

The consequence of such issues, Hutton argues, is the exclusion of groups of people who could be held wholly culpable for their actions, despite their circumstances not being greatly different to those included in the group that are seen as being less or not culpable for their actions. Again, this is held to have implications for the liberal notion (although, as he acknowledges, this may not happen in practice) that all are treated equally before the law, for those outside of the group not held fully culpable for their actions might ask why they are not being treated in the same manner as those included in the group. Hutton concludes that Hudson's ideas would merely lead the law through the expression of particular allegiances to become politics. In this context, and drawing upon Fish (1994), Hutton (1999: 579) argues that 'the discipline of law allows us to forget this [that 'everything is political'] to pretend that the world is not simply about the struggle for power, but that human societies have more lofty humanitarian aspirations'. Hutton (1999: 580) acknowledges that the law often acts in a political manner, but that it 'does not do so explicitly and openly'. However, for Hutton, if the law were to be premised upon a social theory of culpability, it would have to act in a politically explicit and open manner.

Hudson (1999) defends her thesis from Hutton's claims. She is particularly critical of the ways in which he conceptualises responsibility and culpability. Her argument is that Hutton conflates 'culpability' and 'responsibility' as being equivalent. However, for Hudson legal theory is rather limited with regard to culpability, for, she argues (*ibid*.: 584), it 'has difficulty in moving consideration of culpability beyond a fairly narrow discussion of responsibility, with current debate mainly centred on categories such as recklessness, negligence and omission, rather than on choice'. However, because of the acceptance in law of issues such as self-defence and physical coercion, she suggests, that 'for the law culpability involves an act not only having been done, but having been done from choice' (*ibid*.). The problem that this poses, as we have seen, is the way the law conceptualises choice as an absolutist notion; that, providing it is not affected by mental incapacity or physical coercion, action is always freely chosen, thereby conflating freedom and agency.

Second, Hudson argues that while she advocates a *social* theory of culpability she does not advocate a *group* theory of culpability or responsibility as Hutton suggests. In this regard, Hudson uses the concept of the social to indicate the economic, political, spatial and personal environment in which individuals live. In doing so she distances herself from those commentators and theorists (for example, Bazelon 1976; Klein 1990) who argue for exemptions for particular groups of (impoverished) offenders in order to argue that the 'law should be cognizant of the social circumstances in which crimes occur, as well as physical, mental dimensions of actual crime situations' (Hudson 1999: 585).

Third, Hudson argues that Hutton's ideas of sentencing are increasingly inapplicable to England and Wales and other jurisdictions because, first, the amount of discretion that sentencers can exercise has been eroded by legislation and central government direction and, second, and more importantly from our perspective, because of what she describes as the 'reduction of the welfare safety net' (*ibid.*: 588). Her point here is that desert-based notions of law were developed in a period when welfare provision was different from what it is today. Hudson argues that contemporary desert theory was developed at a time when, because basic welfare needs (for instance, food, healthcare and shelter) were met by the state, the presumption that offenders (providing that they were free of physical coercion and mental incapacitation) acted from a position of having at least some choice was reasonable. However, in contemporary societies, where, as we have seen in *Crime and Inequality*, some groups of people do not have an entitlement to a legitimate income, or only a very low income, it is difficult to make such arguments. Hence, Hudson (*ibid.*, original italics) argues that:

> If an offender does not have the opportunity to afford the means of survival by legitimate means, s/he cannot be said to have *chosen* illegitimate means. It is in this case that I would suggest a defence of economic coercion might be admitted which would be analogous to the defence of physical coercion, and depending on circumstances would – rarely – negate or more often diminish responsibility.

For Hudson the main problem is that sentencing policy is essentially offence- rather than offender-orientated. In other words, it does not take enough account of the wider circumstances of the offender. While such arguments obviously apply to all sentencing options available to magistrates and judges, they have a particular resonance with the use of fines, where it is perhaps easiest to conceptualise how the punishment might be shaped by the material circumstances of offenders. Indeed, it is in relation to fines where recent governments of both the right and left have attempted to formalise strategies for taking into account the means of offenders when setting the level of the punishment.

Financial penalties and inequality

As we have seen, fines are the most commonly used form of punishment. Sentencers and policy-makers like them because they are relatively simple and cheap to operate, and they have the: 'potential benefit of hitting where it hurts most – "in the pocket"' (Raine *et al.* 2003: 182). Fines are imposed to punish offenders by depriving them of money to purchase consumables and/or leisure-related activities. In this sense, Easton and Piper (2005: 226) argue that they can be 'theorised as the deprivation of the amount of time, "liberty" required to earn enough to replenish personal savings'. Such arguments though, are problematic because, first, they assume that fines will have little impact upon those items, like food, and utilities (such as electricity, gas, housing and water) that are crucial for subsistence, and, second, that those people being fined are in a position through paid work to recoup the losses incurred because of the fine. However, given that activities such as saving are closely related to the labour market position of people (Summerfield and Babb 2003, Table 5.27), it is clear that people who are unemployed, underemployed in part-time work or who are in low-paid employment are likely to experience a fine financially more harshly than those who are in better paid, more secure work. In other words, financial penalties disproportionately affect those people whose income is limited (Raine *et al.* 2003).

In Britain there has for several decades been an interest in ways of relating fines more closely to the means of offenders. Perhaps the best-known example was the 'unit fine' introduced as part of the 1991 Criminal Justice Act. This Act also allowed for the closely related development of recovering fines that had been defaulted upon from means-tested benefits (see comments of then Conservative MP John Patten, in Standing Committee A 1990: col. 296).

To understand these parallel developments we need to focus upon the general thrust of the 1991 Criminal Justice Act. This Act was premised upon a just-desert philosophy of sentencing (Easton and Piper 2005) that, as we have seen, Hudson argues often operates to the detriment of poorer people. However, its focus upon a bifurcation of punishment, whereby the majority of offenders would be punished using non-custodial sentences, and prison would be reserved for the most serious of offences and most dangerous offenders, actually led to the introduction of a system of fining that Hudson (1999: 588) describes as a 'sentence … clearly designed to reflect the economic circumstances of the offender'. It would appear in this instance that just deserts delivered a more economically just system of fines; something, as we shall see, that was to contribute to its demise.

The White Paper, *Crime, Justice and Protecting the Public* (Home Office 1990a) that preceded the 1991 Criminal Justice Act noted that:

> For most offenders, imprisonment has to be justified in terms of public protection, denunciation and retribution. Otherwise it can be an expensive way of making bad people worse. The prospects of reforming offenders are usually much better if they stay in the community, provided the public is properly protected. (*ibid.*: para. 2.7)

The explanation in the White Paper of offending located in a moral discourse related to the character of the individual is deeply problematic. However, the White Paper also made it clear that imprisonment was an expensive and, for many offenders, ineffective way of punishing them; in fact it was an institution that was held to exacerbate undesirable moral traits among offenders.

In this context of acknowledging that prisons were not particularly useful in preventing further reoffending, it was argued that 'the severity of the sentence of the court should be directly related to the seriousness of the offence' (*ibid.*: para. 1.6). However, to ensure proportionality in sentencing, Cavadino and Dignan (2002) argue that in the White Paper there was a concerted effort – what they describe as 'punitive bifurcation' – to ensure that alternatives to custody were not seen by sentencers as being 'soft options'. Hence, they argue that there was a development of 'a more overtly punitive approach across the whole range of punishments' (*ibid.*: 122). The White Paper certainly argued that there was a need to strengthen fines as a punishment by relating them to the means of offenders, and by introducing administrative measures that would help to ensure their repayment if they were to take their place in a sentencing regime that ensured only the most serious offences and most dangerous of offenders were punished through imprisonment. In this context, policy-makers saw fines as being problematic for at least two reasons. First, the use of fines was decreasing. So, for example, in 1979 50 per cent of indictable offences were punished by fine; by 1989 this had fallen to 39 per cent (Moxon, Sutton and Hedderman 1990; Moxon, Hedderman and Sutton 1990).

Moxon, Sutton and Hedderman (1990) argued that this decrease in the use of fines was related to increasing unemployment in the first half of the 1980s. Drawing upon Softley (1978) and Crow and Simon (1987), Moxon, Sutton and Hedderman (1990) argued that unemployed people were less likely compared to other people to be fined. Also, because unemployed people were more likely to be imprisoned for fine default (Moxon 1983), Moxon, Sutton and Hedderman (1990: 1) inferred that 'through the early eighties the problems of enforcement were increasingly leading courts to switch to other sentences for those on low income'. In particular, they argued that the falling use of fines was offset by increases in community sentences, most notably probation orders and community service orders, although Crow *et al.* (1989) demonstrated that while in some magistrates' courts fines were undoubtedly being replaced by such sentences, in others unemployed people were discharged or ordered to pay compensation only. It was, however, the replacement of fines by 'up-tariff' community sentences that was particularly worrying to the Home Office.

The second reason why fines were deemed to be problematic relates to a fundamental tension of their imposition in an economically and socially unequal society. Moxon, Sutton and Hedderman (1990: 1–2) noted:

> A low fine may give a false impression that the courts take a lenient view of the offence, but a high fine may invite default and indirectly result in imprisonment for an offence for which custody would not be appropriate.

These two issues – the use of punishments further up the penal tariff as a replacement for fines; and the potential for fine default to lead to imprisonment – were problematic in the context of criminal justice policy at the time, because they were at odds with the focus upon cost-effectiveness and proportionality in sentencing. In other words, the declining use of fines was held to be problematic because the alternatives were financially costly and often led to disproportionate sentences compared to the original offence(s) for which they were imposed. In the case of the declining use of fines financially there was a scissor-type action. On the one hand, providing that fines were paid in an unproblematic manner they actually raised revenue for the state.[1] On the other hand, community sentences were expensive. In 1988, for example, the average cost of a completed probation order was £1,300 and a community service order £500 (Home Office 1990b). Furthermore, because fines were, at least partly, being replaced by punishments higher up the penal tariff, there was a risk that on further conviction offenders would receive a more severe, and therefore financially costly, sentence than if they had been fined for their first offence. Financial considerations also structured concerns with the use of custody for fine defaulters – 90 per cent of whom were unemployed (Moxon, Hedderman and Sutton 1990) – given that in 1989 nearly 17,000 people were imprisoned for fine default compared, for example, to less then 4,000 imprisoned for theft and fraud (House of Commons Debates 1991: col. 318)

From such observations it was concluded that the two main components – the level and collection – of fines were problematic if they were to be regarded as a credible form of punishment and offenders were to be kept out of prison. The then Conservative government sought to tackle the level of fines through what was then described as 'unit fines', and the collection of fines from unemployed and other poor people through deductions from benefit income at source. While these two policies were closely related, we shall take them separately.

Relating fines to income

Unit fines

Before the introduction of unit fines[2] in the 1991 Criminal Justice Act there had for several decades been interest in formalising the ways in which courts related fines to the means of offenders. So, for instance, the Advisory Council on the Penal System (1970) examined the Swedish approach of relating fines to means (the 'day fine'). At the time, however, there were thought to be too many practical difficulties in introducing such a system in Britain, although the Advisory Council did recommend that the training of magistrates should emphasise that in calculating the level of fine, the seriousness of the offence and the offender's means to pay the fine should be considered separately (*ibid.*: para. 24).

In the late 1970s the House of Commons Expenditure Committee (1978) recommended that the possibility of introducing day fines in Britain should be re-examined, as did the All-Party Penal Affairs Group (1980). Then in the 1980s several criminal justice-related organisations, including Justice (1989), NACRO (1981; Crow *et al.* 1989), the Penal Affairs Consortium (1990) and the Prison Reform Trust (1990), as well as the Labour Party (1990), argued in support of the principle of relating fines more closely to the means of the offender. Following the floating of the idea of unit fines at the 1987 Magistrates' Association training day (Gibson 1990), the Home Office set up a trial at four magistrates' courts to test how unit fines might work in practice (Moxon, Sutton and Hedderman 1990).

While the experiments 'were constrained by the fact that there were doubts about imposing larger fines on the rich' (*ibid.*: iii) (something that would haunt the short-lived operation of day fines at a national level in the early 1990s), the four courts 'set local norms for the average disposable income they thought an employed person in their area would have' (*ibid.*: iii). Fines were reduced for those people assessed as having less than this norm. Given the context in which the experiments took place, the results were mixed. There was, for example, a decrease in the proportion of those who were imprisoned for fine default, although there was no increase in the use of fines compared to other sentences. In the experiments disparities were reduced between courts in the level of fines imposed on poorer offenders, and among court staff Moxon, Sutton and Hedderman (1990) reported that there was a feeling that unit fines were an improvement on the existing system and they all continued with them after the experiments ceased. This, however, was very different from the experience once unit fines were introduced nationally, for within six weeks they had been abandoned.

Cavadino and Dignan (2002) argue that there were two main reasons why unit fines were abandoned.[3] Their first reason dovetails with issues that, as we saw above, Hutton (1999) raised at a more abstracted level about relating punishments to the material circumstances of offenders. Here, the point was that the unit fine 'incurred the wrath of a vociferous minority of magistrates' (*ibid.*: 128). Their complaint was that unit fines represented a usurping of their discretion (Ashworth 1997). Arguably they overstated the case because, even with the introduction of unit fines, magistrates still had discretion in making decisions about the seriousness of the offence. They could take into account the circumstances of the offence and any mitigating factors in making such decisions. The second reason why unit fines were abandoned, Cavadino and Dignan (2002; see also Mair 1996) argue, related to the role of the mass media that portrayed unit fines as essentially being unfair. It highlighted cases, such as one where two men convicted for fighting in the street received fines of £64 and £640 because of differences in their income (BBC 2005). However, in such cases the media either glossed over or ignored the income differentials of the men involved. The media, reflecting the main problem with imposing fines in an unequal society, also:

> objected to the fact that relatively well-paid, middle class motoring offenders were being fined substantial sums while the unemployed and low paid were in their view 'let off' with derisory fines for offences which they considered to be much more serious. (Cavadino and Dignan 2002: 128–129)

In brief, it was argued that the 1991 Criminal Justice Act was unjust, particularly for the better off. In the examples above the concern was not so much the amount the poorer person was fined, but the amount the middle-class person was. The scale of fine upon which the nationally rolled unit fine was based was the reason for such concerns. In the trial the scale of fine was £3 to £20. However, in the nationally rolled programme it was £4 to £100, meaning that the differences in fine for the same offence between those with low and high incomes was greater. In the trial, for example, the difference between the amount per unit paid by the poorest and wealthiest was a factor of 7 (£20 divided by £3). In the national programme it was 25 (£100 divided by £4). It was this increased disparity in the fine scale that made it appear that middle-class people were being unjustly punished.

Other problems with unit fines reflected some of the practical issues raised by Hutton (1999) and which we discussed above in relation to the potential of linking punishment to the circumstances of offenders. Most notable was the inability of the judiciary to collect reliable information on the income of defendants. So, for instance, in another widely quoted case an unemployed man was fined £1,200 for dropping litter after he was assessed as being in the top income bracket because he failed to provide any financial details (BBC 2005).

Sanders (1998), however, argues that the motivation for abandoning unit fines was more closely related to the politics of Conservative governments in the 1980s and 1990s. His argument was that 'the Government had no understanding of what they had legislated [for in the 1991 Criminal Justice Act] until the reality hit them in 1993' (ibid.: 537). For Sanders, the person responsible for the 1991 Criminal Justice Act was the Deputy Under-Secretary of State at the Home Office, David Faulkner, who 'pulled the wool over his own Government's eyes. Limiting the use of prison, promoting the use of community sentences, and fining people according to their ability to pay are policies which even a One Nation Conservative Government would probably have resisted' (ibid.). Faulkner managed to get these measured introduced, Sanders (ibid.) argued, because Home Secretaries changed so frequently and, therefore, did not have the time or knowledge 'to wrest control of penal policy from Faulkner'. When Kenneth Clarke MP did manage to do this, Sanders (ibid.) suggests there was a 'retrieval of the brutal inegalitarian Tory philosophy which ... characterised the Thatcher years'. Part of this involved the weakened Major government (it only had a 21-seat majority after the

1992 general election) deciding to place 'law and order' at the top of the political agenda (Cavadino and Dignan 2002).

Following the abolition of unit fines the status quo was returned to the imposition of fines, for while magistrates were to be required to 'fully ... consider an offender's means when imposing a fine' (House of Commons Debates 1993: col. 940), how this was to be done was to be left to their discretion, rather than through the 'application of any mathematical formula' (*ibid.*).

Day fines and New Labour

More recently, New Labour indicated a revisiting of unit fines when it announced the introduction of the 'day fine'. Day fines are well known in Scandinavia, continental Europe and the USA and provided the basis for the Conservatives' unit fine discussed in the previous section. In England and Wales it was the Carter (2003) review of 'correctional services' which suggested the reintroduction of fines that were more systematically related to the means of those being punished.

Dobson (2004: 145) outlines how the genesis of the Carter review, named after the businessman Patrick Carter who led it, can be located in tensions between the Home Office, with its 'tough on crime' mantra, and HM Treasury that found it 'difficult to see worthwhile results from its massive and seemingly limitless investment'. Carter's concern with the criminal justice system was two-fold; cost-effectiveness and maintaining public confidence in it. Once again, one of the main problems highlighted in relation to fines was their declining use, particularly for indictable offences, while the use of community-based punishments and imprisonment had increased. Demonstrating similar concerns to those of the early 1990s, Carter argued that imprisonment and community sentences should only be reserved for the most serious of offences and the most persistent and/or dangerous offenders. In this context, Carter (2003: 26) argued that day fines would be an important part of 'targeted and rigorous sentences' that were required for cost-effectiveness and public confidence.

Carter argued that day fines would operate by the judiciary deciding how many days a particular crime should be punished for and then multiplying the number of days by a figure related to the ability of the offender to repay. However, his suggestions were structured through tensions because, although he noted that day fines should be used for those at low risk of reoffending and for less serious offences, he also argued that if the fine was not paid then the offender should face a custodial sentence equivalent to the number of days for which they had not paid their fine. Hence, while the offender may have a low risk of reoffending and have not engaged in a particularly serious form of offending, s/he would face the harshest of punishment for the non-payment of the fine. This was controversial, for after *R v. Oldham Justices and another* ex parte *Cawley and Others* in the mid 1990s, considerable effort had been put into diverting fine defaulters from imprisonment through measures including community service orders, electronic monitoring and the disqualification of drivers (Cavadino and Dignan 2002). With such developments the number of receptions into custody for fine default fell from 22,723 to 3,700 between 1995 and 1999 (*ibid.*: 131), and to 2,040 in 2005 (Office for Criminal Justice Reform 2006, para. 7.6).

New Labour seemed to accept the principle of day fines, outlining them in the 2005 Management of Offenders and Sentencing Bill and producing a Regulatory Impact Assessment (Home Office 2006) related to their potential introduction. It argued that the cost of introducing them (between £2 and £2.8 million) would be outweighed by the benefits of having, and borrowing from Carter, a system of fines that would re-establish their credibility as a punishment. It was argued by the government that day fines would:

> increase sentencer confidence in the use of fines as a disposal and ... reduce the number of low risk offenders being given a community sentence. This, in turn, will allow NOMS [National Offender Management Service] to focus their resources and expertise on higher risk offenders to reduce offending and protect the public. (*ibid.*: 5)

However, the commitment to day fines was arguably weak, for New Labour was unable to find parliamentary time to ensure their successful introduction. This was because:

> [the] Government considers that it is important that our fine system aims to ensure that fines are set at realistic levels and have an equal impact on all offenders but it does not necessarily require legislation to set out a framework for the detailed process of determining the amount of the fine in every individual case. (personal communication from the Ministry of Justice 2007)

While it is unclear why the day fines were dropped, this quote implies that New Labour did not want to face similar accusations related to the discretion of the judiciary to those faced by the Conservatives in the 1990s. In contrast to introducing day fines the Sentencing Guidelines Council (2007) sought views of sentencers upon two approaches to the setting of fines. Neither was along the lines of unit or day fines. One was a variation on the existing practice of relating fines to a proportion of net weekly income, while the other related the level of fines to fixed amounts. Both versions maintained sentencer discretion.

Recent developments, most notably the use of fixed penalties, in financial punishments are also inconsistent with the idea that financial penalties should be related to the offenders' income. What is more, they exclude the judiciary altogether. There are two types of fixed financial penalties: Fixed Penalty Notices (FPNs) and Penalty Notices for Disorder (PNDs). FPNs are perhaps the better known of the two because of their use in punishing motoring offences (for example, for speeding), but they can also be issued for offences such as dropping litter and for not clearing up dog excrement. PNDs can be applied to a wider range of behaviours, including low-value retail theft and destruction and destroying of property, and selling alcohol to people who are drunk. However, since their introduction in the 2001 Criminal Justice and Police Act the majority have been issued for 'causing harassment, alarm and distress' and being 'drunk and disorderly' (Spicer and Kilsby 2004; Halligan-Davis and Spicer 2004). PNDs were introduced following a speech by then Prime Minister, Tony Blair (2000) in which he outlined his thoughts on 'community'. He argued in a populist section emphasising the importance of responsibility to 'communities' that:

> A thug might think twice about kicking in your gate, throwing traffic cones around your street or hurling abuse into the night sky if he [*sic*] thought he might get picked up by the police, taken to a cashpoint and asked to pay an on the spot fine of, for example, £100.

The suggestion was condemned, with representatives of the police arguing that it was yet another politically motivated policy that they had to enforce and that it would detract from front-line policing (the *Independent*, 1 July 2000), and those concerned with civil liberties arguing that it undermined justice by making the police 'judge and jury' in relation to certain offences (the *Guardian*, 1 July 2000). In fact, police opposition was so great that less than a week later it was reported that the plan had been abandoned (the *Times*, 4 July 2000). However, the then Secretary of State for the Home Department, Charles Clarke MP, hinted at further developments when he argued that:

> Actually, the Prime Minister was using a figure of speech when he talked of police officers frogmarching young hooligans to Cashpoints. What the Prime Minister was trying to do was to give an immediacy to his proposition that there needs to be immediate action to address the issue of violence and disorder on the streets. (*ibid.*)

It is widely argued that PNDs were a more acceptable version of what Blair had suggested in 2000. They were, in the words of Liberal Democrat MP Simon Hughes, 'a fallback, intended to give the impression that ... [marching 'thugs' to cashpoint machines] was not a completely barmy idea but only a half-barmy idea' (House of Commons Debates 2001: col. 74). In addition to the deterrent argument used by Blair, PNDs were justified as a measure that it was hoped would help reduce the time police spent away from front-line duties (for example, attending court and doing paperwork), while also delivering 'swift, simple, effective justice' (Home Office 2002, cited in Roberts 2005: 1).

Ashworth (2000) argues that fixed penalties are a compromise between administrative efficiency and equal impact. However, the compromise is more weighted to administrative efficiency because fixed penalties are not related to the means of the offender. This is justified by the argument that fixed penalties are 'set sufficiently low for it not to cause injustice' (Easton and Piper 2005: 230). Such arguments, however, are difficult to defend, for PNDs are set at standard rates which means they cannot possibly have an equal impact upon offenders of differing means. A PND of £80, for instance, represents about 10 days' IS at the single 'adult rate', but just over a day's wage for someone earning the median. In debates concerning the introduction of the 2001 Criminal Justice and Police Bill it was left to Liberal Democrat MP Simon Hughes to raise such issues:

> It is fine for well-heeled, intelligent individuals to get fixed penalty notices if they happen to be messing around on the streets one evening, having been to a posh dining club. It is no trouble to them because they would just write out a cheque the

next day. It would make no difference to their bank accounts and would be just one of those things ... On the other side are people like a lad from my constituency, who I recently tried to help. He was a 19-year-old, sleeping rough in a car and not of high intelligence, who was trying to cope with life and hold down a part-time job. Such people are much less likely to manage if they have to deal with a fixed penalty notice. They would have trouble organising themselves, ensuring they had the money to pay on time and understanding what to do if they wanted to challenge the notice. (Standing Committee F 2001: col. 19; see also his comments in House of Commons Debates 2001: col. 73)

While Hughes's argument is overly pessimistic about the capacities of young roofless people, he makes a trenchant point; fixed penalties impact disproportionately upon poorer people. This is particularly worrying because of, for instance, the high and increasing number of PNDs issued. In 2006 over 180,000 PNDs were issued, a 38 per cent rise on 2005 (the *Times*, 13 August 2007). Furthermore, evidence from the pilot (Halligan-Davis and Spicer 2004) of PNDs suggests that they have a net-widening effect, drawing more people into the criminal justice system. As Roberts (2005: 3) argues, rather than diverting people away from the criminal justice system PNDs actually provide an 'additional entry point and route into it', a route that is likely to be disproportionately taken by poor people.

Fines and social security benefits

As we have noted, the level at which fines were set was just one of the concerns raised about them in the late 1980s. The other was their payment. Alongside the trial of unit fines in the late 1980s, Moxon, Hedderman and Sutton (1990) also studied the potential effects of introducing the power to deduct fine payments from social security benefits. Such powers were consistent with the general thrust of criminal justice policy in the late 1980s; that it should be cost-effective and proportionate to the crime. In addition, Moxon, Hedderman and Sutton (1990) also observed that there were inconsistencies between employed and unemployed offenders in the manner in which they could pay their fines, for it was already possible for those who were employed to have their fines paid through an attachment of earnings, although it was a power that was infrequently used.

Moxon, Hedderman and Sutton (*ibid.*) argued that this was because 'offenders who are in steady employment are those least likely to get into serious difficulties over paying their fines', something confirmed by later research (Whittaker and Mackie 1997). Whittaker and Mackie's (*ibid.*) research, however, also found that magistrates were sympathetic to the concerns of fine defaulters who were employed in small business and who feared that an attachment of earnings would lead to their losing their job.

Moxon, Hedderman and Sutton (1990: 2) acknowledged the 'main objection' to deductions from means-tested benefits: 'that it would be wrong in principle to deprive those who are hardest up of such control as they have over their meagre resources'. However, and somewhat missing the point about having *control* over resources, they rejected such criticism by noting that many people on benefits were fined and managed to pay them. In addition, they quoted research from Scotland (Nicholson and Millar 1990) which suggested that a majority of unemployed people who had been fined welcomed the opportunity to pay their fines through deductions from their benefit because it would save them the costs (for example, bus fares) associated with paying fines and because, for many, fines were not their top priority.

A further objection to deducting fines from benefits was raised in Scotland in research concerning the fines officer scheme. Here, the argument was that making the effort to pay the fine was part of the punishment; 'payment [was] not supposed to be painless' (*ibid.*: 3), a feeling that was later echoed by some magistrates in England and Wales (cf. Whittaker and Mackie 1997). Moxon, Hedderman and Sutton (1990), however, rightly argued that the effort to pay fines was more keenly felt by poorer people who were more likely to have to make small, regular payments than by better off people who might be able to clear the fine in a single payment, or who could pay via an attachment to earnings. More controversially, they argued – drawing upon research from Northern Ireland (Jardine 1986) – that the more difficult and painful it became to pay a fine, the more likely it was that people would accept some time in prison as an alternative to paying it. This was held to be problematic because, they argued (Moxon, Hedderman and Sutton 1990: 3), it was 'clearly undesirable that an offender should consider himself [*sic*] free to choose whether to pay a fine or go to prison'.

Moxon, Hedderman and Sutton (1990) found that if deductions from IS were made when the fine was first imposed, up to 119,000 offenders per year would be eligible for such deductions, while if they were imposed after default some 71,000 offenders per annum would be eligible to have their fine deducted from their benefit. Perhaps most importantly, however, Moxon, Hedderman and Sutton (*ibid*.) found that the number of fine defaulters imprisoned could be reduced by 13,000 if fines could be deducted from their benefits. Following the study, agreement was reached between the Department of Social Security and the Home Office that the option of making deductions from IS should be made available to the courts for those offenders who had defaulted upon their fines. The 1991 Criminal Justice Act made it possible for magistrates to apply to have a set amount deducted from IS (and now also means-tested JSA and Pension Credit).

While the Labour Opposition welcomed the introduction of unit fines in the 1991 Criminal Justice Act, it opposed the deductions of fines from benefit, arguing: 'If fines are deducted from income support, the poor will become even poorer and, putting aside arguments of compassion, that is undesirable as increased poverty may be a stimulus to another offence' (Roy Hattersley MP, then Shadow Home Secretary, House of Commons Debates 1990b: col. 162). However, such arguments were rejected because while the 1991 Act argued that prison should be reserved only for the most serious of offenders, as we have seen, explanations of offending were located in a discourse related to moral failing. In this sense, deduction of fines from benefits can be considered as much part of the Conservatives' desire to tackle the so-called 'dependency culture' as it was a measure to strengthen fines as a punishment, for it reinforced the message that individuals must always take responsibility for their actions, no matter how poor they were. It also reflected a broader belief in Conservative governments that 'there is now no universally agreed standard of poverty' (Secretary of State for Social Services 1985: para. 4.6). If there was no agreed level of income above which claimants should live, the then government could not be accused of pushing people below it in order to repay the fines they had incurred.

In a demonstration of just how far New Labour has travelled in terms of rejecting the socio-economic basis of offending, it has overseen an increase of nearly 80 per cent (from £2.80 to £5 per week) in the level at which fines can be deducted from means-tested benefits. This was a recommendation in the Carter review (Carter 2003) that, as we have seen, wanted to re-establish fines as a credible sentence. Increasing the level of payment of the fine from benefits was held to be consistent with this aim. For example, then 'Courts minister' Christopher Leslie MP, noted that the increase in the level of payment would help maintain the credibility of fines as a sanction and, more generally, help maintain confidence in the criminal justice system (Criminal Justice System 2004). Research has indeed suggested that some magistrates were reluctant to use deduction from benefits because 'the amount that could be deducted was too low' (Whittaker and Mackie 1997: x), with magistrates expecting, for example, unemployed offenders to pay between £3 and £5 per week (Charman *et al.* 1996). However, increasing the payment of fines from benefits dovetailed with New Labour's version of communitarianism that, as we have seen in previous chapters, assumes individual responsibility in all circumstances. This was made clear in the press release announcing the increase, which under the headline 'Ministers Crack Down on Criminals on State Benefits' (Criminal Justice System 2004: 1) recorded 'Benefits Minister' Chris Pond MP, as saying: 'The right to state benefits must be matched by a responsibility to the society which is paying for them' (*ibid.*: 2). However, the point raised by Moxon, Hedderman and Sutton (1990) about benefit recipients having little control over their resources in such circumstances has still not been addressed, for while Carter's proposed day fine linked punishment to income, concern about the ability to pay fines, particularly from benefit-level income, was more about the credibility of fines as a punishment than it was with the ability of poor people to afford the payment of £5 per week.

Community punishments and social security benefits

The theme of balancing rights and responsibilities also structured the 2000 Child Support, Pensions and Social Security Act. This Act enables the Department for Work and Pensions to withdraw (or reduce, if claimants have dependants) for a period of four weeks certain benefits, including IS and JSA, from people who have breached their community sentences. McKeever (2004) traces this policy to a concern with the proportion of people who were not completing their community punishments (Hedderman 1999, 2000). This concern led to another, similar to the one with fines: that the judiciary and public were losing confidence in community-based sentences as a punishment for offending behaviour. In this context, the withdrawal of social security benefits for non-compliance with community punishments was, it was argued by the government, an administrative mechanism that, because of its deterrent effect, would encourage compliance (see comments of Angela Eagle, then

Parliamentary Under-Secretary of State for Social Security, Standing Committee F 2000: col. 621). However, in political terms it was merely an extension of New Labour's rights and responsibilities agenda. As then Secretary of State for Social Security Alistair Darling MP told parliament:

At present, one in five offenders given community sentences is brought back before the courts for failing to comply with the requirement of the sentence. We simply cannot allow that to continue, as those people break their side of the bargain but still claim benefits. I do not believe it right that a community punishment should be regarded as a one-way bet, in which people can do what they want while expecting everyone else to pay for their benefits. (House of Commons Debates 2000c: col. 160)

Reflecting such sentiments, it was argued by Angela Eagle MP in the committee stage of the Child Support, Social Security and Pensions Bill that:

This [the withdrawal of benefits for those breaching community punishments] is about rights and responsibilities and the Government's new contract for welfare. We do not believe that the receipt of benefits should be unconditional. We do not have a problem saying that the receipt of benefits is a contract between the individual and the state, and that benefits should not be seen as being available unconditionally, regardless of the individual's behaviour. (Angela Eagle MP, Standing Committee F 2000: cols. 617–618)

However, Eagle's argument was disingenuous because, as was highlighted in the committee stage of the bill, the withdrawal of benefits for non-compliance with community sentences was a new departure in terms of the responsibilities of benefit recipients. This was because it introduced conditionality that was not linked to the receipt of the benefit, in contrast, for example, to the demand made of JSA claimants that they must be available for, and actively seeking, paid work in order to receive it. The 2000 Child Support, Pensions and Social Security Act, on the other hand, in a similar way to more recent developments in HB policy, demanded a particular behaviour that New Labour held to be desirable. However, the argument that the withdrawal of benefits was merely an extension of responsibilities that benefit recipients must face allowed New Labour to deny that it was a punishment; it was described, therefore, as merely 'additional benefit conditionality'. (Angela Eagle MP, Standing Committee F 2000: col. 618)

While Dwyer (2004) does not mention the 2000 Child Support, Pensions and Social Security Act in his analysis of 'creeping conditionality' in various social policies, it is clear that it was part of the trends he describes, for it too meant that:

> The welfare rights of those deemed 'irresponsible' because they cannot, or will not, meet certain state endorsed standards or regulations may be withdrawn or reduced. This enables politicians to place the blame for the predicament of those whose right to publicly funded welfare is reduced or removed firmly at the door of the individuals concerned. (*ibid*.: 266)

This was made clear by Alistair Darling MP, who in responding to a question about the poverty that would be faced by those people who had their benefits withdrawn or reduced, replied:

> the remedy in cases such as the hon. Gentleman described lies in the hands of the person who breaks a probation order. People are not required to live in poverty or to lose their benefit. They are required only to do what the court tells them to do. If they are not willing to do that, they can have no cause for complaint. (House of Commons Debates 2000c: cols. 160–161)

McKeever (2004: 12) argues that this position is problematic because, not only does it demonstrate an ignorance of the dynamics of poverty, but it also 'ignores the links between social problems and offending'.

The withdrawal of benefits for non-compliance was initially introduced as a pilot in four Probation Service areas and was evaluated by researchers commissioned by the Department for Work and Pensions (Knight *et al.* 2003). If the aim was to deter people from disengaging from their community sentences then the evaluation of the pilot schemes was disappointing because in the pilot areas the fall in the rate of non-compliance that was attributable to the schemes was just 1.8 per cent. This was because the withdrawal of benefit was not felt by offenders involved in the evaluation to be a major influence on their behaviour which, in contrast, was related to a number of administrative issues (the potential to withdraw benefits was not widely known about), the more general attitude of participants to compliance and a range of other factors, including 'unstructured or chaotic lives, problematic drug and alcohol use and confrontational attitudes to probation' (*ibid.*: 3). In many ways, these findings reflected what was already known about the ways in which compliance with community sentences is structured through a complex set of economic, social and personal factors (McKeever 2004).

McKeever (2004) argues that from a criminal justice view the withdrawal of benefits for non-compliance with community punishments was problematic. She rejects New Labour's argument that the withdrawal of benefits was not a punishment. By doing so, and drawing upon the work of von Hirsch (1993), she argues that it was a disproportionate punishment, for the effect of the measure was essentially to 'fine an offender 100 per cent of his or her income, by withdrawing his or her primary income-replacement benefit' (McKeever 2004: 9). For McKeever, this was not a proportionate punishment compared to the original sentence because it represented in von Hirsch's terms more than a 'modest step-up in severity' (*ibid.*). Furthermore, McKeever argued that the withdrawal of benefit was disproportionate in relative terms if offenders were compared. This was because there was no equivalent sanction available for those people not in receipt of benefits. It was something that could only be applied to the very poorest people.

However, perhaps more importantly from our perspective, the withdrawal of benefits from those people failing to comply with their community punishments was problematic because it merely exacerbated the material context of offending behaviour. This concern was raised by the National Association of Probation Officers (NAPO) before the pilots began. As 'NAPO spokesman' Harry Fletcher was reported as saying: 'This is a bizarre sanction. If benefits are taken away, the only alternative source of income will be begging or stealing. This will increase crime' (the *Independent*, 2 April 2001). The concerns of NAPO were reflected in the findings from the pilot areas that noted: 'For some offenders, the main way they reported supporting themselves during the sanction period was through offending' (Knight *et al.* 2003: 57). As one respondent told Knight *et al.* (*ibid.*: 58): 'I just thought "f*** [*sic*] it, I'm going back to burgling." I'd stopped, I hadn't done one for ages.' As Grover (2005a) notes, it is likely that such respondents were offending in order to survive, for they reported having 'problems paying for food, heating and electricity' (*ibid.*) because of the withdrawal of their benefits.

Conclusion

This chapter has focused upon financial penalties and the issues that they raise for people living in poverty. It has demonstrated that financial penalties for such people are problematic. In the case of fines, for example, attempts formally to relate their level to the income of offenders have failed. This is despite the fact, or perhaps more tellingly because of the fact, that the evidence suggests that for the brief period that unit fines operated in the 1990s they met their desired goals; their use compared to other disposals increased, and the average fine for unemployed people fell while it increased for people in paid work (Cavadino and Dignan 2002). However, as we have seen, the success of the unit fines in these respects was central to their abolition; the main opposition came in defence of middle-class people who were seen as being the victims of an unfair system of punishment (cf. Lacey 1994).

Policies that have attempted to formalise relationships between means and levels of fines, however, have not failed just because of middle-class opposition. Perhaps more importantly, there has been an inability in policy-making – as we saw Hudson argue powerfully at a more abstract level – to get beyond a narrow definition of responsibility that currently does not take account of the way in which, for many people living in poverty, agency may be constrained by a lack of money. Indeed, we have seen in this chapter that while there have been moves to relate fines more closely and consistently to income, these have been eroded by a concern with the responsibility of individuals to act as moral agents no matter what their material circumstances are. The problem with this, which we have also seen in relation to the recovery of defaulted fines from means-tested benefits, and the financial punishment of benefit recipients who do not complete their community punishments, is that it exacerbates the socio-structural factors that frame offending. These developments do not attain criminal or social justice because they merely make poor people poorer. If criminal and social justice are to be aimed for, the material circumstances of people must be taken into account when punishments are being decided. This is not a means of 'letting off' poorer people or treating them differently from other offenders. In contrast, it is a recognition that the material circumstances of many poor people necessarily restricts their ability to express the responsibilities expected of them, and all people, in a manner that is currently considered legitimate.

Notes

1 If, however, the payment of fines has to be enforced by the courts then their cost can quite rapidly increase, in which case they 'could easily narrow, if not close' the cost difference between fines and community sentences (Mackie *et al.* 2003: 92). In the early years of the twenty-first century the cost of enforcing the payment of fines was about one-third (32.6 per cent) of the total impositions made by courts (*ibid.*: 7).

2 Under the unit fine system introduced by the 1991 Criminal Justice Act, magistrates were able to assign to an offence a number of units dependent upon its seriousness and any mitigating factors. To calculate the amount of the fine the number of units was then multiplied by a figure that was related to the income of the offender.

3 In Scotland attempts were made to introduce unit fines in the 1990 Law Reform (Miscellaneous Offenders) Scotland Bill. They did not, however, survive the Bill's passage through the Scottish parliament. Supervised Attendance Orders were introduced as an alternative to custody for people defaulting upon their fines (see Levy and McIvor 2001).

Chapter 9

Conclusion

Crime and Inequality has examined relationships between crime and predominantly economic inequality. It has also focused upon the ways in which the state has in recent decades attempted to relieve the needs of the poorest people, and, more recently, has attempted to address (child) poverty, the most unacceptable manifestation of economic inequality. In doing so, we have covered a great deal of conceptual and empirical material. What themes can we draw from this material?

The boundaries of academic disciplines

Soothill *et al.* (2002) warn against criminology becoming a too narrowly defined subject and point to the need for it to take seriously other academic disciplines. In particular, they note that there is a need for criminologists to engage with contemporary configurations of welfare policy that is the focus of social policy. *Crime and Inequality* responds to such concerns, for it has attempted to outline recent development in some areas, particularly social security and labour market policy, that are pertinent to understanding the economic context of offending. However, Soothill *et al.*'s. observations are equally applicable to social policy; it must also be willing to engage with the interconnections between crime and inequality as they provide an opportunity to illuminate, and engage with, the tensions and contradictions that competing demands upon policies, and the assumptions upon which they are premised, create. Soothill *et al.*'s observations have been made more urgent because of the trend we saw in Chapter 1 towards what is conceptualised as the 'criminalisation of social policy'; the incursion and the potential use of social policy in order to reduce crime (cf. Knepper 2007).

In that chapter we warned against the uncritical use of this concept, and throughout *Crime and Inequality* we have seen that there are visible trends in the use of social policy in order to deter and punish offending behaviour. However, the criminalisation of social policy in this sense is only a small element of what are often hugely complex and multifaceted policy areas. The main problem, though, with the criminalisation of social policy thesis is that it is likely to be unsuccessful if, as many commentators argue, its role is to reduce crime. This is because there is a tension between, on the one hand, economic inequality as the most important contextual factor of offending and, on the other hand, the criminalisation of social policy that, in various ways, further impoverishes already poor people.

In many ways, such observations point to one of the more problematic aspects of 'joined-up thinking' or 'joined-up government'. Joined-up thinking is often portrayed as being a positive way of thinking about socially located problems such as crime and poverty and addressing them. New Labour has been particularly keen on such an approach (Cook 2006). However, the criminalisation of social policy thesis suggests that the policy outcomes of such thinking can be deeply problematic because it conjoins areas of policy that often have differing aims and objectives and that are often inconsistent.

Inconsistencies and tensions

The main inconsistency in government policy that *Crime and Inequality* has highlighted and examined is between theoretical and more applied criminology that suggest that economic inequality is an important contextual factor in explaining offending, and social policy interventions that have the potential to exacerbate such inequalities. There are several ways in which this tension operates, although they are all linked to historically enduring concerns with the character of poor people. The main concern since the inception of state-organised welfare benefits and services and their feudal predecessors has been that they merely reproduce the alleged character flaws and failures of the individual that caused their poverty in the first place. Historically, this has meant a particular concern with maintaining labour discipline as paid work has been (and is still) seen by élites as *the* means by which individuals can change their corrupt and corrupting character, and demonstrate that they are responsible. In terms of economic support, it has meant that relief of need should be set at a level that does not discourage people from working at wages being offered in prevailing labour markets. At various times in the distant and more recent past there has also been concern that relieving need should not encourage lone motherhood (what was described as bastardy in earlier historical periods) and other forms of familial 'breakdown', such as young people becoming too independent from their families.

These concerns act to ensure that all non-employed people are kept poor through low levels of out-of-work benefits, with young people (aged under 25) facing a particularly harsh benefit regime of no, or very low, levels of benefits. In addition, with regard to maintaining the incentive to work, we have seen that those people officially defined as unemployed, and increasingly other groups of claimants as well, face benefit sanctions if they are deemed not to be adequately co-operating with the various new deals aimed at getting them to compete for paid work. The consequence of these actions is that many people are forced to live on an income that is less than what many consider to be the *de facto* poverty line (the level at which IS is paid).

Second, and following the theme of the criminalisation of social policy, we have seen that increasingly the state can apply sanctions to the benefits of claimants that do not relate to their behaviour *vis-à-vis* their not being in paid work, but relate to their wider behaviour (for example, the introduction of 'probationary tenancies', the withdrawal of HB for those convicted of anti-social behaviour who are deemed not to be making enough effort to change their ways; the sanctioning of the IS for those people deemed not to be fulfilling their community sentences, and the deductions of fines from IS). However, the impact on people is the same; the reduction of already low income and, in some cases, the loss of their homes.

There is a perverse logic here; that through economically marginalising individuals and their families they can be brought into the normative fold, whether that is in relation to paid work or acting pro-socially in a wider sense. However, criminological theory from Bonger (1916) on relationships between absolute deprivation and crime through to more recent expositions on relationships between relative deprivation and crime suggests that this is likely to have the opposite effect, further alienating people from 'respectable', law-abiding society. The point here is that the expanding sanctioning regime aimed at encouraging paid work, maintaining familial discipline and punishing and deterring crime merely exacerbates economic inequality that we have seen is an important contextual factor in explaining offending. In this sense, the various roles of those social policies we have been concerned with are inconsistent. Most notably, attempting to control crime and maintain the commitment to paid work are at odds with the role of attempting to relieve the needs of the poorest people.

The importance of paid work

We have seen in several chapters that a great deal of emphasis has been placed upon paid work as being the solution to offending and anti-social behaviour. For young men it is held to give them an alternative to offending and a sense of purpose in a rather conservative way of reconstructing the patriarchal family. We have argued that paid work is also held to be important because it is seen as *the* means of enabling lone mothers to furnish their children, particularly their male children, with desirable role models. In addition to such arguments about the alleged importance of paid work in reducing offending there are others; for instance, an increased income negates the need to offend because of either absolute or relative deprivation; and, in a social control sense, those in paid work have a greater vested interest in society. However, the nature of contemporary employment for those people that we have been concerned with in *Crime and Inequality* is arguably not that conducive to tackling offending. Drawing upon Currie (1985), for instance, Downes (1998: 3) argues that:

> unemployment is not simply to be contrasted with employment, as if both were standard units of experience. Insecure under-employment is not better than unemployment as a source of livelihood sufficient to support a family and experience an active sense of citizenship. Short spells of unemployment between rewarding jobs is better than being stuck with work that offers only poor pay, hours, conditions and prospects.

The increase in part-time and particularly low-paid work means that even for many people in paid work they have poverty-level incomes, despite the increasingly widespread subsidisation of low pay through tax credits. If crime can be explained through arguments that focus upon relativities (and even absolutes) then there is little reason to suppose that getting entry-level employment in contemporary Britain will reduce offending. Moreover, the means through which recent governments have attempted to increase employment participation are problematic, for they arguably help reproduce the types of labour markets that Downes, in the quote above, argues help frame offending. Such labour markets also have a tendency to marginalise people from paid work altogether. In the case of the former we can point to the evidence discussed in several chapters that government-sponsored employment-related schemes often force people to take paid work that, if they were not under pressure, they would not normally take, and that the subsidisation of low-paid employment through tax credits may actually trap people in such work. In the case of the latter, we can point to what New Labour has labelled the NEET phenomenon, for in addition to the 10 per cent of 16- and 17-year-olds who are not in employment, education or training there are those who leave the NDYP for unknown destinations, an unknown number of whom are NEET.

What these observations suggest is that current configurations of paid work are criminogenic, for they offer only low wages and casual work. In this sense, they do little to improve the material conditions of workers and little to enhance their sense of 'belonging' – or, as New Labour calls it, 'inclusion' – in society. The filling of such employment through employment-related schemes has a similar effect; impoverishment and marginalisation to the mainstream.

Crime, social policy and 'free' market capitalism

While we can point to the practices of the state as contributing to economic inequality, it would be wrong to argue that the state is the cause of economic inequality; the causes lie in the operation of patriarchal and racialised capitalism. However, whether the state is considered to be a 'committee for managing the common affairs of the whole bourgeoisie' (Marx and Engels 1967: 82) or attempts to balance the demands of capital and labour in a more detached manner (for example, Offe 1984), it undoubtedly has to work within capitalist structures that for reasons of profitability require a plentiful supply of cheap labour. What this means is that the reproduction of economic inequality is central to the work of the state and it provides the context for many of the social problems, including crime, that Britain faces.

When in government in the 1980s and 1990s the Conservatives made it clear that inequality was a desirable phenomenon because, in a version of the eighteenth-century argument that poverty is needed to ensure that people work (see, Poynter 1969), of its potential to spur individuals to be enterprising and hard-working. While New Labour has tended to avoid such claims in order not to alienate its longer-standing supporters, apart from a concern with child poverty, it too has little problem with economic inequality (cf. Grover and Stewart 2002).

While many of the policies discussed in *Crime and Inequality* have been located in a discourse of tackling child poverty, we have seen that there are inherent contradictions within this aim and the enforcing of those behaviours defined by government as being central to the needs of contemporary society. In this sense, it is unhelpful to consider economic organisation in Britain as being a *free* market version of capitalism. The idea that capitalism is free from institutional interventions is, quite frankly, a nonsense. States allow and encourage capitalism to develop through a raft of economic and social policies that range from the tax breaks offered to private enterprise, for example, to set up in locations earmarked for development, to tax relief on research and development, to the types of policies discussed in *Crime and Inequality* that are as much concerned with regulating low-paid work as they are with addressing offending and anti-social behaviour. In this sense, it has been observed (for example, Jessop 1994a, 1994b, 2002) that the shift from the 'planned' Keynesian economy of the post-Second World War period to post-1970s neo-liberalism has involved a reregulation of economic activity and its social basis, rather than its wholesale deregulation. In fact, it is arguably the case that the neo-liberal 'free' market has required greater state intervention than the 'planned' Keynesian economy (Grover and Stewart 2002). Through the policies discussed in *Crime and Inequality*, and others we have not had the space to examine, the aim has been to regulate various aspects of the 'free' market, including low-paid work, often casualised and part-time; the widest ever levels of inequality that modern and late-modern Britain has ever witnessed; the responsibilisation and remoralisation of people so that they can be held responsible for the poor material circumstances in which they live; and the protection of areas of commercial activity, most notably those related to consumption. In brief, the free market capitalism, particularly that premised upon Britain's version of neo-liberalism, has required greater responsibility from its people, their greater discipline and an enhanced level of surveillance.

Social divisions, crime and inequality

Following Fraser (1997, 2000), we have seen in several places in *Crime and Inequality* that cultural assumptions about, and constructions of, people, particularly women and BME people, conjoin with political economic arguments to explain the economic hardship that they face. In this sense, the issue of culture also raises important questions about the nature of relationships between crime and inequality. A focus upon gender makes the point. We saw in Chapter 4 that, generally speaking, women are poorer than men and that their poverty can help us to understand their offending behaviour. However, it cannot help us to understand why men are, according to the official crime statistics at least, more likely to commit crime than women. If we were focusing only upon economic inequality as the contextual factor of offending then obviously this would be problematic because it would be expected that women would commit more crime than men. This, however, is not the case, and therefore, we need to understand economic inequality in relation to other cultural factors, such as the differential socialisation patterns of women and men, and the cultural emphasis placed upon the roles of men and women in society. In brief, we also need to understand that offending is linked to the cultural construction of genders and the ways in which they are at least partly 'produced' through criminal justice and social policy interventions. In this sense, the labelling of offenders is equally important to understanding why so many poor people are engaged with criminal justice agencies and are, according to official figures at least, disproportionately criminogenic. An understanding of the political economy and cultural position of people provides a powerful juncture for addressing why poorer people engage in offending and anti-social behaviour, and why they appear to do so more than other groups in the population. In brief, economic inequality provides an important context for explaining offending behaviour and, in addition, cultural constructions help us to understand why particular groups of poorer people are likely to appear disproportionately in the crime statistics.

Crime, inequality and social policy into the future

It would be nice to finish a book like *Crime and Inequality* on a note of optimism. Current concerns with reducing crime and addressing anti-social behaviour might well give some reasons for being optimistic, for, if the economic basis of offending were to be taken seriously, they would add weight to the moral arguments for tackling inequality and poverty. However, given the trends in both criminal justice and social policy outlined in *Crime and Inequality*, it is difficult to be optimistic about the future, particularly in the short to medium term, for there is no indication that the economic basis of crime in the context in which we have discussed it will be taken seriously in the future at either the political economic or cultural levels.

In labour market and social security policy terms there is likely to be little difference in New Labour's approach under Gordon Brown's premiership from that of Tony Blair. After all, Brown was one of the founders of New Labour and certainly the architect of its social and economic policies, most notably labour market and social security policies. Indeed, we have seen in *Crime and Inequality* that New Labour has committed itself to the Freud Report (Freud 2007) that outlines a future social security policy that is even more closely linked to job search activity for a wider range of benefit claimants; a regime that will see the sanctioning of more benefit claimants for failing to cooperate with the demands placed upon them to search for and find paid work. Closely related, there is little to suggest that the cultural position of many poor people, most notably women and BME people, is to be seriously addressed. In the case of BME people, for example, the current emphasis placed upon being British and 'Britishness' that rejects multiculturalism as a failed approach to 'race relations' suggests that cultural constructions of many BME people, especially Asian people, are likely to contribute to continuing racism against them, thereby denying them access to employment that is secure and better paid, and to a range of benefits and services.

Criminology and, indeed, social policy needs to take these issues seriously and to recognise more clearly that they are political projects and discourses. While a great deal of criticism has been aimed at the radical criminologists (for example, Taylor, Walton and Young 1973) of the 1970s, they were surely correct in their basic approach in criminology that was, according to Muncie (2001: 187), to 'promote a form of radical politics'. The idea that criminology and also social policy are a means of promoting a radical form of politics needs to be recaptured from the midst of individualistic and commonsensical explanations of crime and other social problems. In this sense, the conjoining of criminological and social policy analyses provides a powerful basis for resisting the capitalist logic that impoverishes people and creates the economic and social context of social problems, including offending and anti-social behaviour.

Glossary of terms

Benefit Sanction – These are financial penalties (for example, a withdrawal of, or reduction in, benefits) that are attached to benefits for those people who do not act in the manner in which it is stipulated they need to in order to qualify for the benefit they are claiming. So, for instance, Jobseeker's Allowance will be sanctioned if the claimant is not deemed to be actively seeking work. Increasingly, sanctions are applied for a broader range of behaviours, for instance acting in a manner that is deemed anti-social.

Child Tax Credit – One of two benefits that replaced Working Families Tax Credit in April 2003. It also replaced Income Support for children. It is a benefit for children in poorer households and is the government's main mechanism for tackling child poverty. Claimants with no, or a low enough, income receive the whole amount of CTC irrespective of whether they are in paid work or not. Because of this CTC is also held to aid the transition between non-employment and low-paid work for parents. Once in work CTC is withdrawn as income rises.

Children's Centres – These are part of the wider Sure Start initiative that is supposed to give children the best possible start in life. Providing a range of services (from childcare and early years education to job search and readiness activities), Children's Centres should be a one-stop shop for young children (aged under five) and their parents.

Elizabethan Poor Law – Also known as the Old Poor Law, a system of poor relief that existed from 1601 to 1834 which was premised upon a paternalism towards, and fear of, poor people. The unit of administration was the parish and relief was paid for through a levy of rates on the occupiers of land.

Employment and Support Allowance – A new benefit for sick and disabled – people. For new claimants it will replace Incapacity Benefit from 2008. It has a different structure from Incapacity Benefit, for it does not increase in value over time and the level it is paid at depends upon the ability of the claimant to work and their willingness to engage in activities designed to get them back into paid work.

Ethnic Minority Flexible Fund – Initially introduced as a two-year pilot project, the Ethnic Minority Flexible Fund provides money that can be used by the DWP in those areas where a high proportion of the population is BME people. The fund can be used to pay for local approaches – such as the provision of projects highlighting the under-representation of BME workers in particular occupational sectors – to increasing the closeness of BME people to paid work.

Ethnic Minority Outreach – A DWP initiative that was introduced in 2002 aimed at helping unemployed BME people make the transition into paid work through outreach schemes and working with employers on activities such as diversity training.

Family Credit – A benefit that was only available to people who were in paid work of at least 24 hours (later, 16 hours) a week and who had dependent children. Therefore, it subsidised low wages and/or part-time work. It was introduced in 1988 as a more generous version of Family Income Supplement that was introduced in 1971. Family Credit was replaced by New Labour's Working Families Tax Credit, introduced in 1999.

Family Element – A part of tax credit policy that is paid as a benefit or as tax relief to people with dependent children. It is gradually withdrawn once household income rises above £50,000 per annum.

Housing Benefit – A benefit that is designed to help relieve the housing costs (rent only) of poorer people. It is paid irrespective of whether the claimant is in paid work or not. The amount paid is dependent upon income, the cost of the rent and whether the rent is considered to be reasonable by the local authorities administering it.

Incapacity Benefit – A benefit introduced in 1995 as replacement for Invalidity Benefit and Sickness Benefit for those people who are able to prove they are unable to work because of sickness or disability. It is not means-tested and for new claimants only it is being replaced by the Employment and Support Allowance in October 2008.

Income Support – A means-tested benefit that was introduced by the then Conservative government in 1988 as a replacement for Supplementary Benefit (that itself replaced National Assistance in 1966). It is a means-tested benefit, reserved for the poorest people. Its coverage has been reduced over recent years, with, for example, unemployed people having to claim Income-Based Jobseeker's Allowance from 1996 and from 2008 new sick and disabled claimants having to claim the Employment Support Allowance. In addition, from 2003 children were removed from Income Support. Their needs are now supposed to be relieved through the Child Tax Credit.

In-Work Benefit – Generic term used to describe means-tested benefits and tax credits paid to people in low-paid and/or part-time (providing it is more than 16 hours per week) employment.

In-Work Credit – A benefit of £40 (£60 in London) per week for up to 12 months for lone mothers who have taken paid work, but who had previously been claiming out-of-work benefits for at least 12 months. It is a benefit that it is hoped will increase the financial incentive to take paid work among lone mothers.

Jobcentre Plus – The agency that provides face-to-face services to benefit claimants. As well as administering benefits, it provides details of available job vacancies and attempts to fill those vacancies.

Jobseeker's Allowance – A benefit introduced in 1996 as a replacement for Unemployment Benefit and Income Support for unemployed people. It can be claimed by people who are available for and actively seeking paid work. A Jobseeker's Agreement must be signed by the claimant in order to claim. This does not allow claimants to restrict the work they are looking for or are willing to do to a particular type. There are two elements: Contribution- based JSA that lasts for a maximum of six months and is based upon the claimants' National

Insurance contributions; and Income-based JSA that is means-tested, but not time-limited.

National Childcare Strategy – One of New Labour's flagship policies, the National Childcare Strategy was introduced in 1998 as a mechanism to encourage greater levels of provision for childcare at more affordable rates. Funding was mainly focused upon the demand side through the payment of the Childcare Tax Credit, although there was also some short-term funding aimed at pump-priming childcare providers. It has been usurped by the 10-year childcare strategy outlined in 2004.

National Minimum Wage – The first ever national minimum wage (previously there had been industry- specific minimum wages) was introduced by New Labour in April 1999. It now has three rates: the highest is for those workers aged 22 and over, followed by a 'development rate' for those aged 18 to 21 years, and the lowest rate is for those workers who are no longer classed as being in compulsory education, but are under the age of 18.

Neighbourhood Nurseries Initiative – The aim of the Neighbourhood Nurseries Initiative was to increase the amount of childcare provision in the poorest neighbourhoods in order to allow people, particularly lone mothers, living in those areas to (re)enter paid work. It was introduced in the year 2000, but has since been absorbed into the Children's Centres initiative.

New Deal for Lone Parents – Introduced on a national basis in October 1998. It is supposed to encourage lone mothers into paid work by demonstrating the financial benefits of being in work, providing support in getting into work and keeping lone mothers informed of vacancies. Currently, it is not compulsory for lone mothers to engage with it.

New Deal for Young People – Introduced in 1998, the New Deal for Young People is a mandatory scheme for young people (aged 18 to 24) who have been unemployed for at least six months if they wish to continue to claim Jobseeker's Allowance. It has three stages: a four-month 'gateway' in which conscripts should receive intensive and personalised supporting in order to aid their finding of paid work; the 'options' stage where they have to engage in subsidised paid work, full-time education or training, working in the voluntary sector or working with the Environment Task Force. If they are still unemployed after the 'options' stage they enter the 'follow through' stage during which time they receive support similar to that offered in the 'gateway'. Jobseeker's Allowance can be withdrawn at any time during the New Deal for Young People if it is felt the conscript is not fully cooperating.

New Poor Law – The means of relieving need between 1834 and 1848. Introduced by the 1834 Poor Law Amendment Act, the New Poor Law was premised upon the idea of 'less eligibility'; that the situation of the pauper should always be worse than that of the poorest independent labourer. This aspect of the poor law was to be enforced by the provision of relief in workhouses. In practice, it was often not possible to force paupers into workhouses, but they were often expected to do 'work tests' (such as stone breaking) in order to receive relief. The relief of need provided under the New Poor Law was replaced in 1948 with the introduction of National Assistance.

New Workers Scheme – Introduced in 1983 as an expanded replacement of the Young Workers Scheme. Under it employers were paid a subsidy by the state if they paid new workers (aged under 21 years) a low wage. Employers could claim, for up to 12 months, £15 per week if they paid 18- and 19-year-olds less than £55 per week and 20-year-olds less than £65 per week. The scheme was abolished in 1988.

Out of School Childcare Initiative – This initiative was introduced in 1993 as a mechanism to increase the amount of out- of-school childcare available to parents in order to facilitate their entry or return to paid work. The initiative provided funding (usually up to a year) via Training and Enterprise Councils to help pump-prime out-of-school childcare providers. The National Childcare Strategy broadened the focus on childcare away from out-of-school care only.

Out of Work Benefit – Generic term used to describe those benefits paid to people while they are out of paid work.

Parent Plus – A pilot scheme introduced in 1996 to help support lone mothers to get into paid work through a casework approach. It was replaced in 1998 by the New Deal for Lone Parents.

Rough Sleepers Initiative – Introduced by the Conservative government in 1990, the Rough Sleepers Initiative aimed to help tackle street homelessness in large urban areas, initially London, but was then extended to 26 other areas. Funding was made available for hostel-based and outreach services to encourage people to leave the streets, while Housing Associations were given funding to provide permanent accommodation.

Single Room Rent – A mechanism that local authorities can use to restrict the amount of Housing Benefit paid to single young people (under the age of 25) in private rented accommodation by comparing what they actually pay in rent to 'reasonable market rents' in the same area for accommodation that comprises one bedroom and a shared living room, kitchen, toilet and bathroom.

Social Fund – The social fund is part of the social security system that is supposed to relieve exceptional and unforeseen needs. In particular, it pays for 'lumpy' items (for example, beds and bedding, cookers, fridges and so forth) that it is difficult to budget for out of weekly benefit income. The majority of payments are interest-free loans, the repayment of which is expected to be from benefit income.

Tax credits – Generic term that includes the CTC, WTC and Childcare Tax Credit.

Working Families Tax Credit – A benefit that subsidised low pay and/or part-time employment that was introduced by New Labour in October 1999. It was replaced in April 2003 by the WTC and CTC because it was thought to be too complicated and did not make fully clear its two roles of offering financial incentives to paid work and tackling child poverty.

Working Tax Credit – One of two in-work benefits that replaced Working Families Tax Credit in 2003. It can be claimed by adults only, providing that they are working at least 16 hours per week and have a low enough wage. It is supposed to provide a financial incentive for people to take low-paid and/or part-time paid work. It can be paid in addition to CTC if the claimant also has dependent children.

Young Workers Scheme – A scheme introduced in 1982 that encouraged employers to pay low wages to young people (aged 16–17). Through the scheme employers were paid a subsidy by the state if they employed a previously registered unemployed youngster and paid them a low wage. They were paid £15 per week for up to 12 months if they paid the young person less than £40 per week and £7.50 per week if they paid them between £40 and £45 per week. The Young Workers Scheme was replaced in 1983 by the New Workers Scheme.

Youth Opportunities Programme – The Youth Opportunities Programme was introduced by a Labour government in 1978. It was for unemployed young people (aged 16 to 18 years old) and was supposed to offer them training and work experience opportunities to enhance their potential for securing paid work. Participants were paid an allowance by the state. The Youth Opportunities Programme was replaced in 1983 by the Youth Training Scheme.

Youth Training – Youth Training replaced the Youth Training Scheme in 1990. It was similar to the Youth Training Scheme, except that it offered guaranteed coverage for all 16- and 17-year-olds not in education or employment, was more flexible in its approach to the nature and length of training and had a larger stick to encourage participation; those young people who could still claim Income Support could have it withdrawn if they refused a Youth Training place. Youth Training was replaced by the New Deal for Young People in 1998.

Youth Training Scheme – The Youth Training Scheme was introduced by the Conservatives in 1983 and replaced the Youth Opportunities Programme. However, it had a similar role; to enhance the employability of young people by offering them training and skill development opportunities. Initially, it was introduced as a one-year programme, but in 1986 it was extended to two years. In 1988, alongside the withdrawal of Income Support for 16- and 17-year-olds, the Conservatives pledged that there would be a training place for any 16- or 17-year-old not in education, training or employment. The Youth Training Scheme was replaced by Youth Training in 1990.

References

Adler, F. (1975) *Sisters in Crime: The Rise of the New Female Criminal*. New York: McGraw Hill.

Advisory Council on the Penal System (1970) *Non-custodial and semi-custodial penalties. Report of the Advisory Council on the Penal System*. London: HMSO.

Ainley, P., Barnes, T. and Momen, A. (2002) 'Making Connexions: a case study in contemporary social policy', *Critical Social Policy*, 22(2): 376–388.

Alcock, P. (1987) *Poverty and State Support*. Harlow: Longman.

Alcock, P. (1993) *Understanding Poverty* (1st edn). Basingstoke: Macmillan.

Alcock, P. (2006) *Understanding Poverty* (3rd edn). Basingstoke: Macmillan.

Alexander, C. (2004) 'Imagining the Asian Gang: Ethnicity, Masculinity and Youth After "The Riots"', *Critical Social Policy*, 24(4): 526–249.

Alibhai-Brown, Y. (1999) *True Colours: public attitudes to multiculturalism and the role of the government*. London: Institute for Public Policy Research.

All-Party Penal Affairs Group (1980) *Too Many Prisoners. An examination of ways of reducing the prison population*. Chichester: Barry Rose.

Anderson, S., Kinsey, R., Loader, I. and Smith, C. (1994) *Cautionary Tales: Young People, Crime and Policing in Edinburgh*. Aldershot: Avebury.

Armstrong, D., Hine, J., Hacking, S., Armaos, R., Jones, R., Klessinger, N. and France, A. (2005) *Children, risk and crime: the On Track Youth Lifestyles Surveys*, Home Office Research Study 278. London: Home Office.

Ashworth, A. (1997) *Sentencing in the 80's and 90's: the struggle for power*, 8th Eve Saville Memorial Lecture, Kings College London, http://www.kcl.ac.uk/depsta/rel/ccjs/eighties-sentencing.html [accessed 21 August 2007].

Ashworth, A. (2000) *Sentencing and Criminal Justice* (3rd edn). London: Butterworths.

Ashworth, A. (2005) *Sentencing and Criminal Justice* (4th edn). Cambridge: Cambridge University Press.

Atkinson, A. (1998) 'Social Exclusion, Poverty and Unemployment', in A. Atkinson and J. Hills (eds), *Exclusion, Employment and Opportunity*, CASE paper 4. London: Centre for Analysis of Social Exclusion.

Atkinson, J. and Williams, M. (2003) *Employer Perspectives on the Recruitment, Retention and Advancement of Low-pay, Low-Status Employees*. London: Institute for Employment Studies.

Bagguley, P. and Mann, K. (1992) 'Idle Thieving Bastards? Scholarly Representations of the "Underclass"', *Work, Employment and Society*, 6(1): 113–126.

Ballintyne, S. (1999) *Unsafe Streets. Street Homelessness and Crime*. London: Institute of Public Policy Research.

Balls, E. (1993) 'Danger: Men not at work', in E. Balls and P. Gregg, *Work and Welfare. Tackling the Jobs Deficit*. London: Institute of Public Policy Research.

Bannister, J., Fyfe, N. and Kearns, A. (2006) 'Respectable or Respectful? (In)civility and the City', *Urban Studies*, 43(5/6): 919–937.

Bannister, J., Hill, M. and Scott, S. (2007) 'More sinned against than sinbin? The forgetfulness of critical social policy', *Critical Social Policy*, 27(4): 557–560.

Baqi, L. (1987) 'Talking about YTS: the views of black young people', in M. Cross and D. Smith (eds), *Black Youth Futures – ethnic minorities and the Youth Trainig Scheme*. Leicester: National Youth Board.

Barclay, P. (chair) (1995) *Inquiry into Income and Wealth* (vol 1). York: Joseph Rowntree Foundation.

Barkley, D. and Collett, S. (2000) 'Back to the Future: housing and support for offenders', *Probation Journal*, 47(4): 235–242.

Barlow, A. and Duncan, S. (2000a) 'New Labour's Communitarianism, Supporting Families and the "rationality mistake": Part I', *Journal of Social Welfare and Family Law*, 22(1): 23–42.

Barlow, A. and Duncan, S. (2000b) 'New Labour's Communitarianism, Supporting Families and the "rationality mistake": Part II', *Journal of Social Welfare and Family Law*, 22(1): 129–143.

Barlow, A., Duncan, S. and James, G. (2002) 'New Labour, the rationality mistake and family policy in Britain', in A. Carling, S. Duncan and R. Edwards (eds), *Analysing Families. Morality and rationality in policy and practice*. London: Routledge.

Barlow, A. and Duncan, S. with Edwards, R. (2000) 'The Rationality Mistake: New Labour's Communitarianism and Supporting Families', in P. Taylor-Gooby (ed.), *Risk, Trust and Welfare*. London: Macmillan.

Barnes, H., Hudson, M., Parry, J., Sahin-Dikmen, M., Taylor, R. and Wilkinson, D. (2005) *Ethnic minority outreach: an evaluation*, research report no. 229. London: Department for Work and Pensions.

Bauman, Z. (1987) 'Fighting the wrong shadow', *New Statesman*, 25 September: 20–22.

Bauman, Z. (2004) *Work, consumerism and the new poor* (2nd edn). Maidenhead: Open University Press.

Bazelon, D. (1976) 'The Morality of Criminal Law', *Southern California Law Review*, 49: 385–403.

BBC (1999) *Homeless 'abused by the public'*, http://www.news.bbc.co.uk/1/hi/uk/562151.stm [accessed 18 July 2006].

BBC (2005) *Fine plans echo 1991 Tory Policy*, http://news.bbc.co.uk/1/hi/uk_politics/4173913.stm [accessed 21 August 2007].

Beatty, C. and Fothergill, S. (2002) 'Hidden Unemployment Among Men: A Case Study', *Regional Studies*, 36(8): 811–823.

Beatty, C. and Fothergill, S. (2005) 'The Diversion from "Unemployment" to "Sickness" across British Regions and Districts', *Regional Studies*, 39(7): 837–854.

Beatty, C., Fothergill, S. and MacMillan, R. (2000) 'A Theory of Employment, Unemployment and Sickness', *Regional Studies*, 34(7): 617–630.

Becker, S. and Silburn, R. (1990) *The New Poor Clients. Social Work, Poverty And The Social Fund*. Wallington: *Community Care* and the Benefits Research Unit.

Beechey, V. and Perkins, T. (1987) *A Matter of Hours: Women Part-Time Work and the Labour Market*. Cambridge: Polity Press.

Behrens, R. (1982) 'The Scarman Report: II – a British View', *Political Quarterly*, 53(2): 120–127.

Bell, A. and La Valle, I. (2005) *Early stages of the Neighbourhood Nurseries Initiative: Parents' experiences*, Sure Start Unit Report. Nottingham: Department for Education and Skills.

Bennett, F. (2002) 'Gender Implications of Current Social Security Reforms', *Fiscal Studies*, 23(4): 559–584.

Bentley, T., Oakley, K. with Gibson, S. and Kilgour, K. (1999) *The Real Deal: what young people really think about government, politics and social exclusion*. London: Demos.

Benyon, J. (1984a) 'The riots, Lord Scarman and the political agenda', in J. Benyon (ed.), *Scarman and After. Essays reflecting on Lord Scarman's report, the riots and their aftermath*. Oxford: Pergamon Press.

Benyon, J. (1984b) 'The policing issues', in J. Benyon (ed.), *Scarman and After. Essays reflecting on Lord Scarman's report, the riots and their aftermath*. Oxford: Pergamon Press.

Beresford, P., Green, D., Lister, R. and Woodard, K. (1999) *Poverty First Hand: poor people speak for themselves*. London: CPAG.

Beveridge, W. (1942) *Social Insurance and Allied Services*, Cmd. 6404. London: HMSO.

Biehal, N. and Warde, J. (1999) '"I thought it would be easier" The early housing careers of young people leaving care', in J. Rugg (ed.), *Young People, Housing and Social Policy*. London: Routledge.

Bivand, P. (2002) 'Rights and duties in the New Deal', *Working Brief*, 136: 15–17.

Blackaby, D., Leslie, D., Murphy, P. and O'Leary, N. (1998) 'The ethnic wage gap and employment differentials in the 1990s: Evidence for Britain', *Economics Letters*, 58: 97–103.

Blackaby, D., Leslie, D., Murphy, P. and O'Leary, N. (1999) 'Unemployment Among Britain's Ethnic Minorities', *The Manchester School*, 67(1): 1–20.

Blackaby, D., Leslie, D., Murphy, P. and O'Leary, N. (2002) 'White/Ethnic Minority Earnings and employment differentials: evidence from the LFS', *Oxford Economic Papers*, 54: 270–297.

Blackwell, L. and Guinea-Martin, D. (2005) 'Occupational segregation by sex and ethnicity in England and Wales, 1991 to 2001', *Labour Market Trends*, 113(12): 501–511.

Blair, M. (2001) *Why pick on me: school exclusion and black youth*. Stoke-on-Trent: Trentham Books.

Blair, T. (1998) *The Third Way. New Politics for the New Century*, Fabian Pamphlet 588. London: The Fabian Society.

Blair, T. (1999) Beveridge Speech, Toynbee Hall, 18 March, published as 'Beveridge revisited: A welfare state for the 21st century', in R. Walker (ed.), *Ending Child Poverty: Popular Welfare in the 21st Century*. Bristol: Policy Press.

Blair, T. (2000) *Values and the power of community*, speech to the Global Ethics Foundation, Tübigen University, 30 June, http://www.number10.gov.uk/output/Page1529.asp [accessed 26 September 2007].

Blair, T. (2004) *PM's speech to the Daycare Trust*, http://www.pm.gov.uk/output/Page6564.asp [accessed 20 March 2007].

Blair, T. (2005) *PM reveals plans to help to improve parenting*, speech at the Meridian Community Centre, Watford, http://www.pm.gov.uk/output/Page8123.asp [accessed 30 March 2007].

Blair, T. (2006a) 'Our Nation's Future – Social Exclusion', speech to the Joseph Rowntree Foundation, 5 September, http://www.number-10.gov.uk/output/Page10037.asp [accessed 16 March 2007].

Blair, T. (2006b) 'Big challenges need big changes', speech to the Scottish Labour Conference, http://www.scottishlabour.org.uk/pmconfspeech2006/ [accessed 22 February 2007].

Blair, T. (2006c) *Our Nation's Future – multiculturalism and integration*, speech, 8 December 2006.

Bonger, W. (1916) *Criminality and Economic Conditions*. Bloomington: Indiana University Press.

Born, A. and Jensen, P. (2002) 'A second order reflection on the concept of inclusion and exclusion', in J. Anderson and P. Jensen (eds), *Changing Labour Markets, Welfare Policies and Citizenship*. Bristol: Policy Press.

Borrie, G. (chair) (1994) *Social Justice. Strategies for National Renewal. The Report of the Commission on Social Justice*. London: Vintage.

Bottoms, A., Shapland, J., Costello, A., Holmes, D. and Muir, G. (2004) 'Towards Desistance: Theoretical Underpinnings for an Empirical Study', *The Howard Journal*, 43(4): 368–389.

Bowling, B. and Phillips, C. (2002) *Racism, Crime and Justice*. Harlow: Longman.

Box, S. (1981) *Deviance, Reality and Society* (2nd edn). London: Holt, Rinehart and Winston.

Box, S. (1987) *Recession, Crime and Punishment*. Basingstoke: Macmillan Education.

Box, S. and Hale, C. (1983) 'Liberation and Female Criminality in England and Wales', *British Journal of Criminology*, 23(1): 35–49.

Box, S. and Hale, C. (1984) 'Liberation/Emancipation, Economic Marginalization, or less Chilvary', *Criminology*, 22(4): 473–497.

Box, S. and Hale, C. (1985) 'Unemployment, Imprisonment and prison Overcrowding', *Contemporary Crisis*, 9: 209–228.

Bradley, S. (1995) 'The youth training scheme: A critical review of the evaluation literature', *International Journal of Manpower*, 6(4).

Bradshaw, J., Finch, N., Kemp, P. Mayhew, E. and Williams, J. (2003) *Gender and poverty in Britain*, Working Paper Series No. 6. Manchester: Equal Opportunities Commission.

Braithwaite, J. (1984) *Corporate Crime in the Pharmaceutical Industry.* London: Routledge.

Brewer, M. and Browne, J. (2006) *The Effect of the Working Families Tax Credit on Labour Market Participation*, The Institute for Fiscal Studies Briefing Note No. 69. London: Institute for Fiscal Studies.

Brewer, M., Browne, J., Crawford, C. and Knight, G. (2007) *The lone parent pilots after 12 to 24 months: an impact assessment of In-Work Credit, Work Search Premium, Extended Schools Childcare, Quarterly Work Focused Interviews and New Deal Plus for Lone Parents*, Research Report No. 415. Leeds: Corporate Document Services.

Brewer, M., Goodman, A., Sha, J. and Sibieta, L. (2006) *Poverty and Inequality in Britain*, Commentary no. 101. London: Institute for Fiscal Studies.

Brewer, M., Goodman, A., Muriel, A. and Sibieta, L. (2007) *Poverty and inequality in the UK: 2007*, Briefing Note No. 73. London: Institute for Fiscal Studies.

Broad, B. (1998) *Young People Leaving Care: Life After the Children Act 1989.* London: Jessica Kingsley.

Brown, G. (1999) *Chancellor's Speech to the CBI Conference*, 1 November, Birmingham.

Brown, R. (1997) 'Unemployment, Youth and the Employment Relationship', *Youth and Policy*, 55: 28–39.

Brown, R. and Joyce, L (2007) *New Deal for Lone Parents: Non-participation qualitative research*, Department for Work and Pensions Research Report No. 408. Leeds: Corporate Document Services.

Brown, S. (1998) *Understanding Youth and Crime. Listening to youth?*, Buckingham, Open University Press.

Bryson, A. (1998) 'Lone mothers' earnings', in R. Ford and J. Millar (eds), *Private Lives and Public Responses: lone parenthood and future policy in the UK.* Policy Studies Institute.

Bryson, A., Ford, R. and White, M. (1997) *Lone mothers, employment and well-being*, Social Policy Research 129. York: Joseph Rowntree Foundation.

Burchardt, T., Le Grand, J. and Piachaud, D. (1999) 'Social Exclusion in Britain 1991–1995', *Social Policy and Administration*, 33(3): 227–244.

Burghes, L. (1996) 'Debates on Disruption: what happens to the children of lone parents', in E. Silva (ed.), *Good Enough Mothering? Feminist perspectives on lone motherhood.* London: Routledge.

Burghes, L. and Stagles, R. (1983). *No choice at 16: a study of educational maintenance allowances*, CPAG Poverty Pamphlet No. 57. London: CPAG.

Burnett, J. (2004) 'Community cohesion and the state', *Race and Class*, 45(3): 1–18.

Burney, E. (2002) 'Talking Tough, Acting Coy: What Happened to the Anti-Social behaviour Order, *The Howard Journal*, 41(5): 469–484.

Butcher, T. (2005) 'The hourly earnings distribution before and after the National Minimum Wages', *Labour Market Trends*, 113(10): 427–435.

Byrne, D. (1999) *Social Exclusion*. Buckingham: Open University Press.

Callinicos, A. (2001) *Against the Third Way*. Cambridge: Polity Press.

Cameron, C., Mooney, A. and Moss, P. (2002) 'The child care workforce: current conditions and future directions', *Critical Social Policy*, 22(4): 572–595.

Campbell, B. (1993) *Goliath. Britain's Dangerous Places*. London: Methuen.

Cantle, T. (2001) *Community Cohesion: a report of the Independent Review Team*. London: Home Office.

Carabine, J. (2001) 'Constituting Sexuality Through Social Policy: the case of lone motherhood 1834 and today', *Social and Legal Studies*, 10(3): 291–314.

Carlen, P. (1988) *Women, Crime and Poverty*. Buckingham: Open University Press.

Carlen, P. (1994) 'Gender, Class, Racism and Criminal Justice: Against Global and Gendered-Centric Theories for Poststructuralist Perspectives', in G. Bridges and M. Myers (eds), *Inequality, Crime and Social Control*. Oxford: Wetview Press.

Carlen, P. (1996) *Jigsaw: a political criminology of youth homelessness*. Buckingham: Open University Press.

Carlen, P., Hicks, J., O'Dwyer, J., Christina, D. and Tchaikovsky, C. (1985) (eds), *Criminal Women*. Cambridge: Polity Press.

Carlisle, J. (1996) *The Housing Needs of Ex-Prisoners*, Centre for Housing Policy Research Report. York: University of York.

Carlisle, J. (1997) 'The Housing needs of ex-prisoners', in R. Burrows, N. Pleace and D. Quilgars (eds), *Homelessness and Social Policy*. London: Routledge.

Carmichael, F. and Ward, R. (2000) 'Youth Unemployment and crime in England and Wales', *Applied Economics*, 32: 559–571.

Carr-Hill, R. and Stern, N. (1979) *Crime, the police and Criminal Statistics*. London: Academic Press.

Carter, P. (2003) *Reducing Crime, Managing Offenders: A new approach*. London: Strategy Unit.

Cassidy, J. (1999) *Street Life. Young women write about being homeless*. London: Livewire Books.

Cavadino, M. and Dignan, J. (2002) *The Penal System. An Introduction* (3rd edn). London: Sage.

Chadwick, L. and Scraton, P. (2001) 'Criticial Criminology', in E. McLaughlin and J. Muncie (eds), *The Sage Dictionary of Criminology*. London: Sage.

Chambliss, W. (1964) 'A sociological analysis of the law of vagrancy', *Social Problems*, 12: 67–77.

Chancellor of the Exchequer (1998) *Steering a Stable Course for Lasting Prosperity*, Pre Budget Report November 1998. Cm 4076. London: The Stationery Office.

Charman, E., Gibson, B., Honess, T., and Morgan, R. (1996) *Impositions of fines following the Criminal Justice Act 1993*, Research Findings No. 36. London: Home Office.

Chartered Institute of Housing (2003) *Housing Benefit Sanctions and Anti-Social Behaviour. Response Paper*, http://cih.org/display.php?db=policies&id=404 [accessed 5 April 2007].

Chesney-Lind, M. (1999) 'Girl Gangs and Violence: reinventing the liberated female crook', in M. Chesney-Lind and J. Hagedorn (eds), *Female gangs in America. Essays on girls, gangs and gender*. Chicago: Lake View Press.

Chiricos, T. (1987) 'Rates of Crime and Unemployment: An Analysis of Aggregate Research Evidence', *Social Problems*, 34(2): 187–212.

Clarke, J. (1980) 'Social Democratic Delinquents and Fabian Families: A background to the 1969 Children and Young Persons Act', in National Deviancy Conference (eds), *Permissiveness and Control*. London: Macmillan.

Clarke, T. (2001) *Community Pride Not Prejudice. Making diversity work in Burnley*. Burnley: Burnley Task Force.

Cloward, R. and Ohlin, L. (1960) *Deliquency and Opportunity: A Theory of Delinquent Gangs*. New York: Free Press.

Cohen, A. (1955) *Deliquent Boys: The Culture of the Gang*. New York: Free Press.

Cohen, L. and Machalek, R. (1988) 'A General Theory of Expropriative Crime: An Evolutional Ecological Approach', *American Journal of Sociology*, 94(3): 465–501.

Cohen, R., Coxall, J., Craig, G. and Sadiq-Sangster, A. (1992) *Hardship Britain. Being poor in the 1990s*. London: Child poverty Action Group.

Coleman, R. (2003) 'Images from a Neoliberal City: the state, surveillance and social control', *Critical Criminology*, 12(1): 21–42.

Coleman, R. (2004) 'Watching the Degenerate: Street Camera Surveillance and Urban Regeneration', *Local Economy*, 19(3): 199–211.

Coles, B. (2005) 'Youth Policy 1995–2005: From 'the best start' to 'youth smatters', *Youth and Policy*, 89: 7–19.

Commission on Integration and Cohesion (2007) *Our Shared Future*. Wetherby: Commission on Integration and Cohesion.

Connell, R. (1995) *Masculinities*. Cambridge: Polity Press.

Convery, P. (2002) 'Reforming financial support for 16–18s', *Working Brief* No. 137: 12–23.

Cook, D. (2006) *Crime and Social Justice*. London: Sage.

Coote, A. (1994) (ed.), *Families, Children and Crime*. London: Institute of Public Policy Research.

Cowie, J., Cowie, V. and Slater, E. (1968) *Delinquency in Girls*. London: Heinemann.

CPAG (2003) *Consultation by the Department for Work and Pensions on Housing Benefit Sanctions and Anti-Social Behaviour. Response by the Child Poverty Action Group*, http://www.cpag.org.uk/cro/Briefings/0803_hse_bene_con.htm [accessed 5 April 2007].

CPAG (2006) *Poverty: the facts*, http://www.cpag.org.uk/publications/extracts/PtheFsummary06.pdf [accessed 7 March 2007].

Craine, S. (1997) 'The "Black Magic Roundabout": Cyclical transitions, social exclusion and alternative careers', *Youth, the 'Underclass' and Social Exclusion*. London: Routledge.

Crawford, A. (1997) *The Local Governance of Crime: appeals to community and partnerships*. Oxford: Clarendon Press.

Crawford, A. (1999) 'Questioning Appeals to Community Within Crime Prevention and Control', *European Journal on Criminal Policy and Research*, 7: 509–530.

Criminal Justice System (2004) *Ministers Crack Down On Criminals On State Benefits*, http://www.cjsonline.gov.uk/the_cjs/whats_new/news-3090.html [accessed 22 August, 2007].

Cross, M. and Smith, D. (1987) *Black Youth Futures*. Leicester: National Youth Bureau.

Cross, M., Wrench, J. and Barnett, S., with the assistance of Davies, H. (1988) *Ethnic Minorities and the Careers Service An Investigation into Processes of Assessment and Placement*. University of Warwick: Centre for Research in Ethnic Relations.

Crow, I., Richardson, P., Riddington, C. and Simon, F. (1989) *Unemployment, Crime and Offenders*. London: Routledge.

Crow, I. and Simon, F. (1987) *Unemployment and magistrates' courts*. London: NACRO.

Crozier, G. (2005) '"There's a war against our children": black educational underachievement revisited', *British Journal of Sociology of Education*, 26(5): 585–598.

Cunningham, J. and Cunningham, S. (2007) '"No choice at all": Destitution or deportation? A commentary on the implementation of Section 9 of the Asylum and Immigration (Treatment of Claimants, etc.) Act 2004', *Critical Social Policy*, 27(2): 277–298.

Cunningham, S. and Tomlinson, J. (2005) '"Starve them out": does every child really matter? A commentary on Section 9 of the Asylum and Immigration (Treatment of Claimants, etc.) Act, 2004', *Critical Social Policy*, 25(2): 253–275.

Currie, E. (1985) *Confronting Crime. An American Challenge*. New York: Pantheon.

Dant, T. and Deacon, A. (1989) *Hostels to Homes? The Rehousing of Single Homeless People*. Aldershot: Avebury.

Davies, B. (1986) *Threatening Youth: Towards a National Youth Policy*. Milton Keynes: Open University Press.

Davies, J., Lle, S. with Deacon, A., Law, I., Kay, H. and Julienne, L. (1996) *Homeless young black and minority ethnic people in England*, Department Working

Paper No. 15. Leeds: School of Sociology and Social Policy, University of Leeds.

Davis, J. (1990) *Youth and the Condition of Britain: Images of Adolescent Conflict.* London: Athlone Press.

Davis, M. (1990) *City of Quartz: Excavating the Future in Los* Angeles. London: Verso.

Davis, M. (1999) *Ecology of Fear: Los Angeles and the Imagination of Disaster.* New York: Vintage.

Daycare Trust (1998) *Delivering the National Childcare Strategy – local authorities taking a lead,* Briefing Paper 1. London: Daycare Trust.

Daycare Trust (2006) *Childcare Today: A Progress Report on the Government's Ten-year Childcare Strategy.* London: Daycare Trust.

Deacon, A. (2000) 'Learning from the US? The influence of American ideas upon "new labour" thinking on welfare reform', *Policy and Politics,* 28(1): 5–18.

Deacon, A. (2002) *Perspectives on Welfare.* Buckingham: Open University Press.

Deacon, A. (2004) 'Justifying Conditionality: the Case of Anti-social Tenants, *Housing Studies,* 19(6): 911–926.

Dean, H. (1999) *Begging Questions: Street-level economic activity and social policy failure.* Bristol: Policy Press.

Dean, H. and Gale, K. (1999) 'Begging and the contradictions of citizenship', in H. Dean (ed.), *Begging Questions: Street-level economic activity and social policy failure.* Bristol: Policy Press.

Dean, H. and Melrose, M. (1999) 'Easy pickings or hard profession/Begging as an economic activity', in H. Dean (ed.), *Begging Questions: Street-level economic activity and social policy failure.* Bristol: Policy Press.

Dean, H. and Taylor-Gooby, P. (1992) *Dependency Culture: The explosion of a myth.* London: Harvester Wheatsheaf.

Dean, J. (1982) *Educational choice at 16,* Research Study Final Report, Research and Statistics. London: Inner London Education Authority.

Dennis, N. (1997) *The Invention of Permanent Poverty.* London: Institute of Economic Affairs Health and Welfare Unit.

Dennis, N. and Erdos, G. (1993) *Families Without Fatherhood.* London: Institute of Economic Affairs Health and Welfare Unit.

Department for Education and Skills (2001) 'Help us Bring a 21st century Nursery near you', *Press Release 047,* 26 January.

Department for Education and Skills, Department for Work and Pensions, Women and Equality Unit and Strategy Unit (2002) *Delivering for Children and Families: Inter-departmental Childcare.* London: Department for Education and Skills.

Department for Education and Skills (2003) *Aiming High: Raising the Achievement of Minority Ethnic Pupils.* Nottingham: Department for Education and Skills.

Department for Education and Skills (2006a) *Final Regulatory Impact Assessment for the Education and Inspections Act 2006.* London: Department for Education and Skills.

Department for Education and Skills (2006b) *Ethnicity and Education: The Evidence on Minority Ethnic Pupils aged 5–16*. Nottingham: Department for Education and Skills.

Department for the Environment, Transport and Regions (2000) *Quality and Choice: a decent home for all*. London: Department for the Environment, Transport and Regions.

Department for Work and Pensions (2002) 'New Deal for Young People and Long-term Unemployed people Aged 25+: statistics to September 2002', *First Release*. London: Department for Work and Pensions.

Department for Work and Pensions (2003a) *Housing Benefit Sanctions and Anti-social Behaviour: a consultation paper*. London: Department for Work and Pensions.

Department for Work and Pensions (2003b) *Households Below Average Income (HBAI) 1994/95–2001/02*. London: TSO.

Department for Work and Pensions (2004a) *Housing Benefit Sanctions and Anti-Social Behaviour: An analysis of consultation*. London: Department for Work and Pensions.

Department for Work and Pensions (2004b) *Report on consultation on sanctions against anti-social behaviour published*, Press Release, 27 January.

Department for Work and Pensions (2005) *DWP supports doctors in helping people back to work*, Press release, 8 September.

Department for Work and Pensions (2006a) *Action to tackle nuisance neighbours*, Press release, 5 June 2006.

Department for Work and Pensions (2006b) *Welfare Reform Bill 2006 – Regulatory Impact Assessment*, http://www.dwp.gov.uk/welfarereform/docs/WelfareReformRIA.pdf.

Department for Work and Pensions (2007) *Households Below Average Income (HBAI) 1994/95–2005/06*. London: TSO.

Department of Employment (1981) *New Earnings Survey 1980*. London: HMSO.

Department of Employment (1985) *Employment Gazette*, 93(1). London: HMSO.

Department of Health and Social Security (1974) *Report of the Committee on One-Parent Families*, Cmnd. 5629. London: HMSO.

De Sousa, E. (1987) 'Racism in the YTS', *Critical Social Policy*, 7(20): 66–73.

Dicken, P. (1992) *Global Shift. The Internationalization of Economic Activity* (2nd edn). London: Paul Chapman Publishing.

Dickens, R. and Manning, A. (2004) 'Spikes and spill-overs: the impact of the national minimum wage on the wage distribution in a low-wage sector', *The Economic Journal*, 114: C95–C101.

Dickinson, D. (1995) 'Crime and Unemployment', *New Economy*, 2(2): 115–120.

Dickinson, P. (2001) *Lessons Learned from the Connexions Pilots*, Department for Education and Skills Research Report 308. London: Department for Education and Skills.

Dobson, G. (2004) 'Get Carter', *Probation Journal*, 51(2): 144–154.

Dornan, P. (2004) (ed.), *Ending Child Poverty by 2020. The first five years*. London: Child Poverty Action Group.

Dorsett, R. (2001) *The New Deal for Young People: relative effectiveness of the options in reducing male unemployment*, PSI Research Discussion Paper 7. London: Policy Studies Institute.

Dorsett, R. (2004) *The New Deal for Young People: effect of the options on the labour market status of young men*. London: Policy Studies Institute.

Dorsett, R. (2006) 'A new deal for young people: effect on the labour market status of young men', *Labour Economics*, 13(3): 405–422.

Downes, D. (1998) 'Crime and Inequality: Current Issues in Research and Public Debate Introduction', *The British Criminology Conferences: Selected Proceedings, Volume 1: Emerging Themes in Criminology*. http://www.britsoccrim.org/volume1/014.pdf [accessed 22 February 2007].

Downes, D. and Rock, P. (1998) *Understanding Deviance: A guide to the sociology of crime and rule breaking* (3rd edn). Oxford: Oxford University Press.

Drakeford, M. (1996) 'Parents of Young People in Trouble', *The Howard Journal*, 35(3): 242–255.

Duncan, S. and Edwards, R. (1997) 'Single Mothers in Britain: Unsupported Workers or Mothers', in S. Duncan and R. Edwards (eds), *Single Mothers in an International Context: Mother or Workers?* London: UCL Press.

Duncan, S. and Edwards, R. (1999) *Lone Mothers, Paid Work and Gendered Moral Rationalities*. London: Macmillan.

Duncan, S., Edwards, R., Reynolds, T. and Alldred, P. (2003) 'Motherhood, paid work and partnering; values and theories', *Work Employment and Society*, 17(2): 309–330.

Dwyer, P. (2004) *Understanding Social Citizenship: themes and perspectives for policy and practice*. Bristol: Policy Press.

Easton, E. and Piper, C. (2005) *Sentencing and Punishment: The Quest for Justice*. Oxford: Oxford University Press.

Edwards, R. and Duncan, S. (1996) 'Rational economic man or lone mothers in context?', in E. Silva (ed.), *Good Enough Mothering? Feminist Perspectives on Lone Motherhood*. London: Routledge.

Elliott, C. and Ellingworth, D. (1996) 'The relationship between unemployment and crime – a cross sectional analysis employing the British Crime Survey 1992', *International Journal of Manpower*, 17(6/7): 81–88.

Elliott, C. and Ellingworth, D. (1998) 'Exploring the relationship between unemployment and property crime', *Applied Economic Letters*, 5(8): 527–530.

EMETF (2004) *Equality. Opportunity. Success., Year 1 Progress report*. London: Department for Work and Pensions.

Equal Opportunities Commission (2006) *Facts About Women and Men in Great Britain*. Manchester: Equal Opportunities Commission.

Equalities Review (2007) *Fairness and Freedom: The Final report of the Equalities Review*. London: The Equalities Review.

Erskine, A. and McIntosh, I. (1999) 'Why begging offends: historical perspectives and continuities', in H. Dean (ed.), *Begging Questions: Street-level economic activity and social policy failure*. Bristol: Policy Press.

Essen, J. and Wedge, P. (1982) *Continuation in childhood disadvantages*, SSRC/DHSS Studies in Deprivation and Disadvantage. London: Heineman.

ETHNOS (2006) *The Decline of Britishness: A research report*. London: Commission for Racial Equality.

Etzioni, A. (1993) *The Parenting Deficit*. London: Demos.

Evans, M. (1998) 'Behind the Rhetoric: The Institutional Basis of Social Exclusion and Poverty', *IDS Bulletin*, 19(1): 42–49.

Evans, M., Harkness, S. and Ortiz, A. (2004) *Lone parents cycling between work and benefits*, Research Report No 217. Leeds: Corporate Document Services.

Fairclough, N. (2000) *New Labour, New Language?* New York: Routledge.

Farnsworth, K. and Holden, C. (2006) 'The Business-Social Policy Nexus: Corporate Power and Corporate Inputs into Social Policy', *Journal of Social Policy*, 35(3): 473–494.

Farrall, S. (2002) *Rethinking What Works with Offenders: Probation, Social Context and Desistance from Crime*. Cullompton, Devon: Willan Publishing.

Farrington, D. (2009) *Childhood risk factors and risk-focused prevention*, http://www.number10.gov.uk/output/Page10035.asp [accessed 20 December 2007].

Farrington, D., Gallaghar, B., Morley, L., St Ledger, R. and West, D. (1986) 'Unemployment, School Leaving and Crime', *The British Journal of Criminology*, 26): 335–356.

Feinstein, L. (2002) *Quantitative Estimates of the Social Benefits of Learning, 1: Crime*, Wider Benefits of Learning Research Report No. 5. London: Centre for Research on the Wider Benefits of Learning.

Felstead, A., Gallie, D. and Green, F. (2002) *Workskills in Britain 1986–2001*. Nottingham: Department for Education and Skills Publications.

Field, F. (1989) *Losing Out: the emergence of Britain's underclass*. Oxford: Blackwell.

Field, F. (1995) *Making Welfare Work: Reconstructing Welfare for the Millennium*. London: Institute of Community Studies.

Field, F. (2003) *Neighbours from Hell: The Politics of Behaviour*. London:Politico's.

Field, S. (1990) *Trends in Crime and Their Interpretation: A Study of Recorded Crime in Post-War England and Wales*, Home Office Research Study 119. London: HMSO.

Fieldhouse, E., Kalra, V. and Alam, S. (2002) 'How new is the New Deal? A qualitative study of the New Deal for Young People on minority ethnic groups in Oldham', *Local Economy*, 17(1): 50–64.

Fimister, G. (2001) *Tackling child poverty in the UK: An end in sight?* London: Child Poverty Action Group.

Finn, D. (1987) *Training Without Jobs: New Deals and Broken Promises*. Basingstoke: Macmillan.

Finn, D. (1998) 'The Stricter Benefit regime and the New Deal for the Unemployed', in E. Brunsdon, H. Dean and R. Woods (eds), *Social Policy Review 10*, Social Policy Association. London: Guildhall University.

Fish, S. (1994) *There's No Such Thing as Free Speech: and its a good thing too*. Oxford: Oxford University Press.

Fitzpatrick, S. (2000) *Young Homeless People*. Basingstoke: Macmillan.

Fitzpatrick, S. and Kennedy, C. (2000) *Getting by: Begging, rough sleeping and The Big Issue in Glasgow and Edinburgh*. Bristol: Policy Press.

Fitzpatrick, S. and Kennedy, C. (2001) 'The Links between begging and rough sleeping: a question of legitimacy?' *Housing Studies*, 16(5): 549–568.

Fitzpatrick, S., Kemp, P. and Klinker, S. (2000) *Single Homelessness: an overview of research in Britain*. Bristol: Policy Press.

Flaherty, J., Veit-Wilson, J. and Dornan, P. (2004) *Poverty: the facts* (5th edn). London: Child Poverty Action Group.

Flint, J. (2002) 'Social Housing Agencies and the Governance of Anti-social behaviour', *Housing Studies*, 17(4): 619–637.

Flint, J. and Nixon, J. (2006) 'Governing Neighbours: Anti-social Behaviour Orders and New Forms of Regulating Conduct in the UK', *Urban Studies*, 43(5/6): 939–95.

Flood-Page, C., Campbell, S., Harrington, V. and Miller, J. (2000) *Youth crime: Findings from the 1998/99 Youth Lifestyles Survey*. Home Office Research Study 209. London: Home Office.

Fooks, G. and Pantazis, C. (1999) 'The criminalisation of homelessness, begging and street living', in P. Kennett and A. Marsh (eds), *Homelessness: Exploring the New Terrain*. Bristol: Policy Press.

Fothergill, S. (2001) 'The True Scale of the Regional Problem in the UK', *Regional Studies*, 35(3): 241–246.

Fowles, R. and Merva, M. (1996) 'Wage inequality and criminal activity: An extreme bounds analysis for the United States, 1975–1990', *Criminology*, 34(2): 163–182.

France, A., Hine, J., Armstrong, D. and Camina, M. (2004) *The On Track Early Intervention and Prevention Programme: from theory to action*, Home Office Online Report 10/04. London: Home Office.

Francesconi, M. and Van der Klaauw, W. (2004) *The consequences of 'in-work' benefit reform in Britain: New evidence from panel data*, ISER Working Papers Number 2004–13. Colchester: ISER.

Fraser, N. (1997) *Justice Interruptus, Critical Reflections on the 'Postsocialist' Condition*. New York: Routledge.

Fraser, N. (2000) 'Rethinking Recognition', *New Left Review*, 3: 107–120.

Freud, D. (2007) *Reducing dependency, increasing opportunity: options for the future of welfare to work. An independent report to the Department for Work and Pensions*. Leeds: Corporate Document Services.

Friedman, M. (1962) *Capitalism and Freedom*. Chicago: University of Chicago Press.

Frost, N., Mills, S. and Stein, M. (1999) *Understanding Residential Care*. Aldershot: Ashgate.

Furlong, A. (2006) 'Not a very NEET solution: representing problematic labour market transitions among early school leavers', *Work, Employment and Society*, 20(3): 553–569.

Gadd, D. and Farrall, S. (2004) 'Criminal careers, desistance and subjectivity: Interpreting men's narratives of change', *Theoretical Criminology*, 8(2): 123–156.

Gamble, A. (1988) *The Free Economy and the Strong State: the politics of Thatcherism*. London: Macmillan.

Garland, D. (1997) '"Governmentality" and the problem of crime', *Theoretical Criminology*, 1(2): 173–214.

Garrett, P. (2006) 'Making "Anti-Social Behaviour": A Fragment on the Evolution of "ASBO Politics" in Britain', *British Journal of Social Work*, 37(5): 839–856.

Garrett, P. (2007a) '"Sinbin" Solutions: The "Pioneer" Projects for "Problem Families" and the Forgetfulness of Social Policy Research', *Critical Social Policy*, 27(2): 203–30.

Garrett, P. (2007b) '"Sinbin" research and the "lives of others": A rejoinder in an emerging and necessary debate', *Critical Social Policy*, 27(4): 560–564.

Ghate, D. and Ramella, M. (2002) *Positive Parenting: The National Evaluation of the Youth Justice Board's Parenting Programme*. London: Youth Justice Board.

Gibson, B. (1990) *Unit Fines*. Winchester: Waterside Press.

Giddens, A. (1998) *The Third Way: The Renewal of Social Democracy*. Cambridge: Polity Press.

Giddens, A. (2000) *The Third Way and its Critics*. Cambridge: Polity Press.

Giddens, A. (2001) *The Global Third Way Debate*. Cambridge: Polity Press.

Gillbourn, D. and Mirza, H. (2000) *Educational Inequality: Mapping race, class and gender: a synthesis of research evidence*. London: OFSTED.

Gilling, D. (2001) 'Community Safety and Social Policy', *European Journal on Criminal Policy and Research*, 9: 381–400.

Gilroy, P. (1987a) *There Ain't No Black in the Union Jack*. London: Hutchinson.

Gilroy, P. (1987b) 'The myth of black Criminality', in P. Scraton (ed.), *Law, Order and the Authoritarian State*. Milton Keynes: Open University Press.

Ginsburg, N. (1979) *Class, Capital and Social Policy*. London: Macmillan.

Ginsburg, N. (2005) 'The privatization of council housing', *Critical Social Policy*, 25(1): 115–135.

Godfrey, C., Hutton, S., Bradshaw, J., Coles, B., Craig, G. and Johnson, J. (2002) *Estimating the Cost of Being 'Not in Education, Employment or Training' at Age 16–18*, Brief No. 346. Nottingham: Department for Education and Skills.

Goffman, E. (1962) *Asylums: essays on the social situation of mental patients and other inmates*. Chicago: Aldine Publishing.

Golding, P. and Middleton, S. (1982) *Images of Welfare*. Martin Robertson.

Goldson, B. (1998) *Children in Trouble: Backgrounds and Outcomes. An Investigation into the Social Circumstances and Sentence Outcomes relating to a sample of 'Young Offenders'*. Liverpool: Department of Sociology, Social Policy and Social Work, University of Liverpool.

Goldson, B. and Jamieson, J. (2002) 'Youth Crime, the 'Parenting Deficit' and State Intervention: A Contextual Critique', *Youth Justice*, 2(2): 82–99.

Gordon, A. (1980) 'Leaving School: a question of money', *Educational Studies*, 6: 43–45.

Gordon, P. (1993) 'The Police and Racist Violence in Britain', in T. Bjorgo and R. Witte (eds), *Racist Violence in Europe*. London: Macmillan.

Gottfredson, M. and Hirschi, T. (1990) *A General Theory of Crime*. Stanford: Stanford University Press.

Gough, I. (1979) *The Political Economy of the Welfare State*. London: Macmillan.

Gouldner, A. (1971) *The Coming Crisis in Western Sociology*. London: Heinemann.

Graham, J. and Bowling, B. (1995) *Young People and Crime*, Home Office Research Study No. 145. London: Home Office.

Gray, A. (1998) 'New Labour – new labour discipline', *Capital and Class*, 65: 1–8.

Gray, A. (2001) '"Making Work Pay" – Devising the Best Strategy for Lone Parents in Britain', *Journal of Social Policy*, 30(2): 189–208.

Greater London Authority (2005a) *A Fairer London: The Living Wage in London*. London: Greater London Authority.

Greater London Authority (2005b) *London's Living Wage For Young People*, Current Issue Note 7. London: Greater London Authority.

Greater London Authority (2006) *A Fairer London: The Living Wage in London*. London: Greater London Authority.

Gregg, P. and Harkness, S. (2003) 'Welfare reform and lone parents employment', in R. Dickens, P. Gregg and J. Wadsworth (eds), *The Labour Market Under Labour: State of Working Britain 2003*. Basingstoke: Palgrave.

Gregg, P. and Wadsworth, J. (1996) 'More Work in Fewer Households', in J. Hills (ed.), *New Inequalities: the Changing Distribution of Income and Wealth in the United Kingdom*. Cambridge: Cambridge University Press.

Gregg, P. and Wadsworth, J. (2000) *Two Sides to Every Story: Measuring Worklessness and Polarisation at Household Level*, Centre for Economic Performance Working Paper No. 1099. London: London School of Economics and Political Science.

Grogger, J. (1998) 'Market Wages and Youth Crime', *Journal of Labour Economics*, 16(4): 756–791.

Grover, C. (2003) '"New Labour", welfare reform and the reserve army of labour', *Capital and Class*, 79: 17–23.

Grover, C. (2005a) 'Crime and Inequality', in M. Peelo and K. Soothill (eds), *Questioning Crime and Criminology*. Cullompton: Willan Publishing.

Grover, C. (2005b) 'The National Childcare Strategy: the social regulation of lone mothers as a gendered reserve army of labour', *Capital and Class*, 85: 63–85.

Grover, C. (2005c) 'Living Wages and the "Making Work Pay" Strategy', *Critical Social Policy*, 25(1): 5–27.

Grover, C. (2006) 'Welfare reform, accumulation and social exclusion in the United Kingdom', *Social Work and Society*, 4(1), http://www.socwork. net/2006/1/articles/grover.

Grover, C. (2007) 'The Freud Report on the Future of Welfare to Work: some critical reflections', *Critical Social Policy*, 27(4): 534–545.

Grover, C. and Piggott, L. (2005) 'Disabled people, the reserve army of labour and welfare reform', *Disability and Society*, 20(7): 707–719.

Grover, C. and Piggott, L. (2007) 'Social security, employment and Incapacity Benefit: Critical reflections on a new deal for welfare', *Disability and Society*, 22(7): 733–746.

Grover, C. and Soothill, K. (1996) 'Ethnicity, the Search for Rapists and the Press', *Ethnic and Racial Studies*, 19(3): 568–584.

Grover, C. and Stewart, J. (2002) *The Work Connection: the role of social security in regulating British economic life*. Basingstoke: Palgrave.

Grover, C. and Stewart, J. (2004) 'Care Leavers, Financial Support and the Children (Leaving Care) Act, 2000', *Benefits: a journal of social security research policy and practice*, 12(2): 107–111.

Grover, C., Stewart, J. and Broadhurst, K. (2004) 'Transitions to Adulthood: some critical observations of the Children (Leaving Care) Act, 2000', *Social Work and Social Sciences Review*, 11(1): 5–18.

Groves, W. and Frank, N. (1986) 'Punishment, Privilege and Structured Choice', in W. Groves and G. Newman, *Punishment and Privilege*. Albany: Harrow and Heston.

Haggerty, K. (2001) 'Review of *Crime in Context*', *Canadian Journal of Sociology*, 26(1): 130–132.

Hakim, C. (1982) 'The Social Consequences of High Unemployment', *Journal of Social Policy*, 11(4): 433–467.

Hakim, C. (1995) 'Five feminist myths about women's employment', *British Journal of Sociology*, 46(3): 429–455.

Hale, C. (1998) 'Crime and the business cycle in post-war Britain revisited', *British Journal of Criminology*, 38(4): 681–698.

Hale, C. (2005) 'Economic marginalization, social exclusion and crime', in C. Hale, K. Hayward, A. Wahidin and E. Wincup, *Criminology*. Oxford: Oxford University Press.

Hales, J. and Collins, D. (1999) *New Deal for Young People: leavers with unknown destinations*, Employment Service Research Report 21. Sheffield: Employment Service.

Halligan-Davis, G. and Spicer, K. (2004) *Piloting 'on the spot penalties' for disorder: final results form a one-year pilot*, Findings 257. London: HMSO.

Halsey, A. (1993) 'Foreword', in N. Dennis and G. Erdos, *Families Without Fatherhood*. London: Institute of Economic Affairs Health and Welfare Unit.

Hansen, K. and Machin, S. (2002) 'Spatial crime patterns and the introduction of the UK minimum wage', *Oxford Bulletin of Economics and Statistics*, 64: 677–697.

Harker, L. (2006) *Delivering on Child Poverty: what would it take? A report for the Department for Work and Pensions*, Cm 6951. London: The Stationery Office.

Hartnagel, T. (1982) 'Modernization, female social roles, and female crime: A cross-national investigation', *Sociological Quarterly*, 23: 477–490.

Harvey, J. and Houston, D. (2005) *Research into the Single, Room Rent regulations*. Leeds: Corporate Document Services.

Haworth, A. and Manzi, T. (1999) 'Managing the "Underclass": Interpreting the Moral Discourse of Housing Management', *Urban Studies*, 36(1): 153–165.

Hayward, K. (2002) 'The vilification and pleasure of youthful transgression', in J. Muncie, G. Hughes and E. McLaughlin (eds), *Youth Justice: Critical Readings*. London: Sage.

Hayward, K. and Young, J. (2004) 'Cultural Criminology: Some notes on the script', *Theoretical Criminology*, 8(3): 259–273.

Hayek, F. (1960) *The Constitution of Liberty*. London: Routledge and Kegan Paul.

Hearn, J. (1998) 'Troubled masculinities in social policy discourses: young men', in J. Popay, J. Hearn and J. Edwards (eds), *Men, Gender Divisions and Welfare*. London: Routledge.

Heath, A. (1991) 'The Attitudes of the Underclass', in D. Smith (ed.), *Understanding the Underclass*. London: Policy Studies Institute.

Hedderman, C. (1999) *The ACOP Enforcement Audit – Stage One*. Criminal Policy Research Unit. London: South Bank University.

Hedderman, C. (2000) *Improving Enforcement: The Second ACOP Audit*, Criminal Policy Research Unit. London: South Bank University.

Heidensohn, F. (1968) 'The deviance of women: a critique and an enquiry', *British Journal of Sociology*, 19: 160–175.

Hendessi, M. (1992) *4 in 10 report on young women who become homeless as a result of sexual abuse*. London: CHAR.

Hendrick, H. (1990) *Images of youth: age, class and the male youth problem, 1880–1920*. Oxford: Clarendon Press.

Henricson, C., Coleman, J. and Roker, D. (2000) 'Parenting in the Youth Justice Context', *The Howard Journal*, 39(4): 325–338.

Heron, C. and Dwyer, P. (1999) 'Doing the Right Thing: Labour's Attempt to Forge a New Welfare Deal Between the Individual and the State', *Social Policy and Administration*, 33(1): 91–104.

Hills, J. and Stewart, K. (2005) 'Introduction', in J. Hills and K. Stewart, *A More Equal Society? New Labour, poverty, inequality and exclusion*. Bristol: Polity Press.

Hillyard, P., Pantazis, C., Gordon, D. and Tombs, S. (eds), (2004) *Beyond Criminology: taking harm seriously*. London: Pluto Press.

Himmelfarb, G. (1995) *The De-moralization of Society*. London: Institute of Economic Affairs Health and Welfare Unit.

Hine, J. (2005) 'Early Multiple Intervention: A View from On Track', *Children and Society*, 19: 117–130.

Hirschi, T. (1969) *Causes of Delinquency*. Berkeley: University of California Press.

HM Treasury (1997a) *Securing Britain's Long-Term Economic Future*, Cm 3804. London: The Stationery Office.

HM Treasury (1997b) *Employment Opportunity in a Changing Labour Market*, The Modernisation of Britain's Tax Benefit System Number One. London: HM Treasury.

HM Treasury (1999) *Tackling Poverty and Extending Opportunity*, The Modernisation of Britain's Tax Benefit System Number Four. London: HM Treasury.

HM Treasury (2003) *Pre Budget Report 2003: The strength to take the long-term decisions for Britain: Seizing the opportunities of the global recovery*, Cm 6042. London: The Stationery Office.

HM Treasury (2006) *A Strong and Strengthening Economy: Investing in Britain's Future*, HC 968. London: The Stationery Office.

HM Treasury and Department for Education and Skills (2005) *Support for*

Parents: the best start for children. London: HM Treasury and Department for Education and Skills.

HM Treasury, Department for Education and Skills, Department for Work and Pensions and Department for Trade and Industry (2004) *Choice for parents, the best start for children: a ten year strategy for childcare*. London: HM Treasury.

Hoggarth, L. and Smith D. (2004) *Understanding the Impact of Connexions on Young People at Risk*, Research Report 607. Nottingham: Department for Education and Skills.

Home Office (nd) *Offender Management Caseload Statistics Quarterly Briefing October to December 2005, England and Wales*. London: Home Office.

Home Office (1990a) *Crime, Justice and Protecting the Public*, Cm 965. London: HMSO.

Home Office (1990b) *Probation Statistics England and Wales 1988*. London: HMSO.

Home Office (2006) *Making provision in the Management of Offenders and Sentencing Bill to introduce a 'Day Fine' scheme for adult offenders*. London: Home Office.

Hoogvelt, A. and France, A. (2000) 'New Deal: The Experience and Views of Clients in One Pathfinder City (Sheffield)', *Local Economy*, 15(2): 112–127.

Hopkins Burke, R. (2001) *An Introduction to Criminological Theory*. Cullompton: Willan Publishing.

Hopwood Road, F., Maynard, K. and Sandbach, J. (2007) *Locked out: CAB evidence on prisoners and ex-offenders*. London: Citizens Advice.

House of Commons Debates (1985) *Board and Lodging Payments*, vol. 81 (25 June): cols. 780–791.

House of Commons Debates (1990a) *Child Maintenance*, vol. 178 (29 October): cols. 729–749.

House of Commons Debates (1990b) *Criminal Justice Bill*, vol. 181 (20 November): cols. 139–236.

House of Commons Debates (1991) *Criminal Justice Bill*, vol. 186 (20 February): cols. 287–407.

House of Commons Debates (1993) *Criminal Justice*, vol. 224 (13 May): cols. 939–951.

House of Commons Debates (1997) *Social Security*, vol. 290 (19 February): cols. 930–1018.

House of Commons Debates (2000) *Child Support, Pensions and Social Security Bill*, vol. 342 (11 January): cols. 150–249.

House of Commons Debates (2001) *Criminal Justice and Police Bill*, vol. 362 (29 January): cols. 34–143.

House of Commons Debates (2006a) *Welfare Reform Bill*, vol. 449 (24 July): cols. 616–707.

House of Commons Debates (2006b) *New Deal*, vol. 444 , part 2 (28 March): cols. 940W–943W.

House of Commons Debates (2007) *Raising Expectations: Staying in Education and Training Post-16, written ministerial statements*, issue no. 2093 (22 March 2007) cols: 50WS–52WS.

House of Commons Expenditure Committee (1978) *Reduction of pressure on the prison system*, Report No. 15. London: HMSO.

Howard, M., Garnham, A., Fimister, G. and Veit-Wilson, J. (2001) *Poverty: the facts* (4th edn). London: Child Poverty Action Group.

Hudson, B. (1995) 'Beyond proportionate punishment: Difficult cases and the 1991 Criminal Justice Act', *Crime, Law and Social Change*, 22: 59–78.

Hudson, B. (1998) 'Doing Justice to Difference', in A. Ashworth and M. Wasik (eds), *Fundamentals of Sentencing Theory*. Oxford: Clarendon Press.

Hudson, B. (1999) 'Punishment, Poverty and Responsibility: The case for a hardship defence', *Social and Legal Studies*, 8(4): 583–591.

Hudson, B. (2000) 'Punishing the Poor: Dilemmas of Justice and Difference', in W. Heffernan and J. Kleinig (eds), *From Social Justice to Criminal Justice. Poverty and the Administration of Criminal Law*. New York: Oxford University Press.

Hudson, B. (2003) *Justice in the Risk Society*. London: Sage.

Hudson, M., Phillips, J., Ray, K. and Barnes, H. (2007) *Social cohesion in diverse communities*. York: Joseph Rowntree Foundation.

Hudson, M., Barnes, H., Ray, K., and Phillips, J. (2006) *Ethnic minority perceptions and experiences of Jobcentre Plus*, Department for Work and Pensions Research Report No. 349. Leeds: Corporate Document Services.

Humphries, J. and Rubery, J. (1984) 'The reconstitution of the supply side of the labour market: the relative autonomy of social reproduction', *Cambridge Journal of Economics*, 8(4): 331–346.

Hunt, A. (1975) *Management Attitudes and Practices Towards Women at Work*. London: HMSO.

Hunter, C. and Nixon, J. (2001) 'Social Landlords' Responses to Neighbour Nuisance and Anti-Social Behaviour: From the Negligible to the Holistic?', *Local Government Studies*, 27(4): 89–104.

Hutson, S. and Liddiard, M. (1994) *Youth Homelessness. The Construction of a Social Issue*. Basingstoke: MacMillan.

Hutton, J. (2006) *Welfare Reform: 10 Years on, 10 years ahead*, speech at the Institute for Public Policy Research event, Welfare Reform: 10 Years on, 10 years ahead, 18 December.

Hutton, N. (1999) 'Sentencing, Inequality and Justice', *Social and Legal Studies*, 8(4): 571–582.

Iacovou, M. and Aassve, A. in association with M. Davia, L. Mencarini, S. Mazzucco, D. Mendola and A. Busetta (2007) *Youth Poverty in Europe*. York: Joseph Rowntree Foundation.

Institute of Race Relations (1987) *Policing Against Black People*. London: Institute of Race Relations.

Jamieson, J. (2005) 'New Labour, Youth Justice and the Question of "Respect"', *Youth Justice*, 5(3): 180–193.

Jamieson, J., McIvor, G. and Murray, C. (1999) *Understanding Offending Among Young People*. Edinburgh: TSO.

Jardine, E. (1986) *Fines and Fine Default in Northern Ireland*, PPRU Occasional paper 11. Belfast: Northern Ireland Office.

Jeffs, T. (1997) 'Changing their ways. Youth work and "underclass" theory', in R. MacDonald (ed.), *Youth, the 'Underclass' and Social Exclusion*. London: Routledge.

Jeffs, T. and Spence, J. (2000) 'New Deal for Young People: Good deal or poor deal?', *Youth and Policy*, 66: 34–61.

Jessop, B. (1994a) 'The transition to post-Fordism and the Schumpeterian workfare state', in R. Burrows and B. Loader (eds), *Towards a Post-Fordist Welfare State?* New York: Routledge.

Jessop, B. (1994b) 'Post-Fordism and the State', in A. Amin (ed.), *Post Fordism. A Reader*. Oxford: Blackwell.

Jessop, B. (2002) *The Future of the Capitalist State*. Cambridge: Polity.

Johnsen, S., Cloke, P. and May, J. (2005) 'Transitory spaces of care: serving homeless people on the street', *Health and Place*, 11(4): 323–336.

Johnson, A. (2002) *Job retention and Advancement in Employment: review of research evidence*, In-House Report 98. London: Department for Work and Pensions.

Jones, C. and Novak, T. (1999) *Poverty, Welfare and the Disciplinary State*. London: Routledge.

Jones, S. (2006) *Criminology* (3rd edn). Oxford: Oxford University Press.

Joseph, K. (1976) *Stranded on the Middle Ground*. London: Centre for Policy Studies.

Joyce, L. and Whiting, K. (2006) *Sanctions: Qualitative summary report on lone parent customers*, Department for Work and Pensions Working Paper No 27. Leeds: Corporate Document Services.

Justice (1989) *Sentencing: the way ahead*. London: Justice.

Kalra, V. (2002) 'Riots, Race and Reports: Denham, Cantle, Oldham and Burnley Inquiries', *Sage Race Relations Abstracts*, 27(4): 20–30.

Kalra, V., Fieldhouse, E. and Alam, S. (2001) 'Avoiding the New Deal: A Case Study of Non-participation by Minority Ethnic Young People', *Youth and Policy*, 72: 63–79.

Katz, J. (1988) *Seductions of Crime*. New York: Basic Books.

Kemp, P. (2005) 'Young People and Unemployment: From welfare to workfare?', in M. Barry (ed.), *Youth Policy and Social Inclusion: Critical debates with young people*. London: Routledge.

Kemp, P. and Rugg, J. (1998) 'The impact of housing benefit restrictions on young single people living in privately rented accommodation', *Findings*, 098. York: Joseph Rowntree Foundation.

Kemp, P. and Rugg, J. (2001) 'Young People, Housing Benefit and the Risk Society', *Social Policy and Administration*, 35(6): 688–700.

Kendall, I. and Holloway, D. (2001) 'Education Policy', in S. Savage and R. Atkinson (eds), *Public Policy Under Blair*. Basingstoke: Palgrave.

Kipke, M., Simon, T., Montgomery, S., Unger, J. and Iversen, E. (1997) 'Homeless Youth and Their Exposure to and Involvement in Violence While Living on the Streets', *Journal of Adolescent Health*, 20: 360–367.

Klein, D. (1973) 'The aetiology of female crime', in J. Muncie, E. McLaughlin and M. Langan (eds) (1996) *Criminological Perspectives: A Reader*. London:

Sage. Also reproduced in S. Datesman and F. Scarpitti (eds) (1980) *Women, Crime and Justice.* New York: Oxford University Press.

Klein, M. (1990) *Determinism, Blameworthiness and Deprivation.* New York: Oxford University Press.

Knepper, P. (2007) *Criminology and Social Policy.* London: Sage.

Knight, T., Mowlam, A., Woodfield, K., Lewis, J., Purdon, S. and Kitchen, S. with Roberts, C. (2003) *Evaluation of the community sentences and withdrawal of benefits pilot,* research report 198. Leeds: Corporate Document Services.

Kundnani, A. (2001) 'From Oldham to Bradford: the violence of the violated', *Race and Class,* 43(2): 105–110.

Kundnani, A. (2002) 'The death of multiculturalism', *Race and Class,* 43(4): 67–72.

Kundnani (2004) 'The rise and fall of British multiculturalism', in G. Titley (ed.), *Resituating Culture.* Strasbourg: Council of Europe.

Kundnani, A. (2007) 'Integrationism: the politics of anti-Muslim racism', *Race and Class,* 48(4): 24–44.

Labour Party (1990) *A safer Britain: labour's White Paper on criminal justice.* London: Labour Party.

Lacey, N. (1994) 'Government as Manager, Citizen as Consumer: The Case of the Criminal Justice Act 1991', *The Modern Law Review,* 57(4): 534–554.

Lakey, J., Parry, J., Barnes, H. and Taylor, R. (2002) *New Deal for Lone Parents: A Qualitative Evaluation of the In-Work Training Grant Pilot (IWTG).* London: Policy Studies Institute.

Land, H. (1980) 'The Family Wage', *Feminist Review,* 5: 55–77.

Land, H. (1999) 'New Labour, New Families?', in H. Dean and R. Woods (eds), *Social Policy Review 11.* Luton: Social Policy Association

Laub, J. and Sampson, R. (2001) 'Understanding Desistance from Crime', in M. Tonry (ed.), *Crime and Justice: An Annual Review of Research,* 26: 1–69, Chicago: University of Chicago.

Lea, J. (2000) 'The MacPherson Report and the Question of Institutional Racism', *Howard Journal of Criminal Justice,* 39(3): 219–233.

Lea, J. and Young, J. (1984) *What is to be done about law and order? Crisis in the Eighties.* Harmondsworth: Penguin.

Lee, D., Marsden, D., Rickman, P., and Duncombe, J. (1990) *Scheming for Youth. A study of YTS in the enterprise culture.* Milton Keynes: Open University Press.

Legard, R., Woodfield, K. and White, C. (2001) *Staying Away or Staying On? A Qualitative Evaluation of the Education Maintenance Allowance,* Research Report 256. London: Department for Education and Employment.

Levitas, R. (1996) 'The Concept of social exclusion and the new Durkheimian Hegemony', *Critical Social Policy,* 16: 5–20.

Levitas, R. (1998) *The Inclusive Society? Social Exclusion and New Labour.* Basingstoke: Macmillan.

Levy, L. and McIvor, G. (2001) *National Evaluation of the Operation and Impact of Supervised Attendance Orders.* Edinburgh: The Stationery Office.

Lewis, J. (1984) *Women in England 1870–1950: Sexual Divisions and Social Change*. Hemel Hempstead: Harvester Wheatsheaf.

Lewis, J. (2002) 'Individualisation, Assumptions About the Existence of an Adult Worker Model and the Shift Towards Contractualism', in A. Carling, S. Duncan and R. Edwards (eds), *Analysing Families: Morality and Rationalisty in Policy and Practice*. London: Routledge.

Lewis, J. Mitchell, L., Woodland, S., Fell, R. and Gloyer, A. (2000) *Employers, lone parents and the work-life balance*, working age research report 64. Leeds: Corporate Document Services.

Lilley, P. (1994) *Widening Pay Differentials: Causes, consequences and cures*. London: Conservative Political Centre.

Lissenburgh, S. (2004) 'New deal option effects on employment entry and unemployment exit – An evaluation using propensity score matching', *International Journal of Manpower*, 25(5): 411–430.

Lister, R. (2004) *Poverty*. Cambridge: Polity.

Lister, R. (ed.) (1996) *Charles Murray and the Underclass. The Developing Debate*. London: Institute of Economic Affairs, Health and Welfare Unit.

Lister, S. (2004) 'Housing benefit sanctions for anti-social behaviour', *Benefits. The journal of benefits and social justice*, 12(2): 102–106.

Lombroso, C. and Ferrero, W. (1895) *The Female Offender*. London: Fisher Unwin.

Long, S. and Witte, A. (1981) 'Current economic trends: implications for crime and criminal justice', in K. Wright (ed.), *Crime and Criminal Justice in a Declining Economy*. Massachusetts: Oelgeschlager, Gunn and Hain.

Lord Chancellor, Secretaries of State for Scotland, Social Security and Northern Ireland, and Lord Advocate (1990) *Children Come First: The Government's proposals on the maintenance of children*, Cm 1264. London: HMSO.

Low Pay Commission (2001) *The National Minimum Wage. Making a Difference. Third Report of the Low Pay Commission*, 1, Cm 5075. London: The Stationery Office.

Low Pay Commission (2003) *The National Minimum Wage: Building on Success. Fourth Report of the Low Pay Commission*. London: The Stationery Office.

Low Pay Commission (2004) *Protecting Young Workers. The national minimum wage. The Low Pay Commission Report 2004*, Cm 6152. London: The Stationery Office.

Low Pay Commission (2005) *National Minimum Wage, Low Pay Commission Report 2005*, Cm 6475. London: HMSO.

Low Pay Commission (2006) *National Minimum Wage, Low Pay Commission Report 2006*, Cm 6759. London: The Stationery Office.

Lowe, S. (1997) 'Homelessness and the law', in R. Burrows, N. Pleace and D. Quilgars (eds), *Homelessness and Social Policy*. London: Routledge.

Lydon, R. and Walker, I. (2005) 'Welfare to Work, Wages and Wage Growth', *Fiscal Studies*, 26(3): 335–370.

Lyng, S. (1990) 'Edgework: A Social Psychological Analysis of Voluntary Risk-Taking', *American Journal of Sociology*, 95(4): 876–921.

MacDonald, R. (ed.), (1997) *Youth, the 'underclass' and Social Exclusion*. London: Routledge.

MacDonald, R. and Marsh, J. (2001) 'Disconnected Youth?', *Journal of Youth Studies*, 4(4): 373–391.

MacDonald, S. (2006) 'A Suicidal Woman, Roaming Pigs and Noisy Trampolinist: refining the ASBO's definition of 'Anti-Social Behaviour', *The Modern Law Review*, 69(2): 182–213.

Machin, S. and Meghir, C. (2004) 'Crime and economic incentives', *Journal of Human Resources*, 39(4): 958–979.

Machin, S. and Marie, O. (2006) 'Crime and Benefit Sanctions', *Portuguese Economic Journal*, 5(2): 149–165.

Mackie, A., Raine, J., Burrows, J., Hopkins, M. and Dunstan, E. (2003) *Clearing the Debts: the Enforcement of Financial Penalties in Magistrates' Courts*, Home Office Online Report 09/03. London: Home Office.

Macnicol, J. (1987) 'In Pursuit of the Underclass', *Journal of Social Policy*, 16(3): 293–318.

Macpherson, Sir W. (1999) *The Stephen Lawrence Inquiry. Report of an Inquiry by Sir William MacPherson of Cluny*, Cm 4262-1. London: TSO.

Maguire, S. and Rennison, J. (2005) 'Two Years On: The Destinations of Young People who are Not in Education, Employment or Training at 16', *Journal of Youth Studies*, 8(2): 187–201.

Mair, G. (1996) 'Criminal Justice Policy and Practice: rhetoric, reality and research', *The Liverpool Law Review*, 18(1): 3–18.

Malpass, P. and Murie, A. (1994) *Housing Policy and Practice* (4th edn). Basingstoke: Macmillan.

Mann, K. (1994) 'Watching the defectives: Observers of the underclass in the USA, Britain and Australia', *Critical Social Policy*, 14(2): 79–99.

Maruna, S. (2006) 'Desistance (from crime)', in E. McLaughlin and J. Muncie (eds), *The Sage Dictionary of Criminology*. London: Sage.

Marx, K. and Engels, F. (1967, originally 1888 version) *The Communist Manifesto*, with an Introduction by A.J.P. Taylor, Harmondsworth: Penguin.

Massey, D. (1984) *Spatial Divisions of Labour. Social structure and the geography of production* (2nd edn). Basingstoke: Macmillan.

Matza, D. (1964) *Delinquency and Drift*. New York: Wiley.

May, J., Cloke, P. and Johnsen, S. (2005) 'Re-phasing neo-liberalism: New Labour and Britain's crisis of street homelessness', *Antipode*, 37(4): 703–730.

McCalla, D., Grover, C. and Penn, H. (2001) *Local Nurseries for Local Communities*. London: National Children's Bureau.

McCarthy, B. and Hagan, J. (1991) 'Homelessness: a criminogenic situation?', *British Journal of Criminology*, 31(4): 393–410.

McKeever, G. (2004) 'Social Security as a Criminal Sanction', *Journal of Social Welfare and Family Law*, 26(1): 1–16.

McKeown, É. and Ghate, D. (2004) *The National Evaluation of On Track, Phase Two: Theoretical overview of the programme and its evaluation*. London: Policy Research Bureau.

McLaughlin, E. (2006) 'Hate Crime', in E. McLaughlin and J. Muncie (eds), *The Sage Dictionary of Criminology* (2nd edn). London: Sage.

McLaughlin, E. and Murji, K. (1999) 'After the Stephen Lawrence Report', *Critical Social Policy*, 19(3): 371–385.

Merriman-Johnson, A. (2005) *Black And Minority Ethnic People In The New Deal From Practice To Policy*. London: Black Enterprise and Training Group.

Merton, R. (1938) 'Social Structure and Anomie', *American Sociological Review*, 3: 672–682.

Messerschmidt, J. (1993) *Masculinities and crime: critique and reconceptualization of theory*. Lanham: Rowman and Littlefield.

Messerschmidt, J. (1997) *Crime as structured action: gender, race, class and crime in the making*. Thousands Oaks: Sage.

Metropolitan Police Association (2004) *Report of the MPA Scrutiny on MPS Stop and Search Practice*. London: Metropolitan Police Association.

Middleton, S., Maguire, S., Ashworth, K., Legge, K., Allen, T., Perren, K., Battistin, E., Dearden, L., Emmerson, C., Fitzsimons, E. and Meghir, C. (2003) *The Evaluation of Education Maintenance Allowance Pilots: Three years evidence. A Quantitative Evauation*, Research Report 499. Nottingham: Department for Education and Skills.

Middleton, S., Perren, K., Maguire, S., Rennison, J., Battistin, E., Emmerson, C. and Fitzsimons, E. (2005) *Evaluation of Education Maintenance Allowance Pilots: Young People Aged 16 to 19 Years Final Report of the Quantitative Evaluation*, Brief No. RB678. Nottingham: Department for Education and Skills.

Millar, J. (2000) 'Lone Parents and the New Deal', *Policy Studies*, 21(4): 333–345.

Ministerial Group on Public Order and Community Cohesion (2001) *Building Cohesive Communities*. London: Home Office.

Mizen, P. (2004) *The Changing State of Youth*. Basinstoke: Palgrave Macmillan.

Morgan, P. (1999) *Farewell to the Family? Public policy and family breakdown in Britain and the USA* (2nd edn). London: Institute of Economic Affairs.

Moxon, D. (1983) 'Fine default: unemployment and the use of imprisonment', *Research Bulletin*, 16: 38–41. London: Home Office.

Moxon, D., Hedderman, C. and Sutton, M. (1990) *Deductions from benefit for fine default*, Home Office Research and Planning Unit Paper 60. London: Home Office.

Moxon, D., Sutton, M. and Hedderman, C. (1990) *Unit fines: experiments at four courts*, Home Office Research and Planning Unit Paper 59. London: Home Office.

Mulgan, G. (1993) 'Foreword', in A. Etzioni (1993) *The Parenting Deficit*. London: Demos.

Mullins, D. and Murie, A. (2006) *Housing Policy in the UK*. Basingstoke: Palgrave Macmillan.

Muncie, J. (1999) *Youth and Crime: A critical introduction*. London: Sage.

Muncie, J. (2001) 'New Criminology', in E. McLaughlin and J. Muncie (eds), *The Sage Dictionary of Crime*. London: Sage.

Muncie, J. (2004) *Youth and Crime* (2nd edn). London: Sage.

Muncie, J. and Hughes, G. (2002) 'Modes of youth governance: political rationalities, criminlization and resistance', in J. Muncie, G. Hughes and E. McLaughlin (eds), *Youth Justice: Critical Readings*. London: Sage.

Mungham, G. (1982) 'Workless youth as moral panic', in T. Rees and P. Atkinson (eds), *Youth Unemployment and State Intervention*. London: Routledge and Kegan Paul.

Murphy, J. (2007) *Welfare Reform – Challenges for the next 10 years*, speech to The Work Foundation, 12 February 2007.

Murray, C. (1984) *Losing Ground: American Social Policy 1950–1980*. New York: Basic Books Inc.

Murray, C. (1990) *The Emerging British Underclass*. London: Institute of Economic Affairs Health and Welfare Unit.

Murray, C. (1994) *Underclass: The Crisis Deepens*. London: Institute of Economic Affairs Health and Welfare Unit.

NACAB (1990) *Hard Times For Social Fund Applicants*. London: NACAB.

NACRO (1981) *Fine default: report of a NACRO Working Party*. London: NACRO.

Naffine, N. and Gale, F. (1989) 'Testing the Nexus: Crime, Gender, and Unemployment', *British Journal of Criminology*, 29(2): 144–156.

National Audit Office (2002) *The New Deal for Young People*, HC 639, session 2001–2002. London: The Stationery Office.

National Statistics (2004) *New Earnings Survey 2003*. London: The Stationery Office.

National Statistics (2005) *Annual survey of hours and earnings 2005*. London: The Stationery Office.

National Statistics (2006a) *Social Trends 36*. Basingstoke: Palgrave Macmillan.

National Statistics (2006b) *Labour Market Trends*, 114(10). London: The Stationery Office.

National Statistics (2006c) *Work and worklessness among households*, First Release. London: National Statistics.

National Statistics (2006d) *Child and Working Tax Credits Statistics Finalised annual awards, 2004–05*. London: National Statistics.

National Statistics (2006e) *Labour Market Trends*, 114(12). London: The Stationery Office.

National Statistics (2007) *DWP Quarterly Statistical Summary*. London: Department for Work and Pensions.

Neale, J. (1997) 'Homelessness and theory reconsidered', *Housing Studies*, 12(1): 47–61.

Nelken, D. (2002) 'White-collar crime', in M. Maguire, R. Morgan and R. Reiner (eds), *The Oxford Handbook of Criminology*. Oxford: Oxford University Press.

Nicholson, L. and Millar, A. (1990) *A survey of fine defaulters in Scottish courts*. Edinburgh: Scottish Office.

Nightingale, C. (1993) *On the Edge*. New York: Basic Books.

Niner, P. (1989) *Homelessness in nine local authorities: case studies of policy and practice*. London: HMSO.

Nixon, J. and Hunter, C. (2004) *Taking a stand against anti-social behaviour? No, not in these shoes*, www.york.ac.uk/inst/chp/hsa/papers/spring%2004/Nixon&Hunter.pdf [accessed 20 March 2007].

Norman, J. and Ganesh, J. (2006) *Compassionate Conservatism. What it is. Why we need it*. London: Policy Exchange.

Norris, C. and Armstrong, G. (1999) *The Maximum Surveillance Society*. Oxford: Berg.

Novak, T. (1988) *Poverty and the State: An Historical Sociology*. Milton Keynes: Open University Press.

O'Brien, M. (2005) 'What is *cultural* about cultural criminology', *British Journal of Criminology*, 45: 599–612.

O'Brien, M. and Penna, S. (2007) 'Social exclusion in Europe: some conceptual issues', *International Journal of Social Work*, advance online publication.

Offe, C. (1984) *Contradictions of the Welfare State*. London: Hutchinson.

Office for Criminal Justice Reform (2005) *Criminal Statistics 2004* (2nd edn). London: Home Office.

Office for Criminal Justice Reform (2006) *Criminal Statistics 2005 England and Wales*. London: Home Office.

Office of the Deputy Prime Minister (1999) *Coming in from the Cold: the Government's strategy on rough sleeping*, http://www.communities.gov.uk/index.asp?id=1150097 [accessed 10 July 2007].

OFSTED (2007) *The Annual Report of Her Majesty's Chief Inspector of Education, Children's Services and Skills 2006/07*, HC 1002. London: The Stationery Office.

Ogbonna, E. and Noon, M. (1999) 'A new deal or new disadvantage? British ethnic minorities and Government training', *International Journal of Manpower*, 20(3/4): 165–178.

Osborne, K. and Nichol, C. (1996) 'Patterns of pay: results of the 1996 New Earnings Survey', *Labour Market Trends*, November: 477–485.

Ouseley, H. (2001) *Community Pride. Making Diversity Work in Bradford*. Bradford: Bradford Vision.

Øyen, E. (1997) 'The contradictory concepts of social exclusion and social inclusion', in C. Gore and J. Figueiredo (eds), *Social Exclusion and Anti-Poverty Policy*. Geneva: International Labour Organization.

Pain, R. (2000) 'Place, social relations and the fear of crime: a review', *Progress in Human Geography*, 24(3): 365–387.

Pain, R. and Francis, P. (2005) 'Living with crime: spaces of risk for homeless young people', *Children's Geography*, 2(1): 95–110.

Palmer, G., MacInnes, T. and Kenway, P. (2006) *Monitoring Poverty and Social Exclusion 2006*. York: Joseph Rowntree Foundation.

Papps, P. (1998) 'Anti-social Behaviour Strategies – Individualistic or Holistic?', *Housing Studies*, 13(5): 639–656.

Paylor, I. (1992) *Homelessness and Ex-offenders: a case for reform*, social work monograph 111. Norwich: University of East Anglia.

Paylor, I. (1995) *Housing Needs of Ex-offenders*. Aldershot: Avebury.

Payne, L. (2003) 'Anti-Social Behaviour', *Children and Society*, 17(4): 321–324.

Pearson, G. (1983) *Hooligan: A History of Respectable Fears*. Basingstoke: Macmillan.

Peck, J. (1999) 'New Labourers? Making a New Deal for the "workless class"', *Environment and Planning C – Government and Policy*, 17(3): 345–372.

Peelo, M., Stewart, J., Stewart, G. and Prior, A. (1992) *A Sense of Justice: offenders as victims of crime*. Wakefield: Association of Chief Officers of Probation.

Penal Affairs Consortium (1990) *Means-related fines*. London: Penal Affairs Consortium.

Penna, S. (2001) 'Policy Contexts of Social Work in Britain: the wider implications of New Labour and the New Legal Regime', *Social Work and Society*, 1, http://wwww.socwork.net/penna.html.

Performance and Innovation Unit (2001) *In Demand: Adult skills in the 21st century*. London: Performance and Innovation Unit.

Peters, M. and Joyce, L. (2006) *A review of the JSA sanctions regime: Summary research findings*. Leeds: Corporate Document Services.

Phillips, C. (2005) 'Ethnic inequalities under New Labour: progress or entrenchment?', in J. Hills and K. Stewart (eds), *A More Equal Society? New Labour, Poverty, Inequality and Exclusion*. Bristol: Policy Press.

Phillips, C. and Bowling, B. (2007) 'Ethnicities, Racism, Crime and Criminal Justice', in M. Maguire, R. Morgan and R. Reiner (eds), *Oxford Handbook of Criminology* (4th edn). Oxford: Oxford University Press.

Phoenix, J. (1999) *Making Sense of Prostitution*. London: Methuen.

Phoenix J. (2003) 'Rethinking Youth Prostitution: National Provision at the Margins of Child Prostitution and Youth Justice', *Youth Justice*, 3(3): 152–168.

Pierson, P. (1994) *Dismantling the Welfare State? Reagan, Thatcher and the Politics of Retrenchment*. Cambridge: Polity Press.

Piven, F. and Cloward, R. (1972) *Regulating the Poor. The Functions of Public Welfare*. London, Tavistock.

Platt, L. (2002) *Parallel Lives?* London: Child Poverty Action Group.

Platt, L. (2007) *Poverty and ethnicity in the UK*. Bristol: Policy Press.

Pleace, N. (1998) 'Single Homelessness and Social Exclusion: The Unique and the Extreme', *Social Policy and Administration*, 32(1): 46–59.

Pleace, N. (2000) 'The New Consensus, the Old Consensus and the Provision of Services for People Sleeping Rough', *Housing Studies*, 15(4): 581–594.

Pleace, N., Burrows, R. and Quilgars, D. (1997) 'Homelessness in contemporary Britain: conceptualisation and measurement', in R. Burrows, N. Pleace and D. Quilgars (eds), *Homelessness and Social Policy*. London: Routledge.

Pleace, N. and Quilgars, D. (2003) 'Led rather than leading? Research on homelessness in Britain', *Journal of Community and Applied Social Psychology*, 13: 187–196.

Policy Studies Institute (2007) 'Community Cohesion policy must tackle poverty', *Press Release*, 29 May, http://www.psi.org.uk/news/pressrelease.asp?news_item_id=204 [accessed 11 June 2007].

Powell, M. and Hewitt, M. (2002) *Welfare State and Welfare Change*. Buckingham: Open University Press.

Poynter, J. (1969) *Society and Pauperism. English Ideas on Poor Relief 1795–1834*. London: Routledge and Kegan Paul.

Priemus, H. and Kemp, P. (2004) 'The Present and Future of Income-related Housing Support: Debates in Britain and the Netherlands', *Housing Studies*, 19(4): 653–668.

Prison Reform Trust (1990) *Tackling fine default*. London: Prison Reform Trust.

Pyle, D. and Deadman, D. (1994) 'Crime and Unemployment in Scotland – some further results', *Scottish Journal of Political Economy*, 41(3): 314–324.

Rafter, N. and Heidensohn, F. (1995) (eds.) *International Feminist Perspectives in Criminology: Engendering a Discipline*. Buckingham: Open University Press.

Raine, J., Dunstan, E. and Mackie, A. (2003) 'Financial penalties as a sentence of the court: Lessons for policy and practice from research on the magistrates' courts of England and Wales', *Criminal Justice*, 3(2): 181–197.

Rake, K. (2001) 'Gender and New Labour's Social Policies', *Journal of Social Policy*, 30(2): 209–231.

Randall, G. and Browne, S. (2002) *Helping rough sleepers off the streets*. London: Office of the Deputy Prime Minister.

Ray, L. and Smith, D. (2004) 'Racist Offending, Policing and Community Conflict', *Sociology*; 38(4): 681–699.

Ray, L., Smith, D. and Wastell, L. (2004) 'Shame, rage and racist violence', *British Journal of Criminology*, 44(3): 350–368.

Remy, J. (1990) 'Patriarchy and fratriarchy as forms of androcracy', in J. Hearn and D. Morgan, *Men, Masculinities and Social Theory*. London: Unwin Hyman.

Respect Task Force (2006) *Respect Action Plan*. London: Respect Task Force.

Rice, P. (1987) 'The Demand for Post-Compulsory Education in the UK and the Effects of Educational Maintenance Allowances', *Economica*, 54: 465–475.

Ritchie, D. (2001) *Panel report. Oldham Independent Review*. Oldham: Oldham Independent Review.

Roberts, K. (1984) 'Youth unemployment and urban unrest', in J. Benyon (ed.), *Scarman and After: Essays reflecting on Lord Scarman's report, the riots and their aftermath*. Oxford: Pergamon Press.

Roberts, R. (2005) 'More penalties, less justice', *Harm and Society*, http://www.crimeandsociety.org.uk/articles/mplj.html [accessed 3 September 2007].

Rodger, J. (2006) 'Antisocial families and withholding welfare support', *Critical Social Policy*, 26(1): 121–143.

Rose, N. (2000) 'Government and Control', *British Journal of Criminology*, 40(2): 321–339.

Roseneil, S. and Mann, K. (1996) 'Unpalatable choices and inadequate families: lone mothers and the underclass debate', in E. Silva (ed.), *Good Enough Mothering? Feminist perspectives on lone motherhood*. Routledge: London.

Rough Sleepers Unit (2000) *Blocking the Fast Track from Prison to Rough Sleeping*, http://www.communities.gov.uk/index.asp?id=1150098 [accessed 18 July 2007].

Rusche, G. (1933) reprinted as 'Labour Market and Penal Sanction: thoughts on the sociology of criminal justice', in I. Taylor (ed.), (1998) *Crime and Political Economy*. Aldershot: Ashgate.

Rusche, G. and Kirchheimer, O. (1939) *Punishment and Social Structure*. New York: Russell and Russell.

Rutherford, A. (2002) 'Youth Justice and Social Inclusion', *Youth Justice*, 2(2): 100–107.

Rutter, J. and Giller, H. (1983) *Juvenile Delinquency. Trends and Perspectives*. Harmondsworth: Penguin.

Sales, R. (2002) 'The deserving and the undeserving? Refugees, asylum seekers and welfare in Britain', *Critical Social Policy*, 22(3): 456–478.

Sales, R. (2007) *Understanding immigration and refuge policy: Contradictions and continuities*. Bristol: Policy Press.

Sanders, A. (1998) 'What Principles Underlie Criminal Justice Policy in the 1990s?', *Oxford Journal of Legal Studies*, 18(3): 533–542.

Scarman, Lord (1981) *The Brixton Disorders 10–12 April 1981*, Cmnd. 8427. London: HMSO.

Scourfield, J. and Drakeford, M. (2002) 'New Labour and the "problem of men"', *Critical Social Policy*, 22(4): 619–640.

Seccombe, W. (1986) 'Patriarchy stabilized: the construction of the male breadwinner wage norm in nineteenth-century Britain', *Social History*, 11(1): 53–76.

Secretaries of State for Education and Employment and Social Security and Minister for Women (1998) *Meeting the Childcare Challenge*, Cm 3959. London: The Stationery Office.

Secretaries of State for Employment, Education and Science, Scotland and Wales (1981) *A New Training Initiative*, Cmnd. 8455. London: HMSO.

Secretary of State for Education and Employment (1999) *Learning to Succeed. A new framework for post-16 learning*, Cm 4392. London: The Stationery Office.

Secretary of State for Education and Skills (2005) *Youth Matters*, Cm 6629. London: The Stationery Office.

Secretary of State for Education and Skills (2007) *Raising Expectations: staying in education and training post-16*, Cm 7065. London: The Stationery Office.

Secretary of State for Social Services (1985) *Reform Of Social Security*, 1, Cmnd. 9517. London: HMSO.

Secretary of State for the Home Department (1997) *No More Excuses – A New Approach to Tackling Youth Crime in England and Wales*, CM 3809, http://www. homeoffice.gov.uk/documents/jou-no-more-excuses?view=html [accessed 13 November 2006].

Secretary of State for the Home Department (1998) *Supporting Families. A Consultation Document*. London: Home Office.

Secretary of State for the Home Department (2003) *Respect and Responsibility – Taking a Stand Against Anti-Social Behaviour*, Cm 5578. London: The Stationery Office.

Secretary of State for Work and Pensions (2007) *In-Work, Better Off: Next Steps to Full Employment*, Cm. 7130. London: The Stationery Office.

Sentencing Guidelines Council (2007) *Magistrates' Court Sentencing Guidelines, Draft for Consultation*. London: Sentencing Guidelines Council.

Shaw, C. and McKay, H. (1942) *Juvenile Delinquency and Urban Areas*. Chicago: University of Chicago.

Shaw, S. (1989) 'Monetary penalties and imprisonment: the realistic alternatives', in P. Carlen and D. Cook (eds), *Paying for Crime*. Milton Keynes: Open University Press.

Simon, R. (1975) *Women and Crime*. Massachusetts: Heath.

Sivanandan, A. (2001) 'Poverty is the New Black', *Race and Class*, 43(1): 1–5.

Sivanandan, A. (2006) 'Race, terror and civil society', *Race and Class*, 47(3): 1–8.

Slipman, S. (1994) 'Would you take one home with you?', in C. Murray, *The Emerging British Underclass*. London: Institute of Economic Affairs Health and Welfare Unit.

Smart, C. (1977) *Women, Crime and Criminology*. London: Routledge and Kegan Paul.

Smart, C. (1979) 'The new female criminal: reality or myth', *British Journal of Criminology*, 19(1): 50–59.

Smith, D. (1995) *Criminology for Social Work*. Basingstoke: Macmillan.

Smith, D. and Stewart, J. (1997) 'Probation and Social Exclusion', *Social Policy and Administration*, 31(5): 96–115.

Smith, D., Ray, L. and Wastell, L. (2002) 'Racist Violence And Probation Practice, *Probation Journal*, 49(3): 3–9.

Smith, R. (2005) 'Welfare versus justice – Again!', *Youth Justice*, 5(3): 11–16.

Smith, T. and Lee, C. with Braswell, S., Coxon, K., Smith, G., Sylva, K. and Tanner, E. (2005) *Early Stages of the Neighbourhood Nurseries Initiative: Opening the Nurseries*. Nottingham: Department for Education and Skills Publications.

Snow, D., Baker, S. and Anderson, L. (1989) 'Criminality and Homeless Men: An Empirical Assessment', *Social Problems*, 36(5): 532–49.

Social Exclusion Unit (1998) *Rough Sleeping*, Cm 4008. London: Social Exclusion Unit.

Social Exclusion Unit (1999) *Bridging the Gap: New Opportunities for 16–18 year olds not in education, employment or training*, Cm 4405. London: The Stationery Office.

Social Exclusion Unit (2002) *Reducing Re-offending by Ex-prisoners*. London: Social Exclusion Unit.

Softley, P. (1978) *Fines in magistrates' courts*, Research Study No. 46. London: HMSO.

Soothill, K., Peelo, M. and Taylor, C. (2002) *Making Sense of Criminology*. Cambridge: Polity.

Spencer, A. and Hough, M. (2000) *Policing Diversity: Lessons from Lambeth*, Policing and Reducing Crime Unit paper 121. London: Home Office.

Spicer, K. and Kilsby, P. (2004) *Penalty notices for disorder: early results from the pilot*, Findings 232. London: Home Office.

Standing Committee A (1990) *Criminal Justice Bill*, 10th Sitting, 18 December. London: HMSO.

Standing Committee B (2002) *Housing Benefit (Withholding of Payment) Bill*, 1st sitting, 18 June. London: The Stationery Office.

Standing Committee F (2000) *Child Support, Pensions and Social Security Bill*, 20th sitting, 29 February. London: The Stationery Office.

Standing Committee F (2001) *Criminal Justice and Police Bill*, 1st sitting, 6 February. London: The Stationery Office.

Statewatch (nd.) *ASBOwatch. Monitoring the use of Anti-Social Behaviour Orders*, http://www.statewatch.org/asbo/asbowatch-puborder.htm [accessed 18 July 2007].

Statewatch (2005) 'UK: Stop and search: Ethnic injustice continues unabated', *Statewatch*, 15(1): 15–16.

Stedward, G. (2000) 'New Labour's education policy', in D. Coates and P. Lawler (eds), *New Labour in Power*. Manchester: Manchester University Press.

Stephens, M. (2005) 'An Assessment of the British Housing Benefit System', *European Journal of Housing Policy*, 5(2): 111–129.

Stewart, G., Lee, R. and Stewart, J. (1986) 'The Right Approach to social security – the Case of the Board and Lodging Regulations', *Journal of Law and Society*, 13(3): 371–399.

Stewart, G. and Stewart, J. (1988) 'Targeting' youth or how the state obstructs young people's independence', *Youth and Policy*, 25: 19–24.

Stewart, G. and Stewart, J. (1993) *Social Circumstances of Younger Offenders Under Supervision*. London: Association of Chief Officers of Probation.

Strategy Unit (2003) *Ethnic Minorities and the Labour Market*. London: Strategy Unit.

Summerfield, C. and Babb, P. (eds) (2003) *Social Trends No. 33* (2003 edn). London: The Stationery Office.

Sunley, P., Martin, R. and Nativel, C. (2001) 'Mapping the New Deal: local disparities in the performance of welfare-to-work', *Transactions of the Institute of British Geographers*, 26(4): 484–512.

Sutherland, E. (1961, originally published 1949) *White Collar Crime*, with forward by Donald R. Cressey. New York: Holt, Rinehart and Winston.

Tarling, R. (1982) 'Unemployment and Crime', *Home Office Research Bulletin* No. 14: 28–33.

Taylor, C. (2001) 'The Relationship between Social and Self-Control: Tracing Hirschi's Criminological Career', *Theoretical Criminology*, 5(3): 369–388.

Taylor, I. (1997) 'The Political Economy of Crime', in M. Maguire, R. Morgan and R. Reiner (eds), *The Oxford Handbook of Criminology* (2nd edn). Oxford: Oxford University Press.

Taylor, I. (1999) *Crime in Context. A critical criminology of market societies*. Cambridge: Polity Press.

Taylor, I., Walton, P. and Young, J. (1973) *The New Criminology*. London: Routledge and Kegan Paul.

Taylor, M. (1998) *Work Incentives*, The Modernisation of Britain's Tax and Benefit System Number Two. London: HM Treasury.

Taylor, S. (1984) 'The Scarman Report and explanations of riot', in J. Benyon (ed.), *Scraman and After. Essays reflecting on Lord Scarman's report, the riots and their aftermath*. Oxford: Pergamon Press.

Thane, P. (1978) 'Women and the Poor Law in Victorian and Edwardian England', *History Workshop Journal*, 6: 29–51.

Thomas, A. and Niner, P. (1989) *Living in Temporary Accommodation: a survey of homeless people*. London: HMSO.

Thomas, W. (1967, originally 1923) *The Unadjusted Girl*. New York: Harper and Row.

Thompson, E. (1963) *The Making of the English Working Class*. London: Victor Gollancz.

Tidsall, K. (2006) 'Antisocial behaviour legislation meets children's services: challenging perspectives on children, parents and the state', *Critical Social Policy*, 26(1): 101–120.

Tikly, L., Osler, A. and Hill, J. (2005) 'The ethnic minority achievement grant: a critical analysis', *Journal of Education Policy*, 20: 283–312.

Tikly, L., Haynes, J., Caballero, C., Hill, J. and Gillbourn, D. (2006) *Evaluation of Aiming High: African Caribbean Achievement Project*, Research Report No. 801. Nottingham: Department for Education and Skills.

Tomlinson, S. (2005) 'Race, ethnicity and education under New Labour', *Oxford Review of Education*, 31(1): 153–171.

Tonry, M. (1994) 'Proportionality, parsimony and interchangeability of punishments' in A. Duff, S. Marshall, R. Dobash and R. Dobash (eds), *Penal theory and practice: tradition and innovation in criminal justice*. Manchester: Manchester University Press.

Tonry, M. (1996) *Sentencing matters*. Oxford: Oxford University Press.

Toynbee, P. (2006) 'Compassionate Conservatism', the *Guardian*, 13 June.

TUC (2002) 'New Deal Sanctions', *Briefing Document* No. 47. London: TUC.

Unsworth, C. (1982) 'The Riots of 1981: Popular Violence and the Politics of Law and Order', *Journal of Law and Society*, 9(1): 63–85.

Utting, D. (1995) *Family and Parenthood. Supporting Families, Preventing Breakdown*. York: Joseph Rowntree Foundation.

Utting, D., Bright, J. and Henricson, C. (1993) *Crime and the family: Improving child-rearing and preventing delinquency*. London: Family Policy Studies Centre.

Veit-Wilson, J. (1986) 'Paradigms of poverty: a rehabilitation of B. S. Rowntree', *Journal of Social Policy*, 15(1): 69–99.

Veit-Wilson, J. (1998) *Setting Adequacy Standards: how governments define minimum incomes*. London: Polity Press.

Verma, G. and Darby, D. (1987) *Race, Training and Employment*. Lewes: Falmer Press.

Vincent, J. and Dobson, B. (1997) *Jobseeker's Allowance Evaluation: Qualitative Research on Disallowed and Disqualified Claimants*, Research report No. 15. London: Department for Education and Employment.

Vincent, J., Deacon, A. and Walker, R. (1995) *Homeless Single Men: roads to resettlement?* Aldershot: Avebury.

von Hirsch, A. (1993) *Censure and Sanctions.* Oxford: Clarendon Press.

Wachholz, S. (2005) 'Hate crimes against the homeless: warning-out new England style', *Journal of Sociology and Social Welfare*, December, XXXII(4): 141–163.

Wagner, D. (1993) *Checkerboard Square: culture and resistance in a homeless community.* Boulder: Westview.

Walker, A. (1990) 'Blaming the Victims', in C. Murray, *The Emerging British Underclass.* London: Institute of Economic Affairs Health and Welfare Unit.

Wardhaugh, J. (2000) *Sub City: young people, homelessness and crime.* Aldershot: Ashgate.

Wells, W. (1983) *The Relative Pay and Employment of Young People*, Research Paper No. 42. London: Department of Employment.

Welshman, J. (2006) *Underclass: A History of the Excluded, 1880–2000.* London: Hambledon Continuum.

Whittaker, C. and Mackie, A. (1997) *Enforcing financial penalties*, Home Office Research Study 165. London: Home Office.

Wilkinson, R. (2004) 'Why is violence more common where inequality is greater', *Youth Violence: Scientific Approaches to Prevention*, 1036: 1–12.

Williamson, H. (1997) 'Status Zero youth and the "underclass"', in R. MacDonald (ed.), *Youth, the 'underclass' and Social Exclusion.* London: Routledge.

Willott, S. and Griffin, C. (1999) 'Building your own lifeboat: working-class male offenders talk about economic crime', *British Journal of Social Psychology*, 38(4): 445–460.

Wilson, D., Sharp, C. and Patterson, A. (2006) *Young People and Crime: Findings from the 2005 Offending, Crime and Justice Survey.* London: Home Office.

Wilson, J. and Kelling, G. (1982) 'Broken Windows', *The Atlantic Monthly*, March: 29–38.

Wilson, W. (1987) *The Truly Disadvantaged: the inner city, the underclass and public policy.* Chicago: Chicago University Press.

Witt, R., Clarke, A. and Fielding, N. (1998) 'Crime, Earnings Inequality and Unemployment in England and Wales', *Applied Economics Letters*, 5: 265–267.

Witt, R., Clarke, A. and Fielding, N. (1999) 'Crime and Economic Activity: A Panel Data Approach', *British Journal of Criminology*, 39(3): 391–400.

Work and Pensions Committee (2002) *The Government's Employment Strategy*, Third Report, HC 815. London: TSO.

Work and Pensions Committee (2005) *Department for Work and Pensions: Delivery of Services to Ethnic Minority Clients*, 4th report, 1, HC268-1. London: The Stationery Office.

Work and Pensions Committee (2007) *The Government's Employment Strategy, Third Report of Session 2006–07*, HC63-I. London: The Stationery Office.

Wylie, T. (2004) 'How connexions came to terms with youth work', *Youth and Policy*, 83: 19–29.

Yar, M. and Penna, S. (2004) 'Between Positivism and Post-modernity? Critical Reflections on Jock Young's *The Exclusive Society*', *British Journal of Criminology*, 44: 533–549.

Young, J. (1992) 'Ten points of realism', in J. Young and R. Matthews (eds), *Rethinking Criminology: the realist debate*. London: Sage.

Young, J. (1999) *The Exclusive Society*. London: Sage.

Young, J. (2002) 'Crime and Social Exclusion', in M. Maguire, R. Morgan and R. Reiner (eds), *The Oxford Handbook of Criminology* (3rd edn). Oxford: Oxford University Press.

Young, J. (2003) 'Merton with energy, Katz with structure: The sociology of vindictiveness and the criminology of transgression', *Theoretical Criminology*, 3: 389–414.

Young, J. (2004) 'Crime and the Dialectics of Inclusion/Exclusion: Some Comments on Yar and Penna', *British Journal of Criminology*, 44(4): 550–561.

Young, J. (2006) 'Relative Deprivation', in E. McLaughlin and J. Muncie (eds), *The Sage Dictionary of Criminology* (2nd edn). London: Sage.

Author index

Subject index

4785

DATE DUE
